Gothic Fiction and the Writing of Trauma, 1914–1934

For Jerrold E. Hogle, in gratitude

Gothic Fiction and the Writing of Trauma, 1914–1934

The Ghosts of World War One

Andrew Smith

EDINBURGH
University Press

Edinburgh University Press is one of the leading university presses in the UK. We publish academic books and journals in our selected subject areas across the humanities and social sciences, combining cutting-edge scholarship with high editorial and production values to produce academic works of lasting importance. For more information visit our website: edinburghuniversitypress.com

© Andrew Smith 2022, 2024

First published in hardback by Edinburgh University Press 2022

Edinburgh University Press Ltd
The Tun – Holyrood Road
12(2f) Jackson's Entry
Edinburgh EH8 8PJ

Typeset in 10.5/13 Sabon LT Pro by
Cheshire Typesetting Ltd, Cuddington, Cheshire, and
printed and bound by CPI Group (UK) Ltd, Croydon, CR0 4YY

A CIP record for this book is available from the British Library

ISBN 978 1 4744 4343 2 (hardback)
ISBN 978 1 4744 4344 9 (paperback)
ISBN 978 1 4744 4345 6 (webready PDF)
ISBN 978 1 4744 4346 3 (epub)

The right of Andrew Smith to be identified as the author of this work has been asserted in accordance with the Copyright, Designs and Patents Act 1988, and the Copyright and Related Rights Regulations 2003 (SI No. 2498).

Contents

Acknowledgements	vi
Introduction: The Ghosts of War	1
1. The Psychology of War: Gothic and the Redirection of the Uncanny	21
2. The Ghosts of War: Writing Trauma	64
3. Spiritualism, War and the Modernist Gothic	110
4. Aftershock: Malevolent Ghosts and the Problem of Memory	157
Conclusion: Ghostly Afterlives	201
Bibliography	210
Index	219

Acknowledgements

This book was begun during a period of research leave from the University of Sheffield in the Spring term of 2018 and completed during a period of research leave in the Autumn term of 2021. I am very grateful for the support I received from the English Research Strategy Committee for these sabbaticals. Many thanks to the Faculty Librarian, Peter Barr, in helping me access relevant online primary material and more generally to the library staff for generously purchasing some core primary texts that I required. In particular I wish to thank Professor Jerrold E. Hogle for his invaluable suggestions on the directions of the book and for his meticulous critical reading of a manuscript version. I would also like to thank Professor Kate McLoughlin and Professor Gill Plain for their insightful comments on an early version of the full manuscript. Many thanks also to Dr Jackie Jones at Edinburgh University Press for her enthusiasm for the project. Parts of this book were delivered as conference papers at 'Haunted Studies: The Ghost Stories of M. R. James', at Leeds Library in 2016, 'Remembering 1916' at the University of Sheffield in 2016, the International Gothic Association conference at Manchester Metropolitan University in 2018 and as a Keynote address at 'The Remains of the Body' conference at the University of Warwick in 2021. I am grateful for the feedback that I received from the delegates at these events.

Both of my grandfathers were wounded in the First World War and although I knew neither of them I would like to acknowledge that they were part of this journey. Finally, and as always, I would like to thank my wife, Joanne Benson, for her love, tolerance and support during the writing of this book.

Introduction: The Ghosts of War

To hear the thin beating of the gas tom-toms for many an acre, when the night mist lay heavily in the moonlight, traversing a silence and solitude beyond ordinary life, was fantastic enough. It was all a ghost story.
Edmund Blunden, *Undertones of War* (1928) (Blunden 2015a: 42)

At Béthune, I saw the ghost of a man named Private Challoner.
Robert Graves, *Goodbye to All That* (1929) (Graves 1967: 102)

It was all in the day's work – an exhausted Division returning from the Somme Offensive – but for me it was as though I had watched an army of ghosts.
Siegfried Sassoon, *Memoirs of an Infantry Officer* (1930) (Sassoon 1997: 76)

Good night, Phantom …
Vera Brittain, *Testament of Youth* (1933) (Brittain 2014: 205)

Ghosts haunt accounts of World War One, appearing in memoirs, novels, short stories and poems. These ghosts have a diverse range of functions as they variously reflect the experience of the battlefield and life on the home front, as well as shaping more metaphysical considerations about life and death. Superficially, these ghosts appear as Gothic figures devoid of traditional Gothic intent. In war memoirs, ghosts rarely generate horror, often appearing as battlefield guides, or as seemingly benign presences behind the frontline, or as metaphors for exhaustion. Often the ghost is employed to capture the unreality of the battlefield, as in Blunden's *Undertones* above. No-man's-land becomes figured as a dead landscape inhabited by the living who await their possible imminent death. Or, as in Graves, sometimes the dead come back, with Private Challoner spied peering in through a window as a group of officers, celebrating their safe return from the front, embark on an epic meal of 'new potatoes, fish, green peas, asparagus, mutton chops, strawberries and cream, and three bottles of Pommard' (Graves 1967: 102). Challoner, excluded on metaphysical grounds (and quite possibly those of rank), salutes and moves on, leaving behind 'nothing except a fag-end smoking on the pavement' (102). There is something of survivor guilt here, but also a lament for a lost comrade who does not seem to resent his exclusion. For Sassoon the ghosts are seen *en masse* as 'with an almost spectral appearance, the lurching brown figures flitted past with slung rifles and heads bent forward under basin-helmets' (Sassoon 1997: 76). They are simultaneously tangible, with 'rifles' and 'basin-helmets', and intangible, 'spectral' figures who have 'flitted past'. The sense that they are there but not there is also reflected in the closing lines of a letter, quoted above, that Vera Brittain received from her fiancé, Roland Leighton, in early December 1915 (the Roland who would die of wounds on 23 December). She becomes a ghost to him, an absent presence who haunts his feelings, even while at this moment he is expressing a quotidian irritation that Vera and his mother have been attempting to interfere spectrally in his affairs.

These phantoms might seem to be non-Gothic entities but this study argues that the Gothic plays a key role in shaping these representations of ghosts because the Gothic ghost helps to contain what otherwise appears as unfettered anxiety and trauma. Representing trauma in the guise of the ghost establishes a way of understanding, rather than provoking, anxiety. This is one function of the ghost at this time. Other ghosts are not so easy to divest of their war-induced trauma, and other strategies, centred on exclusion, are deployed. My central argument is that these diverse ghosts are all familiar from a Gothic tradition which has its origins in the spectres which haunt Walpole's *The Castle of Otranto* (1764). Crucially, these Gothic ghosts underpin later formations of a highly troubled, divided and doubled, spectral subjectivity that we find in Freud's 'The Uncanny' (1919), which bears a close relationship to many of the texts discussed here in which the uncanny ghost is either successfully exorcised or construed as a continuing source of horror. This is not to say that these war-produced spectres do not, on occasion, challenge conventional ideas about literary ghosts but, as we shall see, the reasons why accounts of trauma (in both fiction and non-fiction) evoke the Gothic and either develop, or move beyond, the traditional Gothic ghost are related to quite specific cultural reasons. This study thus attempts to advance our understanding of the cultural representation of the ghost significantly. The ghost becomes the key figure here (rather than, say, the vampire or the werewolf, although even they will have some say in this emerging Gothic imaginary) because the ghost functions to help manage trauma.

A central ambition of this book is to demonstrate how to read critically the cultural representations of trauma in World War One era ghost stories, which requires an analysis of the textual strategies (not always successful) made to represent and decode traumatic states. Representations of trauma are explored across various literary and non-literary contexts which also deploy forms of spectrality – including poems, war memoirs, spiritualist publications and therapeutic accounts of shell-shock. It is important to acknowledge that these ways of managing trauma are derived from different disciplines and contexts – the psychoanalytical, the literary, the quasi-religious. There is, however, a shared cultural impulse at work that unites them as they all attempt to make sense of the trauma of war. As we shall see, a specific version of the subject is shared across these different contexts; indeed, a fundamental claim of this book is that a Gothic version of the self exists in both the field of psychology and the ghost story. Whilst these models of the subject come from different contexts (clinical and literary), they historically coincide in numerous literary accounts of uncanniness and trauma, as witnessed in how Freud grants a special significance to the literary text in 'The Uncanny':

> The uncanny as it is depicted in *literature*, in stories and imaginative productions, merits in truth a separate discussion. Above all, it is a much more fertile province than the uncanny in real life, for it contains the whole of the latter and something more that cannot be found in real life. (Freud 1990b: 372, italics in original)

The symbiotic relationship between literature and disciplines such as psychology, after all, is a longstanding one, and the specific links between accounts of feeling and the Gothic can be traced as far back as Edmund Burke's *Philosophical Enquiry into the Origin of our Ideas of the Sublime and Beautiful* (1757), which modelled a symbiosis between sublimity and terror – including deep, pre-conscious fears – that underpinned the late eighteenth-century Gothic. Freud's 'The Uncanny' inherits much from Burke's thesis, and Freud's focus on the uncanny double echoes images of the divided self that repeatedly appear in the late nineteenth-century Gothic.[1] Languages of trauma thus have literary, philosophical and psychoanalytical points of contact even as they exist within disciplines which are specific to them.

This book seeks to enrich an understanding of both the Gothic and the literature of World War One by illustrating how the figure of the ghost was used to manage and control images of trauma, even when the spectre was making visible cultural fears about death. This type of Gothic seeks to understand, to control and to alleviate trauma by focusing such emotions through familiar Gothic devices centred on how lost selves can be regenerated. The uncanny, as we shall see, is a fundamentally Gothic category even when it is employed in stories which are not otherwise obviously Gothic.

The uncanny is crucial to this study as it informs certain tales (and, as we shall see, many of their authors were clearly familiar with Freud's work), and was often reworked through clinical therapeutic processes at the time. The uncanny represents an anxiety that the home becomes ghosted by its dead and is shaped by concerns about how helpless the domestic world feels in relation to that prospect. 'The Uncanny' articulates war-inflected anxieties, but it is also important to establish more broadly Freud's model of trauma.

Freud's Traumatic Self

How to make psychological, cultural and political sense of death and mourning is central to this book, and it was just as central to Freud's 'The Uncanny'.[2] There he reflects on home front anxieties about living dead soldiers (physically present but psychologically missing) through an anticipatory discourse of mourning, building upon his *Mourning and Melancholia* (1917), which tried to demarcate a healthy sense of mourning from unhealthy feelings of perpetual melancholia. That thoughts about death and dying were focusing much of his writing during this period is also evidenced by *Beyond the Pleasure Principle* (1920), in which Freud addresses the function of the death drive and how it relates to a model of trauma. The ghost provides one way of trying to rationalise war experiences, and Freud attempts a similar strategy to rationalise, and so contain, often violent death and the trauma of the still-living who have confronted it. It is therefore important to outline Freud's view of trauma in *Beyond the Pleasure Principle*, since it has strongly influenced theoretical accounts of shock and anxiety, and is regarded as a major point of origin for the classic Western model of trauma.[3]

Freud begins Section Two of *Beyond the Pleasure Principle* by acknowledging that the prevailing model of trauma had been developed to account for neuroses generated in response to 'severe mechanical concussions, railway disasters and other accidents involving a risk to life' (Freud 1991a: 281). Freud then notes that:

> The terrible war which has just ended gave rise to a number of illnesses of this kind, but it at least put an end to the temptation to attribute the cause of the disorder to organic lesions of the nervous system brought about by mechanical force. (281)

Freud argues that trauma is generated by surprise, so that the trauma produced by an exploding shell is similar to the type of trauma caused by a railway accident. No matter how well one is prepared, the actual shock of impact under shell-fire takes the subject by surprise. Freud claims that such traumatic experiences are largely replayed in dreams but are not manifested with the same intensity in waking life. These dreams are largely non-symbolic and simply take 'the patient back into the situation of his accident' (282). Freud sees trauma as linked to the death drive, which is backward-looking and in opposition to the life-enhancing, forward-looking sexuality of the pleasure principle (*Thanatos* versus *Eros* in ancient Greek). Freud also notes that a specific trauma is prone to repetition until it is relived and therapeutically managed. Freud proceeds to explore repetition in the game of *fort-da*, in which children play out their temporary separation from their mother in a scene that prefigures, and is revisited in, the type of loss associated with mourning and trauma. Such a moment illustrates how the subject is haunted by feelings of loss, but the wider problem confronted by Freud is to account for why a self-destructive death drive exists at all, since its presence is more difficult, evolutionarily speaking, to explain than the sex drive. Freud finds his solution in a discussion of sado-masochism.

Freud argues that sado-masochism occurs when a narcissistic infantile erotic hostility towards the sex-object (such as the mother who may leave the child) is transformed, in later life, into a sadistic 'function of overpowering the sexual object' (327). Freud thus attempts to merge violence with a form of pleasure in order to argue for how the two might be related. However, Freud is not convinced by this bridge over the chasm between *Thanatos* and *Eros* because 'this way of looking at things is very far from being easy to grasp and creates a positively mystical impression' (327–8). Freud is working through ideas as they come to him, only to find himself stumbling upon solutions which are, for him, highly provisional and frequently unconvincing. He consequently realises that he is trying to marry two worlds which are described by different disciplines. The body, with its propensity to degeneration, is rooted in a quasi-Darwinian model of physical biology, whereas the complex symbolic forms of *Eros* reflect advancements in sexual psychology. At the end of *Beyond the Pleasure Principle*, Freud admits that this problem might be solved by psychology adopting other scientific terms because 'The deficiencies in our description would probably vanish if we were already in a position to replace psychological terms by physiological or chemical ones,' leading him to conclude that 'Biology is truly a land of unlimited possibilities' (334). Here, Freud seemingly elevates the physiological over the psychological; this might seem at odds with his earlier view that trauma cannot be attributed to 'organic lesions of the nervous system', but he is making the point that psychology has yet to develop scientifically robust descriptions of either trauma or *Eros*, and may need to co-opt some biological terms to help frame emerging psychoanalytical observations about the relationship between mind and body. He is also making a more abstract point about evolution (and how it relates to minds and bodies), which should be seen within the context of the war. For Freud, the horror generated by the war indicates that the world has not spiritually or intellectually evolved. He goes so far as to claim that the view of humanity as evolving constitutes a 'benevolent illusion': 'The present development of human beings requires, as it seems to me, no different explanation from that of animals' (314). Freud struggles to articulate what this new model of the subject looks like. The human subject that he conceives of here is a divided one, torn between *Thanatos* and *Eros*, impulses which are, paradoxically, both opposed and merged. Freud attempts to resolve this impasse through recourse to Aristophanes' account in Plato's *Symposium* of the myth in which Zeus had divided complex bodily forms (with four arms and opposing sexes) into two, so that each half now desperately searches for its lost other half. The idea that the subject is incomplete and mourns for this missing part of the self tacitly asserts the idea of the ghosted subject who is aware of an absent presence which, as in the game of *fort-da*, needs to be ritualistically reached out for. The subject is therefore defined by what they have lost and what they mourn. They are haunted by feelings of loss and are ghost-like because they are implicitly aware that something is missing: the need to become fully re-embodied, which can be achieved only through psychological and physical integration.

For Freud, trauma is dogged by the issue of belatedness. The attempt to understand the traumatic event can take place only outside that event and requires a return to it, which is impossible to achieve completely and needs to be diverted from the original shock. Freud notes that 'dreams occurring in traumatic neuroses have the characteristic of repeatedly bringing the patient back into the *situation* of his accident' (282, my italics), not the full pain of it. The return to the site of trauma is a repetition, then, that works to numb the experience – as in the child's game of *fort-da*, in which ritualised repetitions of the mother's disappearance provide a way of defusing feelings of loss – so that 'there are ways and means enough of making what is in itself unpleasurable into a subject to be recollected and worked over in the mind' (286). Repetition is thus both a sign of trauma and a signal that the subject is trying to manage trauma through this revisiting *and* revising of the moment. This traumatic subject, after all, is torn between then (the instance of trauma) and now (the repetition of trauma). The instinct to repeat cannot be accounted for by Freud in purely biological terms because for him it has, psychologically speaking, a 'mystical' quality which links it to a Gothic sentiment that the subject feels powerless to control: 'what they are afraid of at bottom is the emergence of this compulsion with its hint of possession by some "daemonic" power' (308). Freud's attempt to make sense of a death drive and an associated trauma should be read as an act of interpretive containment in which rebellious feelings of anxiety and loss are brought under safe therapeutic control. The issue of what constitutes forms of 'containment' – therapeutic processes and fictional plot devices – is central to this book.

Beyond the Pleasure Principle, with its focus on 'The terrible war which has just ended' (Freud 1991a: 281), thus functions as a cultural document which tries to make sense of the war, a feature that it shares with the ghost story as it too attempts to make sense of the war by reconstructing the wartime experiences of the ghostly combatant. How to plot the experience of the returning soldier emphasises the importance of turning trauma into a narrative form, so that their experience can be explained, managed and moved beyond. The chief problem confronted by the analyst and the short story writer (as well as the poet, novelist and memoirist) is how to analyse feelings of trauma which are still being worked through. During the war and in the immediate post-war period, there was no point of belatedness at which an interpretation could be made. The ghost in this context functions as the figure *par excellence* for trauma. Like partly remembered trauma, the ghost is there and not there, a liminal figure which makes present what a culture cannot clearly see and fears to revisit. Freud explicitly engages with just that kind of figure in 'The Uncanny' when he argues that the spirits of the dead seem to typify uncanniness because 'Many people experience the feeling in the highest degree in relation to death and dead bodies, to the return of the dead, and to spirits and ghosts' (Freud 1990b: 364). The divided subject in *Beyond the Pleasure Principle* is also ghosted by what it does not have, and the closest that Freud can come to making this lack visible is Plato's *Symposium* and its rendering of complex life forms as split into simpler, internally unified ones.

This study is indebted to accounts of trauma in which the issue of figuration has played an important role, at least in the deconstructive turn granted it by the Yale School in the 1990s. It is important to note the significance of the work of Cathy Caruth in helping to establish trauma studies as an area of critical enquiry. In *Unclaimed Experience: Trauma, Narrative, and History* (1996), she explores the relationship between trauma and literature, which is central to this project. Although not explicitly addressing the figure of the ghost, she acknowledges that Freud turns to literature for his models of subjectivity 'because literature, like psychoanalysis, is interested in the complex relation between knowing and not knowing', since 'it is at the specific point at which knowing and not knowing intersect that the language of literature and the psychoanalytic theory of traumatic experience precisely meet' (Caruth: 1996: 3). In theories of trauma, she argues, literature 'stubbornly persists in bearing witness to some forgotten wound' (5) that functions like a ghost because, *pace* Freud, 'What returns to haunt the victim [...] is not only the reality of the violent event but also the reality of the way that its violence has not yet been fully known' (6). Her discussion of Freud's account of trauma's belatedness chimes with how the ghost functions in war memoirs and in the ghost story. The dilemma is whether, in trauma, death, conceptually speaking, is what lives on whilst psychic life dies because the subject cannot gain access to the moment of trauma, despite repetitive attempts to do so. As suggested earlier, this displacement reflects the position of both the traumatised individual and the traumatised culture which uses literature, such as the ghost story, to attempt to make sense of the past. For Caruth, *Beyond the Pleasure Principle* asks one fundamental question: '*What does it mean to survive?*' (60, italics in original). To survive seems to be impossible because the traumatic moment recalled belatedly is always beyond understanding and so, in Freudian terms, beyond abreaction, the release of a repressed emotion through reliving the experience that caused it.

While Caruth's account of trauma has not gone unchallenged, what is valuable in her analysis is the focus on the cultural reproduction of trauma.[4] Caruth's account of the problem of belatedness views storytelling as a way of trying to manage shell-shock culturally and so provides a productive way of considering the issue of narration and how it relates to trauma.[5] Her reading of the classic Freudian and Western tradition and her focus on the problem of narration are helpful because it is this tradition which underpins the shared context of memoirs, the ghost story, and versions of trauma that are articulated in accounts of shell-shock. Caruth's approach addresses how texts reference emotion through a type of textual absence. How to find a narrative form for trauma is key and many of the texts discussed here attempt to narrate trauma, no matter how partially and problematically, as a way of finding the ground on which trauma might be made to appear, and so to disappear. The post-trauma narrative and its associations with therapeutic improvement through the retrospective refilling of a traumatic absence appear in the use of plot and narrative structure in many of the tales discussed here. The traumatic moment ceases to retain its emotional impact when it becomes expressed in a coherent narrative form, which is employed to manage, because it makes sense of, emotional turmoil. These issues of narration take us back to the Gothic text, which also lies at the centre of this study.

Gothic Literature: Fragments

At the beginning of this chapter brief reference was made to Walpole's *The Castle of Otranto* and how its spectres are either developed or moved beyond in ghost stories about World War One. Walpole is a key figure in this book as his novel provides a way of thinking about subjectivity which is echoed in the images of incompletion that underpin ideas of belatedness in accounts of trauma. It is also the case that Walpole's spectres invite questions about how one can belong in a world in which the return of the past (the return, perhaps, of trauma) is highly problematic when the past appears to lack continuity and so undoes Enlightenment notions of certainty. This is a past which is associated with memory and Shakespearean formations of spectrality which gave shape to Walpole's ghosts.

The Castle of Otranto addresses how the sins of the past need to be appeased in the present. Manfred is the illegitimate heir to the principality of Otranto and he is ultimately deposed by the insistent presence of the past, which demands both restitution and recollection. Manfred is confronted by a past that he cannot forget and this is built upon Walpole's explicit referencing of *Hamlet*, in which Hamlet's father's ghost seeks revenge, restitution and remembrance. This is a key framework for understanding our soldier-ghosts. Dale Townshend has noted that the lessons about death raised by *Hamlet* are twofold. First, crucially, 'death, however resistant, must be drawn into an intimate and enduring relation with truth' (Townshend 2008: 73). The ghost thus must be associated with a concealed truth; it is not a figure of fancy or unreality. Second, 'the dead in Gothic need to be adequately remembered, memorialized and mourned' (75). These types of ghost inform both Walpole's model of the spectre and, subsequently, the representation of dead soldiers who, like Hamlet's father, command 'Remember me' (I, v, 91). As we shall see, these soldier ghosts are often (especially in spirit novels 'dictated' by dead soldiers) trapped in a purgatory that echoes the plight of Hamlet's father, who is:

confined to fast in fires,
Till the foul crimes done in my days of nature
Are burnt and purged away (I, v, 11–13)

The ghost's liminality is manifested in this in-between space in which Hamlet's father is both a purveyor of secrets and, through insisting on revenge, dictates how he should be remembered. As Townshend notes, *Hamlet* is also, repeatedly, about the failure of rituals of mourning (such as the unceremonious burial of Polonius and the only partial Christian burial of Ophelia, but also, powerfully, in the truncated mourning of Hamlet's father). Townshend notes that the play emphasises the consequences of 'thwarted mourning' (Townshend 2008: 75), so that it 'serves the Gothic, in a decidedly more modern and psychological sense, as horrific testament to the ghosts and spectres that issue forth when any failed, curtailed or prohibited act of mourning is at stake' (76). Walpole's novel inherits this, and although the legitimate heir, Theodore, is restored to power, he is grieving the death of Matilda and trapped within an emotional narrative of loss rather than a political narrative centred on gain. These acts of curtailed mourning in *Hamlet* are developed in Walpole's novel, which was, in turn, highly influential in establishing the key forms of representation of the British Gothic tradition. These incomplete rituals of mourning recur repeatedly in stories about World War One soldier-ghosts, who culturally configure the need for mourning, even while their violent death and often hasty burials conform to the patterns of 'thwarted mourning' noted by Townshend. These war ghosts are also often out for revenge, demand forms of remembrance, and unsettle the ambitions of a post-war world which cannot move into a new peace until these ghosts have been appropriately appeased. These issues also relate to ideas about subjectivity (what Freud inherits from a Gothic tradition inaugurated by Walpole) and models of history.

The Walpolean subject is as discontinuous as the divided shell-shocked spectre, whose new personality is seemingly an acquired aberration. However, this is only an aberration (indeed, a sign of illness) according to a Freudian version of subjectivity, mapped, for example, in *The Interpretation of Dreams* (1899), which emphasises that selves are continuous, even while Freud's war writings, such as 'The Uncanny' and *Beyond the Pleasure Principle*, identify a new and troubling subjectivity which appears to echo the irrationality of the war itself – reflected in the emergence of a new, seemingly discontinuous, subject. This is an issue which, despite its ostensibly psychological origins, is related to competing models of history.

Jonathan Dent, in his account of how the Gothic challenges Enlightenment models of historiography (associated with, for example, David Hume), argues that 'Whereas Enlightenment historiography gives the impression that progress and rationality ultimately drive the historical process, the Gothic shows how violence and irrationality frequently dictate the ruthless sweep of history' (Dent 2016: 16), which is a similar conclusion to that which Freud reached when reflecting on the war in *Beyond the Pleasure Principle*. Historical writing, of a strictly Enlightenment kind, asserts 'coherence and continuity' (Dent 2016: 31), reflecting many of the tales discussed here, which try to work beyond the troubled doubled self of the uncanny (one who even Freud cannot, ultimately, rationalise) as they too seek for continuity and coherence. Dent argues for 'the presence of history in the human psyche' (Dent 2016: 23), so that discontinuous versions of the subject exist as projections of historical problems. In this context the belatedness of the analytical scene can be conflated with a post-war culture which belatedly tries to make sense of the war through images of the not-as-yet cured soldier who struggles to get to grips with their not-as-yet exorcised ghost. Walpole plays a pivotal role in these forms of representation.

The Castle of Otranto can be read as addressing ideas of political legitimacy as Manfred attempts to shore up his dynasty through a strategic marriage. However, Manfred is the illegitimate heir of the principality of Otranto and the repressed legitimate history becomes manifested when the marriage is disrupted – with Manfred's son, the fifteen-year-old groom Conrad, crushed by a gigantic helmet. The legitimate line of the usurped Alfonso is ultimately restored and his descendant, Theodore, inherits the principality. The novel appears to suggest that political order is re-established but Dent notes the seemingly random nature of how the past is presented – through the intervention of a gigantic helmet and through ancestral figures who step out of paintings. For Dent this is a model of history which 'fall(s) outside the scope of Enlightenment history' (Dent 2016: 43), which Hume had associated with progress and continuity, and not with the type of seemingly violent irruptions which punctuate Walpole's novel. Dent notes that Hume, in *The History of England* (1754–61), avoids any discussion of war precisely because conflict cannot be accommodated within a model of rational progress (Dent 2016: 54). This means that, while Hume focuses on continuity and models of civilisation and their forms of development, 'the Gothic probes the uncivilised aspects of the past that remain in the shadow' (Dent 2016: 55). Read in these terms, *Otranto* is a war story with a militaristic air to it (there are lots of combative knights and violent deaths), which articulates forms of violence repressed through omission from Hume's historiography. However, as Freud claims, the repressed always returns and Dent elaborates how Freud's terms from 'The Uncanny', the *heimlich* and the *unheimlich*, represent the retrospective positions of Hume and Walpole, with Walpole articulating the type of national, war-torn trauma that Hume sought to deny (Dent 2016: 59, 54). It is therefore little surprise that Walpolean ghosts haunt accounts of trauma and conflict in the tales discussed here and their uncanny presence constantly evokes the type of order and control which tries to contain, manage and ultimately repress them.

A key issue to consider in this context is the ambivalent way in which the past ghosts the present. In *Otranto*, order is seemingly re-established when Theodore is restored as the heir to the principality; however, this political narrative is undone by a private drama focused on the family. Manfred is married to Hippolita, with whom he has a daughter, Matilda; after the death of Conrad, Manfred needs another male heir to hold on to his position. He tries to force himself upon Isabella, to whom Conrad was to be married, because he does not believe that Hippolita can give him another son. Manfred's rapacious pursuit of Isabella is disrupted by the spectral intervention of Manfred's grandfather, in which his portrait 'uttered a deep sigh and heaved its breast' (Walpole 1998: 26), before stepping out of the frame and leading Manfred away from Isabella. The ghost of his grandfather registers disappointment at Manfred's behaviour and indicates how ghosts formulate ethical interventions. However, the cosmology of *Otranto* is not thereby freighted with a clear providential structure which supports the punishment of the wicked and defends the innocent. Manfred accidently kills Matilda, believing her to be Isabella, who is secretly meeting with Theodore. Manfred and Hippolita, now childless, withdraw from the narrative and take holy orders. Theodore, who had fallen in love with Matilda, is left to marry Isabella, but while this shores up the future of the principality, it brings him no personal happiness. Political plots and family narratives cannot be reconciled and this is in a novel which repeatedly emphasises the protean, unstable nature of reality, in which portraits and statues come alive, characters are killed by mistake, and the revelation of one's true social standing (Theodore is a peasant at the start of the novel) does not bring happiness. The whole premise of the importance of blood lines and the aristocracy is caustically critiqued by the figure of Father Jerome (who acts as Manfred's conscience) – '"what is blood? what is nobility? We are all reptiles, miserable sinful creatures"' (58) – before revealing that Theodore is next in line to inherit the principality.

The issue about concealed family dramas will underpin Freud's model of the subject and that Walpole can be read as a precursor to Freud is also suggested in the function of the novel's two Prefaces. The book was first published in 1764 and purported to be a translation by William Marshall of a sixteenth-century edition of an Italian manuscript by one Onuphriro Muralto, which had originally been composed some time between 1095 and 1243. The past thus seems to ghost the present in the current manuscript. The first Preface indicates that the text is a genuine medieval romance, a found document, but the second Preface (to the 1765 edition) makes a more radical claim. In the latter (in which Walpole admits authorship) the claim is made that the novel 'was an attempt to blend two kinds of romance, the ancient and the modern. In the former all was imagination and improbability: in the latter, nature is always intended to be, and sometimes has been, copied with success' (9). Walpole thus states that, beneath the veneer of the older romance, lurks a version of a recognisable reality in which characters function 'according to the rules of probability' (9), so that his characters 'think, speak and act, as it might be supposed mere men and women would do in extraordinary positions' (10). The fantastical narrative harbours a more psychological narrative which works against formal interventions, such as providence, and any ostensible political dramas. Manfred, for example, is a Gothic villain but he is not devoid of compassion:

> Manfred was not one of those savage tyrants who wanton in cruelty unprovoked. The circumstances of his fortune had given an asperity to his temper, which was naturally humane; and his virtues were always ready to operate, when his passion did not obscure his reason. (33)

The problem is that passion tends to take over here, but that leads to self-destruction. The line of Alfonso might triumph but we witness the symbolic giant of Alfonso at the end as he destroys the Castle of Otranto before his spirit ascends to heaven. Images of violence and destruction are pervasive and, at the end, the triumph of the line of Alfonso is at best ambivalent, given the focus on Theodore, who can only share with Isabella 'the melancholy that had taken possession of his soul' (115) as he grieves for Matilda. The ghosts of Walpole thus register the persistence of the past through spectres who are figures of admonishment or revenge familiar from *Hamlet*. Their ghostly messengers may triumph, but in their wake a new form of despair is registered. The human drama that Walpole acknowledges in the second Preface articulates the feelings of loss that underpins Freud's 'The Uncanny', which reflects feelings of grief and melancholy. The ghosts come back, but with an ambivalent, effect and it is this type of spectre that we find appearing so frequently in ghost stories about the First World War.

The Gothic represents, at least in the case of Walpole, an anti-Enlightenment impulse, which can also be related to accounts of war. Kate McLoughlin has also noted how representations of returning veterans in the work of Rebecca West and Virginia Woolf (whose work is discussed here in Chapters 1 and 3) 'resist the Enlightenment's relentless onward surge', by emphasising that veterans constitute 'figures of unknowing'

(McLoughlin 2018: 233). McLoughlin's ambition is ultimately to 'value silences' as a move 'towards a respectful not knowing, which attends to the not said' (3). The tales discussed in this book are approached through a Gothic critical lens which indicates that the *unheimlich* world of the veteran is confronted by the *heimlich* tendencies of a culture which tries to make the veteran speak, not as an act of respect but as a way of banishing the ghosts of war by subjecting them to Enlightenment analytical scrutiny. These tales demonstrate tensions between Enlightenment and anti-Enlightenment impulses which characterise the Gothic and its often paradoxical approach to science. As we shall see, other Gothic texts which evoke images of bodily and textual fragmentation (and science), such as *Frankenstein* (1818), *Strange Case of Dr Jekyll and Mr Hyde* (1886) and *Dracula* (1897), also haunt accounts of the war. These Gothic texts foreground a need for knowledge, understanding and narrative coherence, even while they assert the presence of violence, death and divided selves.

Narrative form is closely related to the difficulty of representing trauma and this has its roots within a Gothic tradition. Robert Louis Stevenson's *Strange Case of Dr Jekyll and Mr Hyde* has a multi-narrative structure which, in its various sensational chapter titles, including 'Story of the Door', 'Incident of the Letter', 'Dr Lanyon's Narrative' and 'Henry Jekyll's Full Statement of the Case', evokes Victorian newspaper crime reportage. However, within this attempt to get at the truth there are complicating stylistic tics. The slippery pronouns of 'Jekyll's Full Statement', for example, which move from first to third person and back again, make ownership of the final line 'I bring the life of that unhappy Henry Jekyll to an end' (Stevenson 2006: 66) ambivalent, as we cannot be sure whether Jekyll or Hyde is narrating at that point.[6] Bram Stoker's *Dracula* may seem to assert a more confident ending because of the collective response to defeating the vampire, which turns the narrators into a team of readers. The multi-narrated structure of the novel does not end merely in fragments, however, but in the final note written by Jonathan Harker, in which 'there is hardly one authentic document! nothing but a mass of type-writing' (Stoker 1996: 351) among the foregoing papers and so no one should expect the novel's story to be believed. Arthur Machen's *The Great God Pan* (1894) records the suicidal dissolution of Helen Vaughan in a chapter titled 'The Fragments', where a baffled Dr Matheson observes 'the body descend to the beasts whence it ascended' (Machen 2010: 70) as Helen's body recapitulates a model of evolutionary development at the point of death. The inconclusive aspects of these narratives reflect a *fin-de-siècle* sensibility in which everything feels uncertain, and the two concluding suicides in Stevenson and Machen act out ideas about the self-destructive society that also appeared in contemporary theories of degeneration which anticipate representations of war as a self-destructive enterprise.[7]

The *fin-de-siècle* Gothic is shaped by specific social pressures that had changed by the 1910s, but its repeated emphasis on a lack of credible evidence, decaying bodies, self-destruction and the importance of bearing witness are inherited by authors (all of whom were Victorians by birth) who incorporate the Gothic in writing about the war *and* in models of the subject that we find in Freud and other war psychologists such as W. H. R. Rivers and Wilfred Bion. These intertextual links are not coincidental. The occult deliberations of psychology at this time (Freud, Jung, Ferenczi, Myers) demonstrate that versions of the paranormal (from telepathy to ghosts) were helping to shape what psychologically constituted the subject.[8] The uncanny, for example, is freighted by a model of the divided self that is indebted to a familiar Gothic tradition of doubling. Roger Luckhurst's assessment of the double notes its presence in writings by Poe, Dostoevsky, Stevenson, Maupassant, Wilde, Conrad and Henry James. He also notes that Stevenson's correspondence about *Jekyll and Hyde* with the psychologist and spiritualist F. W. H. Myers, concerning subliminal consciousness, indicates how Stevenson contributed to the production of theories of the mind during the period, meaning that 'Stevenson's work did not merely *reflect* these developments, but actually helped *constitute* them' (Luckhurst 2006: xvii, italics in original). In turn, these theories shaped Freud's idea of the doubled self in 'The Uncanny'. Luckhurst summarises 'the literature of the double became one of the privileged ways of exploring the mysteries of the modern self, a subjectivity marked less by rationality, order, and coherence than by dream, nightmare, and psychical multiplicity' (Luckhurst 2006: xv). Psychoanalysis is thus ghosted by the Gothic, as Townshend notes in his account of Shakespeare's influence on *Otranto*; 'the symptom is replaced by the spectre – precisely the psychoanalytic point to which *Hamlet*, as cultural artefact, attests' (Townshend 2008: 78).

The Critical Context

This book is the first full-length study to explore both Gothic literature and literature indebted to the Gothic that was produced during and shortly after World War One, although there have been several important contributions to Gothic and war scholarship which have touched on the period. Martin Tropp's *Images of Fear: How Horror Stories Helped Shape Modern Culture* (1990) includes a chapter on the First

World War, in which Tropp claims that in 'Examining the diaries, letters, and memoirs of [...] the soldiers who suddenly found themselves in the surreal landscape of the Great War, we hear echoes of the imaginative literature that helped the participants give form to otherwise unimaginable fears' (Tropp 1990: 180). For Tropp, the ruined landscape functions as a corollary to the ruined Castle that populates the late eighteenth-century Gothic novel. He also argues that the Gothic provided a way both to articulate fear and to control it, so that by 'giving the soldiers who had lived vicariously with fear in the tale of terror something to use to make an otherwise lunatic landscape comprehensible, the pattern of horror provided a way, paradoxically, to remain sane' (217). Tropp is somewhat synoptic on this point, and even as I acknowledge the crucial dimension of this language of containment, this study explores how the figure of the ghost provides different forms of consolation for those directly involved in the war.

There have been studies which have attempted to explore the psychological significance of World War One ghosts as the product of feelings of profound loss. George M. Johnson's *Mourning and Mysticism in First World War Literature and Beyond: Grappling with Ghosts* (2015) applies object relations and attachment theory, derived from D. W. Winnicott among others, in order to construct psychobiographies of a diverse range of writers, including Wilfred Owen, Virginia Woolf and J. M. Barrie. Such an approach, if inevitably speculative, helpfully explores the wider context of spiritualism and how it undergirded a general discourse of mourning at the time. The literary provenance of the ghost is, however, somewhat lost in these deliberations, but the relationship between spiritualism and modernism, in which spiritualism is considered as a literary affect, is usefully explored later in this study. From an historical perspective, meanwhile, Tim Cook has examined how soldiers' stories about helpful frontline ghosts, who provide premonitions of danger, constituted a popular belief at the time. For Cook, such beliefs were a spiritual counterpoint to the materiality of the machine-driven war because 'In this war of machines, industrial power, and dehumanization, the magical, uncanny, and supernatural found a place in soldiers' lives and their belief systems' (Cook 2013: 523). These beliefs, which also included an optimistic adherence to superstitious ritual, frequently, and paradoxically, combined with a pessimistic view of fate, thus providing yet another way of managing anxiety. Cook notes that these beliefs

> were a method [...] by which the soldiers ordered the mind and framed their experiences in the trenches. And while some soldiers believed in magical

forces or the power of rituals, many were also making real their fears in an attempt to combat, contain, or at least make sense of them. (542)

More recently, too, Owen Davies, in *A Supernatural War: Magic, Divination, and Faith During the First World War* (2018), has explored how rituals and amulets were used by soldiers, and those at home, to help ward off danger.[9] The ghost functions in such rituals as a means of containment, at least among those directly caught up in the war, and is later transformed into a figure of ambivalent mourning which will not allow the culture to forget. W. Scott Poole's *Wasteland: The Great War and the Origins of Modern Horror* (2018) provides a broad overview of the multi-media and transnational developments in the Gothic which were prompted by the war and also looks at Freudian ideas within the context of war trauma. However, my focus is specifically upon ghosts in a British literary tradition and explores how representations of subjectivity provide new ways of thinking about how the Gothic relates to other forms of cultural memorialisation.

Building on all these studies but concentrating on the Gothic mentality in all such memorialisations, this book is divided into four chapters which explore the different ways in which images of spectrality, including the often liminal figure of the shell-shocked soldier, were represented either during the conflict or within a period of post-war reflection. Chapter 1, 'The Psychology of War: Gothic and the Redirection of the Uncanny', reads Freud's essay 'The Uncanny' as an account of World War One that is centred on anxieties about the return of the dead into the home. The distance between the home and the battle front is conceptually erased in such moments, and the uncanny can be read as a liminal no-man's-land in which the spectral presence of the dead soldier provides a post-mortem completion of the family. A number of short stories are explored, many of which were published in *The Strand* during the war. Some of these tales make explicit use of the ghost story as a way of containing trauma by emphasising the use of familiar ghost-story plots. Other tales are not specifically tales about ghosts *per se*, but explore how the shell-shocked soldier has become ghost-like through an apparent loss of identity. Such tales indicate that the return home is a return to a safe domestic space in which a soldier is fictively brought back to life and reincorporated into the family. The traumatised soldier represents an alternative self who both is and is not the old subject. These tales are shaped by narrative arcs and pervasive mind-sets which are indebted to the Gothic, although they are not obviously Gothic tales in themselves. However, their tacit engagement with that key Gothic category, the uncanny, influences how the missing are portrayed. How to bring the dead back to life provides an alternative language of spectrality to that encountered in formal ghost stories and, ultimately, dissipates the emotional anxieties associated with the uncanny.

Chapter 2, 'The Ghosts of War: Writing Trauma', explores representations of ghosts in memoirs, short stories and novels that are not contained within familiar plots. These ghosts are more problematic to explain and typically represent moments of traumatic crisis in accounts of the war by Blunden, Graves, Sassoon, Brittain (among other memoirs discussed in this chapter), and various novels and short stories. Such ghosts personify no-man's-land as a liminal zone associated with both death and life. These ghosts sit outside the narrative demands of the ghost story and appear as lost, or without a role, and so challenge the possibility of coherent meaning. They are not ghosts who can be brought back to life within domestic spaces. The lack of a literary plot for the aimless ghost implicates a failure in narrative composition. That failure is reflected in self-conscious meditations upon the problem of writing about the experience of war. The ghost without a ghost story is central to contemplations of the wider story of the war itself and underpins many of the more traumatic versions of shell-shock, which are different in kind to those treatable cases discussed in Chapter 1.

In the modernist context, how to write about ghosts is closely tied to how to write about the war. For the modernists, such as Virginia Woolf, T. S. Eliot and David Jones, the ghost poses a problem for interpretation just as the war poses a challenge to conventional narrative form. Chapter 3, on 'Spiritualism, War and the Modernist Gothic', examines how these issues of writing are linked to how ghosts (or, technically, spirits) attempt to communicate with the living in spiritualist publications. Early articles on the war in *The Occult Review* focused on the horoscopes of the chief protagonists and the esoteric writings of figures such as Nostradamus. Once the heavy casualties began to mount, the journal shifted its emphasis to the figure of the ghostly combatant who patriotically continues the fight. *The Occult Review* came to be interested as much in how messages are communicated as they were in their content, and this chapter explores various examples, including novels supposedly dictated by dead soldiers and Oliver Lodge's account of communicating with his dead officer son in *Raymond* (1916). This chapter ultimately argues that it is the testimony of the dead soldier that plays an important role in developing the fragmented nature of the modernist aesthetic.

Chapter 4, 'Aftershock: Malevolent Ghosts and the Problem of Memory', explores a number of tales from the post-war period which suggest that the war produced vengeful and malevolent ghosts impossible to accommodate within the home. Whilst this resurgence of Gothic hauntings suggests the uncanny, it also complicates such narratives by reflecting on how the ghost functions as a disruptive figure when tied to ambivalent accounts of mourning and memory. The ghost story provides the space for a reflection on war which is quite different from the tales explored in Chapter 1 because these malevolent ghosts reflect a cultural desire to cast off the war dead by consigning them to the past. This chapter thus explores a truly Gothic representation of the ghost which seeks to contain, but also demonise, the war dead. Tales by E. F. Benson and M. R. James, among others, suggest that survivors of the war have irrevocably lost their sense of identity, that what is required is a new strategy by which one might lay the ghosts of the conflict finally to rest – also a feature of the poetry of Richard Aldington and Robert Graves during this period. The horror of the war and how to overcome it are also explored in Dennis Wheatley's *The Devil Rides Out* (1934), which, if not a ghost story, does, through its use of the myth of Osiris, explore how anxieties about the fragmented bodies of the war dead haunt the culture of the 1930s. Dorothy L. Sayers, in *The Nine Tailors* (1934), also highlights strategies for laying to rest the ghosts of the war and the memories that they provoke. My 'Conclusion: Ghostly Afterlives' explores more recent representations of the war in writing by Susan Hill, Pat Barker and others, which interrogates how the war is still commemorated within competing models of cultural memory.

This study argues that ghosts played an important role in the cultural imaginary of the period during and just after World War One. They are complex figures employed to address a diverse range of contexts which are all related to trauma. The ghost story shapes the representation of the seemingly traumatised amnesiac who is brought back to life in the home. Ghosts also functions as a source of terror because they will not leave the post-war world alone and so continue to traumatise it. Ultimately, the ghost makes visible what a culture struggles to accept, define and move beyond – the trauma of the war itself.

Notes

1. See Terry Castle's 'The Spectralization of the Other in The Mysteries of Udolpho', in *The Female Thermometer: Eighteenth-Century Culture and the Invention of the Unconscious* (Oxford: Oxford University Press, 1995), pp. 120–39.
2. W. Scott Poole also explores Freud's 'The Uncanny' within the context of war trauma in *Wasteland: The Great War and the Origins of Modern Horror*

(Berkeley: Counterpoint, 2018), 107–13, as well as making brief reference to shell-shock, which is discussed in depth in Chapters 1 and 2 of my study.
3. This classic model of trauma has been challenged by critics who engage with colonial, post-colonial and more conceptually nuanced gender contexts. See Gert Buelens, Sam Durrant and Robert Eaglestone, eds, *The Future of Trauma Theory: Contemporary Literary and Cultural Criticism* (London: Routledge, 2014), and Michelle Balaev, ed., *Contemporary Approaches in Literary Trauma Theory* (Basingstoke: Palgrave, 2014).
4. See Ruth Leys, *Trauma: A Genealogy* (London: University of Chicago Press, 2000), pp. 266–97.
5. It is important to acknowledge that Caruth's approach says much about the continental influences on critical theory in the 1990s and that her work has been accused of overlooking the political and national contexts of specific elaborations of trauma. Roger Luckhurst, in *The Trauma Question* (London: Routledge, 2008), rightly points out that Freud's model of trauma should be seen as the product of pre-existing scientific theories, which are largely overlooked by Caruth's emphasis on close readings of texts.
6. Whom we see as the narrator at this point determines how we read the text. If Jekyll kills Hyde, then the forces of order triumph; if Hyde kills Jekyll, then the negative forces of social and sexual repression, which have created Hyde, prevail.
7. Theories of degeneration were popular at the time; Edwin Lankester, in *Degeneration: A Chapter in Darwinism* (1880), and Max Nordau, in *Degeneration* (1892), are just two such prominent examples. See also Elaine Showalter's *Sexual Anarchy: Gender and Culture at the Fin de Siècle* (London: Virago, 1992).
8. See Roger Luckhurst's *The Invention of Telepathy, 1870–1901*, (Oxford: Oxford University Press, 2002).
9. See also Leo Ruickbie's *Angels in the Trenches: Spiritualism, Superstition and the Supernatural During the First World War* (London: Robinson, 2018).

Chapter 1

The Psychology of War: Gothic and the Redirection of the Uncanny

This chapter explores how plots centred on family togetherness or romance were used to manage representations of trauma in stories about soldiers returning from World War One. The focus is on stories that encapsulate anxieties around homecoming. These stories both evoke the Freudian uncanny and move beyond it by emphasising that the home becomes the place where identity is restored. These restorations take place within reassuring, textually familiar plots about positive family ties which undo the otherwise radical potential of the disruptive Gothic ghost. The ghost story haunts accounts of traumatised soldiers, but the soldier's return to health casts off the ghost-like figures that they have become.

It was noted in the Introduction that the ghosts of war bear some imprint from ghosts who are familiar from the Walpolean tradition. Like the ghost of Hamlet's father, they demand to be remembered and are often seeking revenge. In Walpole there are also family dramas and political dynasties which become haunted by figures from the past. The family is disrupted by the demands of the political plot which illustrates that private and public worlds are hostile to each other. This is a tension which underpins many of the tales discussed here about soldiers returning from dangerous duty to enter the private world of the home. These soldiers need to be demobilised to enable their entry into the home, even while the home functions to help restore their pre-war selves. These narratives also reflect the anti-Enlightenment ethos of Walpole's novel as they place the emphasis on emotional loss and psychological disorientation, even while they advance some model of a cure. The return to the pre-war self is, as we shall see, a difficult restoration because the war-produced self is often a stubborn figure who is difficult to consign to the past – like Walpole's ghosts, they articulate a grievance, although one which love might resolve. Walpole's ghosts, like Freud's uncanny, are culturally evoked, but for specific cultural reasons become repudiated. Laying the past to rest requires an exorcism.

This chapter argues that the uncanny plays an important role in a certain type of ghost story which centres on the return of traumatised soldiers. The uncanny is a key concept in Gothic Studies, where it is critically employed to explore the feelings of unease provoked by the ghost. In tales about ghostly, psychologically missing, soldiers the uncanny is unconsciously developed and frequently challenged. Such tales often evoke a Gothic framework about lost selves and emotional disorientation, and they frequently establish familiar Gothic structures based on the ghost story, before attempting to move beyond them.

Before discussing tales which centre on the homecoming soldier-ghost it is necessary to spend some time examining how the literary context relates to psychoanalysis (and vice versa) as this underpins the conceptual space where these cultural exorcisms take place.

Uncanny Contexts

The Introduction outlined how World War One shaped Freud's writings on trauma. Freud's 'The Uncanny' (1919) plays a key role in his attempt to understand the relationship between the living and the dead, especially whether thoughts of the dead are inevitably traumatic because they focus on lost loved ones. There is ambivalence here because, while the dead generate feelings of grief, the ghost suggests that the dead do not quite die. The ghost as a purely Gothic entity represents a horror that the dead will not stay dead, whereas the non-malevolent ghost provides reassurance that love survives.

It is important to note how Freud accepts from the outset that there are problems with defining the uncanny; indeed, he admits that it 'is not always used in a definable sense, so that it tends to coincide with what excites fear in general' (Freud 1990b: 339). The experience is particularly difficult to locate in time; as Freud acknowledges, 'It is long since he has experienced or heard anything which has given him an uncanny impression,' so much so that 'he must start by translating himself into that state of feeling, by awakening in himself the possibility of experiencing it' (340). This purposeful regression leads him to conclude that the uncanny is found in the past and linked to often painful memories because 'the uncanny is that class of the frightening which leads back to what is known of old and long familiar' (340). It is also topographically difficult to locate because the term *heimlich*, which relates to the home, has been infiltrated by the *unheimlich* place of the non-home so that '*Unheimlich* is in some way or other a sub-species of *heimlich*' (347). That the home becomes reconfigured by the presence of uncanniness implicitly reworks, as we shall see, concerns about the returning soldier. As I noted in my Introduction, Freud concludes that 'The uncanny as it is depicted in *literature*, in stories and imaginative productions […] is a much more fertile province than the uncanny in real life' (Freud 1990b: 372, italics in original). Literature constitutes the fictional form through which real experience is communicated; that experience is one which, in Freud's essay, typically centres on ghosts and the return of the dead, which turns his essay into a type of ghost story (to the degree that it tells a story about ghosts). The reference to literature also, paradoxically, implicates the idea of plot as one way of attempting to manage a return to *heimlich* forms of familiarity. It is for this reason that his essay critically reads Hoffmann's 'The Sandman' (1817) as a narrative expression of an uncanny return. His reading of the tale addresses it as a disrupted love story by posing the question 'why does the Sand-Man always appear as a disturber of love?' (Freud 1990b: 353), before noting all the romantic and familial relationships that the Sandman destroys. Freud answers his question by arguing that the Sandman represents a fear of the castrating father whose presence unsettles all forms of emotional ties – and so makes the home an *unheimlich* place. The tales discussed in this chapter critically nuance the literary expression of a Gothic uncanniness by making the home a safe place after all, frequently by introducing romance as a way of moving beyond the Gothic uncanny – and yet the restored soldier, symbolically brought back to life in the home, has, in their traumatised form, posed a particular *unheimlich* problem for the home. How plots indebted to the Gothic employ romantic plot devices as an attempt to manage trauma is related to restoring, or emplotting, the traumatised subject back into the home – or back into love. A new complex form of the Gothic romance is thereby produced as a way of challenging the lack of emotional consolation that we find in the uncanny. Ann-Marie Einhaus notes that romance stories were popular during the war because they made the war 'both more bearable and easier to grasp within the framework of well-known generic formulae' (Einhaus 2013: 91). The tales described below indicate how frequently the Gothic and the romance became blurred as romance provided reassuring resolutions to Gothic plots centred on trauma.

The ambivalences and ambiguities of Freud's essay (about unhomely homes and the metaphysical status of the living dead) enable us to read it as a war story focused on the idea of home. This elision between the living and the dead and the past and the present was also a feature of Walpole's ghosts. Freud's concern that the unhomely and homely might become elided, combined with the lack of clarity about whether the dead are really dead, blurs the distinction between home front and battle front precisely because of familial anxieties about the welfare of loved ones involved in the fighting (including Freud's concerns about his own sons). At the centre of Freud's analysis is his reading of Hoffmann's 'The Sandman'; however, this is not the only text analysed in 'The Uncanny'. Freud notes:

> In the middle of the isolation of war-time a number of the English *Strand* Magazine fell into my hands; and, among other somewhat redundant matter, I read a story about a young married couple who move into a furnished house in which there is a curiously shaped table with carvings of crocodiles on it [...] the table causes ghostly crocodiles to haunt the place, or [...] the wooden monsters come to life in the dark [...]. It was a naïve enough story, but the uncanny feeling it produced was quite remarkable. (Freud 1990b: 367)

The tale that Freud refers to is 'Inexplicable' by L. G. (Lucy Gertrude) Moberly, a popular novelist, short story writer and poet, who wrote the war poem 'Commandeered' (1914). 'Inexplicable' was published in *The Strand* in December 1917 and appears between an article by the war correspondent Ellis Ashmead-Bartlett titled 'Life on a Battleship' and an equally lavishly illustrated, multi-authored piece on 'What is the Greatest Deed of Valour?'[1] The idea of the invaded home is central to Moberly's tale and Freud's formulation of the uncanny. The tale is worth discussing in some depth as it demonstrates how the uncanny, as Freud defines it, is shaped by anxieties around the war in which a narrative about ghostly forms takes precedence.

The story is told from the point of view of an unnamed woman looking to rent a house for herself and her husband, Hugh, in a London suburb. The houses in the area are substantial but tinged with decay, with 'a generally unkempt air about the whole place' (Moberly 1917: 572). One property seems to stand out as 'a very delightful house, well arranged, well built, with a nice piece of garden at the back, and plenty of accommodation' (572). The interior, however, tells a story of neglect. The narrator and her husband find themselves 'literally wading through seas of dust, for never in the whole course of my existence have I seen any house so dusty as that house. Our feet sank into a thick powder' (573). The house becomes associated with death as they find themselves wading through the epidermal remains of previous tenants. The discovery of an ornate table with embossed alligators (not crocodiles, as Freud would have it) represents a point of life in this house of the dead. The narrator notes of these figures that 'as the light fell full on the scaly bodies they had an extraordinary look of life, and the little sinister heads with the small evil eyes seemed to move' (572). This savage, definitively *unheimlich* object represents all that is wild and which cannot be accommodated within the 'homely' (Freud 1990b: 342). This is a story without any recognisable plot elements that explain the presence of these alligators and invites a psychoanalytical approach to the tale because no obvious social or historical meaning appears. In 'Inexplicable', the house agent's clerk who shows them round tells them that 'The table goes with the house [...] it is really like a fixture, it goes with the house' (Moberly 1917: 572). For the narrator, this suggestion becomes mysteriously horrific when she records that 'in the dimness that had temporarily descended upon my brain I thought he went on repeating, like a parrot-cry, "It goes with the house. It goes with the house"' (573). Repetition is a feature of the uncanny: the urge to repeat identifies the place where a repression has occurred and needs to be worked through (Freud 1990b: 359–60). That 'Inexplicable' explores the presence of death in life is evident from the observations of Hugh, who detects 'a sort of smell in here of decaying vegetation' (Moberly 1917: 574). A visit from a friend, Jack, emphasises the otherworldly presence in the house when he associates the strange smell with a swamp in New Guinea that he had once crossed in the night on a journey when one of his party was killed by an alligator. This story within the story indicates the presence of a narrative about colonial conflict, which, as we shall see, implicates the war. The servants leave the property as they see strange creatures crawling through it, and the narrator and her husband become aware of alligator forms that predatorily roam through their suburban house until Hugh burns the table and order is restored.

John Zilcosky reads 'Inexplicable' as a war narrative which is both specific and general. The specific reference to Jack's experiences in New Guinea represents 'the political unconscious' in which 'The colonies will strike back. England's sons will die in New Guinea. If they return at all, it will be as corpses, rankly "decaying" like the swamps themselves' Zilcosky 2013: 475). It is notable that in the immediate years following the war, *The Strand* published several items about Lawrence of Arabia and short stories that represented British triumph in orientalist contexts. However, in 1917, British authority in both European and non-European contexts (especially after Gallipoli) is not so clear. The general war anxiety that Zilcosky observes in the tale is related to Freud's reference in 'The Uncanny' to Hauff's fairy story 'The Severed Hand' (1826), in which Freud notes the images of 'Dismembered limbs, a severed head, a hand cut off at the wrist' and in another tale 'feet which dance by themselves' (Freud 1990b: 366). Zilcosky convincingly reads this moment as reflecting the 'uncanny amputated, quivering bodies wavering between life and death' (2013: 476) which shaped the immediate post-war world and consequently underpin Freud's model of the uncanny.[2] Such a view of wounded soldiers is reflected in Virginia Woolf's account in 1920 of amputee veterans at Waterloo station, 'dreadful looking spiders propelling themselves along the platform' (Woolf 1980: 93). The pervasive mood of anxiety which colours 'Inexplicable' also reflects these issues, but here with a specific focus on the inanimate becoming animate. The coming to life of the inanimate alligators resembles Freud's discussion of the coming to life of the doll of Olympia in Hoffmann's 'The Sandman' with uncanny feelings being evoked 'when an inanimate object becomes too much like an animate one' (Freud 1990b: 354); this is also reflected in how statues and paintings in *The Castle of Otranto* come to life. The fear of castration that he sees as central to Hoffmann's tale reflects the concern of becoming unmanned during the war. Jack's recollection about New Guinea in Moberly's tale leaves him in a very fragile state, so that Hugh says '"I'll help you into bed. You've had a bit of shaking,"' to which Jack replies with '"Yes – a bit of shaking"' as they leave the room (Moberly 1917: 578).

While Zilcosky reads the tale as representing anxieties about shell-shock, which would reappear in 'The Uncanny', an issue explored later in this chapter, the return of the dead represented by the alligators is also significant. In 'The Uncanny', Freud claims that it is feelings about the return of the dead, often in spectral form, which constitutes a key characteristic of the uncanny. In 'Inexplicable', not only does the house smell of death; it evokes, in Jack, the memory of a specific death which is imaginatively brought back to life. The idea that the dead may become alive is also recalled through images of the ghost, which Luke Thurston has helpfully discussed in relation to ideas about hospitality.

For Thurston, the radical elements within a ghost story subsist when the plot fails to explain the presence of the ghost. Thurston sees narrative structure, or plot, as like a 'host' who entertains the presence of a troubling 'guest' who disrupts the comparative calm induced by familiar narrative props. In this way, ghost stories are guest stories which assert an unresolvable tension between 'narrative reality and an absolute otherness' (Thurston 2012: 3). The ghost represents an ontologically challenging version of a post-mortem life which cannot be made explicable and so defies narrative attempts to contain it. This blurring of the living with the dead (the inanimate with the animate) to create a new version of life (those ghostly alligators) appears to be a radical challenge to ideas of meaning. This raises questions about the limits of psychoanalysis when confronted by the apparently inexplicable, which explains why Freud found Moberly's tale uncanny. That psychoanalysis might provide a way of decoding the ghost and so make meaning appear within otherwise seemingly cryptic symbolic forms (such as roving alligators) explains why psychoanalytical processes appear so often in ghost stories of the time. The uncanniness of psychoanalysis is worth exploring in depth as it indicates how forms of analysis were closely related to reading, and making sense of, the spectre.

Reading Ghosts and Lost Selves

The tales of war trauma explored in this chapter invite a psychoanalytical explanation which cannot always be produced. The reaching out for reason can be regarded as an Enlightenment impulse even while the cause of disruption, the war, can be attributed to the type of anti-Enlightenment mentality which Jonathan Dent observed in *The Castle of Otranto*. The ambition to decode, contain and so manage trauma is what lies at the heart of these stories, and it is reflected in the ending of Moberly's tale. 'Inexplicable' concludes in a moment which reaches out to the reader. The narrator, at a loss to account for the strange occurrences which have taken place in the house, states that 'it was many a long day before I could live down those weird experiences, and even now they are to me quite inexplicable. Does any explanation of it all occur to you?' (Moberly 1917: 581). This inexplicability could be linked to the war itself, or it could be that the turn to the reader is simply rhetorical, since on one level the tale seems to make no sense. Indeed, it appears to entertain the radically elusive properties of the spectral that Thurston sees as beyond conventional models of meaning. The tale poses the same difficulties of interpretation and analysis which Freud sees as central to an analysis of the uncanny. The invitation to read and make sense should, however, be seen as an invitation to try to force the tale to surrender its symbolic reality. Freud's interest in Moberly's story is, in part, generated by this ambition, seeing as he too, in 'The Uncanny', attempts a symbolic decoding of various fantastical narratives. This leads Freud to conclude that the results produced by a positive psychoanalytical examination seem to bestow a magical status on psychoanalysis, so that 'I should not be surprised to hear that psychoanalysis, which is concerned with laying bare [...] hidden forces, has itself become uncanny to many people for that very reason' (Freud 1990b: 366). During the period, psychoanalysis represents a specific manifestation of the ghostly as its seemingly occult processes are employed to explain what the ghost represents. As Dale Townshend notes, 'In Gothic, as in psychoanalysis, spectrality threatens whenever the dead remain unsatisfied, whenever the time of grief is even slightly out of joint' (Townshend 2008: 78). The uncanny constitutes a meta-narrative about ghosts which appears in ghost stories that reflect directly on psychoanalytical procedure and which relate to feelings of loss.

Published in *The Strand* in 1919, 'The Living Ghost' by Burton Kline is not about war, but it is about how to decode ghosts and has points of contact to 'lost memory' war stories which were popular in *The Strand* at the time. The narrator is Dr Carver, a psychologist who, at a social gathering on a yacht owned by a surgeon, Dr Viall, is taunted by Viall about the comparatively unscientific status of his profession when compared to surgery. Viall states:

> 'your science is fashioned out of disease. We surgeons are taught anatomy on fairly normal bodies. But the very name of your study is a misnomer. It should be spelled, as I've sometimes heard it pronounced – sickology. Your examinations are all of sick minds.' (Kline 1919: 450)

Viall (whose name suggests 'vial', but also that he is vile) presents Carver (whose name suggests that he is a surgeon of the mind) with a problem. Viall recounts that, some years before, he had attended an ailing MP and had taken up residence in a nearby old house in order to be on call as necessary. While there, he claims to have woken from his dreams to find himself transported back into the Walpolean era of the eighteenth century, which appears to him as a material vision in which 'My very bed had been transformed. Above it all was a silken canopy, and draped from it were lacy curtains. To make sure that I was not deceived I even reached out to touch them' (451). Over successive nights he sees a young woman murdered by a man, possibly a servant, at the behest of his wife in order to steal some jewels. The young woman's body is dragged downstairs and placed in a grave prepared for her in the kitchen. When the man attempts to place a heavy flagstone on top, his wife pushes him in so that he shares the grave, and she keeps the jewels to herself. Theft replaces inheritance, a theme familiar from *The Castle of Otranto*.

Viall asserts a supernatural provenance for these visions and, in a common type of ghost story, the resolution would have plausibly involved a journey to the house and a raising of the flagstone to confirm the reality of the vision. Viall taunts Carver that he must be 'stumped' by such a problem, and Carver's mulling takes the tale in a psychological, rather than supernatural, direction:

> I was stumped, as he put it, and for a far better reason than he himself imagined. To anyone trained to observe it, Dr. Viall had just bared his secretmost self in his dream; yet how was it possible for me to betray him before a merry party at dinner? A man who has dreams like that has himself done murder. He may not have vulgarly put a human being to death, as I was sure Dr. Viall

had not; but I gazed at my eminent host and wondered what it was he had done. (456)

Carver denies the reality of the experience and sees it solely as a highly symbolic dream. However, his analysis indicates that what the dream articulates is a 'secretmost self' that is clearly different from the conscious self. This hidden version of the subject is, to Carver's mind, capable of murder and manifests as a repressed set of desires which the conscious Viall is clearly incapable of relating to himself. However, at another level, Kline's story suggests that these impulses are not repressed because they are symbolically recollected within the dream. Displacement into dream symbolism thus constitutes a form of remembering something which Viall has forgotten. The murderous impulse identified by Carver does not manifest as a classic instance of repression, which would typically present itself in psychosomatic ways. His dream concerns memory as it relates both to an earlier experience and also to another present self who disguises the past in the familiar narrative form of a mystery story.

The dream reads like a fairly conventional ghost story, one which requires an explanation to resolve the plot which the anticipated resurrection of the ghost would complete. As in Walpole, the ghost is the bearer of secrets and these secrets are related to Viall's alternative self, which at this stage he is unable to acknowledge. What is contained within the self (that play on vial) is what the completed narrative will reveal. Carver is aware of the disjunction between the dinner party and the act of murder but is also conscious that, at heart, the vision represents a confession.

Carver is forced into decoding the dream. He advances an argument that the vision reflects Viall's guilty rejection of a former lover, one who was a bit old-fashioned in her views: hence the eighteenth-century setting. He notes Viall's hesitation in confirming this reading and interprets that as a sign of a guilty conscience – but also as a concealed longing for this now long-lost woman whose unfair rejection he regrets. It is revealed that Viall had knowingly falsely accused a woman of an infidelity in order to bring the relationship to an end, and this is why she appears in the narrative as a victim who has been the subject of a crime (a defamation). In effect, Viall has murdered his love for her. He is forced to recognise the reality of the analysis and admits:

> 'Now nothing is left me but the thought of her; the thought of that lonely lovely ghost I sent into the world, to haunt me all my life. I have passed my life in holding out my hand to a ghost. Now it is too late.' (Kline 1919: 459)

However, it transpires that the guests on the yacht, who were selected by a friend of Viall's, include 'a charming young widow' (450), who, at the end, appears to be the woman in the story; she says Viall's name and faints – and so the plot is completed.

'The Living Ghost' takes a certain type of ghost story grounded in a supernatural tradition and decodes it by employing psychoanalytical techniques. Psychoanalysis, as a procedure, thus becomes part of a narrative *about* ghosts which indicates the strange reciprocal relationship between the ghost story and psychoanalysis in 1919. As Townshend notes, 'Etched deeply into the unconscious of Gothic discourse' there is 'the reality of thwarted mourning and the inevitable return of the ghostly dead' (Townshend 2008: 79), which is also a characteristic of psychoanalysis at this time. The optimistic conclusion of Kline's tale affirms that love will triumph in the end, and it is the curative possibilities of love that so many of these psychological stories champion as a way of decoding and so laying the ghost to rest. Freud's reading of 'The Sandman' is procedurally emulated in Carver's reading of Viall's dream and both conclude with the identification of a disavowed love as being the chief reason for symbolic displacements. Identifying the reasons for this displacement brings into focus an older self which 'is known of old and long familiar' (Freud 1990b: 340). How to engage with that apparently lost self is an issue that appears repeatedly in stories about psychologically missing, although physically present, traumatised soldiers. Kate McLoughlin has noted that representations of returning soldiers assert their ghost-like liminality because 'the veteran is, inescapably, no longer what he was, and so has a built-in *has-been-ness*' which disrupts conventional 'ideas regarding the persistence and stability of the self' (McLoughlin 2018: 77, italics in original). The tales discussed below both reflect and deny this oxymoronic state by asserting that the temporary discontinuous self can be eradicated. Soldiers who are represented as 'missing' rather than dead provide a way of nuancing the liminality of the ghost, since they become subjects who are also absent, but with the potential to be present at a later date. The home plays a key role in this and its uncanny status is worth exploring as it provides a key context for a number of our stories.

Uncanny Homes

By reading Freud's essay as a ghost story about the war it becomes possible to regard the collapsing of the 'homely' with the 'unhomely' as generated out of the erasure between the home and the battlefield.

This elision appears in Sassoon's *Memoirs of an Infantry Officer* (1930), where the front becomes ghosted by the home and the home by a version of the front. On the eve of battle, Sassoon recalls being in 'a narrow chamber (which) contained a foggy mirror and a clock. The clock wasn't ticking, but its dumb face stared at me, an idiot reminder of real rooms and desirable domesticity' (Sassoon 1997: 151). Conversely, when he returns home to stay with an aunt he notes that 'At one end of the garden three poplars tapered against the stars; they seemed like sentries guarding a prisoner. Across the orchard grass, Aunt Evelyn's white beehives glimmered in the moonlight like bones' (200). Sassoon comes to inhabit an uncanny, conceptual no-man's-land in which the home is taken to the front and the front taken to the home, symbolically articulating a dystopian version of the soldier's return.[3]

For Freud, the experience of the uncanny is one in which the subject seems to be lost as they work through sensations which are metaphysically present but epistemologically absent. The sensations of uncanniness cannot be turned into knowledge other than that of a strictly intuitive kind, in which it is difficult to verify the main point of reference. 'The Uncanny' is shaped by an implicit discourse about those who are missing (and not confirmed as killed) and those who miss them. As noted in the Introduction, for Freud, 'Many people experience the feeling in the highest degree in relation to death and dead bodies, to the return of the dead, and to spirits and ghosts' (Freud 1990b: 364). It is these restless spirits who reflect the idea of the missing. They are not dead but are an absent presence who may be alive in some other form. The spirit represents a liminal presence who may be brought back to life and so reanimated. If the missing soldier can be seen as in a symbolic limbo, then this is also reflected in those who hope for their return. Freud notes that the uncanny is also characterised by 'wish and fulfilment' (Freud 1990b: 371), especially in relation to the dead whom we wish to see returned to us. Freud's essay is about loss, but it is also about a possible reconnection with the dead. Death is not quite the end for Freud, and decoding the ghost provides a way of trying to understand how a culture regards death, but also how a culture reflects on the symbolic function of the home.

The representation of the home and the way that it draws upon feelings of the uncanny is crucial to exploring how it is evoked and challenged in tales which use the home as the place where a symbolic resurrection takes place. Freud's essay draws upon cultural anxieties about the war because the war dead are constituted as figures of the uncanny. The home, romance and family togetherness represent attempts to overcome the feelings of anxiety, and forms of mourning that characterise the uncanny. The spectral soldier who is therapeutically resurrected in the home is a complex figure – a mixture of surface (tics, forgetfulness, silence) and depth (the need for love, reassurance, the desire to belong). A key issue is how the soldier comes to re-engage with the pre-war self. In order to do this, they need to reconnect with love as a way of banishing their new uncanny self.

Loving the Ghost

'A Case of Lost Memory' (1919), by the American science fiction and mystery writer Edwin Balmer, centres on a wealthy English-born American socialite, Captain Paul Railsford, who has been posted as missing in action whilst fighting in France. The telegram announcing this arrives in Chicago before his fiancée, Corinna, has received final letters from him. Corinna, unsure whether Paul is alive or not, carries on writing to him because 'not to write was to give up on him' (Balmer 1919: 426). In one of his last letters, Paul refers to being wounded and helped to safety by one of his men, Stanley Merkowitz, who subsequently dies. He asks Corinna to help Merkowitz's family, who live in a rundown part of Chicago. Much of the story addresses Corinna's nervousness about visiting such a poor part of the city, and when she goes there she finds herself followed by a man whom she decides is not a 'tramp' nor a 'criminal' but possibly a 'Socialist' or 'Anarchist' and perhaps a member of the revolutionary group, the Industrial Workers of the World, which was established in Chicago in 1905 (429). This man attempts a sexual assault on Corinna, but she is rescued by Paul, who has lost his memory but recalled the address of Merkowitz, and has been living rough in the neighbourhood. However, just before the assault she had already encountered Paul – alive, after all – who, at this point, does not know who she is. Corinna's encounter with Paul is tinged with feelings of loss and erotic abandonment:

> She drew back from him, her pulses pressing as though they would burst the beating thing in her breast. Her face, her hands, all her body was hot and wet. To have Paul back from beyond the seas, from the battle, and from the shell-hole where he had lain stunned, back from the hospital, back from 'missing' – to be able to see him, touch him, hold him, and yet not to have him; for him not to know her, or to know himself! (432)

The erotic connections between his war experiences, his physical self and her aroused body are all too clear. At this point, he is still 'missing' because he does not know who she is and therefore who he is. His ghost-like state is closely aligned with his now scruffy appearance, which suggests a downward social slide into a form of social invisibility. His identity is restored when he sees Corinna attacked, and his coming to life in the fight prompts a rejuvenated manliness which he had lost in his wounded state. This is a repeated trope in many of these war stories, in which emasculated men are required to reconnect with their latent masculinity. Love becomes the means through which the self is restored, but there is also a more primitive narrative here which centres on sexual competition over Corinna. Her sexualised response on seeing Paul is the key uncanny element in the story as it contravenes other narrative forms chastely centred on romantic love. The ostensible realist mode, in which Paul is discovered, saved and returned, is at odds with the narrative about sexuality and Freud notes that uncanny affect often appears within an aesthetic of 'common reality' (Freud 1990b: 374), which in the tale is visibly established by the urban character of the neighbourhood and narratively structured through the redemptive tale of romantic feeling. What is uncanny for Freud is the return of primitive feelings which civilisation had seemingly banished – or the presence of the unreal within the context of the real (rather like Walpole's statues and paintings). It is Corinna's sexual yearning for Paul which brings him back to life, but this is at odds with the romantic narrative structure of the story which ultimately rests on the ambition to domesticate Paul by bringing him back to the home.

Corinna's emotional disturbance is also reflected in the suggested social disturbance manifested in the fight between the wealthy Paul and the rapacious socialist. Emotional and social realities are disorientating and these feelings of turmoil can be related to the war. Vera Brittain, in *Testament of Youth* (1933), notes of the immediate post-war period that 'now the universe had become irrational, and nothing was turning out as it once seemed to have been ordained' (Brittain 2014: 259). This type of disruption is in keeping with the anti-Enlightenment intervention associated with war. Conventional models of progress (social, economic, cultural) no longer work. Jonathan Dent notes how the focus of eighteenth-century Gothic on war and attendant moments of unrest 'draws attention to the repression of violent incidents' (Dent 2016: 58), in Enlightenment historiographies. The Gothic represents 'a return of the repressed' (Dent 2016: 57), which forces a culture to acknowledge what it would rather dismiss. This new reality is thus indebted to an older form of the Gothic, as it appears within narratives of the uncanny. 'A Case of Lost Memory' retains many key aspects of the uncanny, but ultimately it is a story of return and reconciliation. It incorporates references to sexuality and lost selves which are familiar from the inception of a Gothic tradition founded upon tabooed desires and conflicted models of subjectivity – a tradition which both feeds into the uncanny and is symbiotically shaped by it. However, the tale also rejects this disorientation. The socialist loses his fight and Paul comes home, but not before other elements of the uncanny have appeared.

While the tale focuses on the return of a psychologically restored Paul, nevertheless a new version of the self appears. This version of Paul may seem dazed and confusedly attached to a notion of place associated with one of his men, but it also represents an alternative version of Paul, who has cast off his privileged life in order to participate in the social world of an impoverished urban district (a social concern which he had addressed in his letters to Corinna). Superficially, this lost version of Paul glosses Freud's idea about an uncanny 'doubling, dividing and interchanging of the self' (Freud 1990b: 356), but it is one without any obvious agency (both socially and psychologically) as Paul's 'other' self is clearly not meant to be him. His return sidesteps this issue of the double and his return to his true self follows an alternative symbolic arc of the uncanny in which 'the re-animation of the dead' (Freud 1990b: 369) becomes a key factor. Ultimately, romantic love and a return to the home eradicates the uncanny by restoring Paul to himself.

'A Case of Lost Memory' addresses the issue of how society treats the psychologically damaged returning soldier, a figure who appears to be ghost-like, as he is physically present but mentally absent. Paul has come home but not in any obviously Freudian way, since his restoration through romantic love undoes the uncanny place of the home and overcomes his symbolic ghostly identity. Significantly, the specific incident that led to his memory loss does not seem to require a therapeutic intervention. Rather, it is love which is most important, seeing as the story of a ghostly lost self transforms into a tale about romance and redemption. The story thus invokes the war in its use of the uncanny and at the end turns away from the uncanny due to specific cultural ambitions for the healthy restoration of the returning soldier.

The idea of 'missing' as a notably liminal condition appears in 'The Unbolted Door' by Marie Belloc Lowndes, and again it is love, although of a different kind, which plays an important role.[4] This story, published in the *Fortnightly Review* in 1929, focuses on the marital problems of grieving parents, Mr and Mrs Torquil, whose son, John, was posted missing in 1918. The tale is set in 1924 on the night before the Armistice commemoration. An old servant explains to a new servant that '"Mrs. Torquil knew well enough what 'missing' meant. But the master, he just couldn't bring himself to believe his son – his heir, too, mind you – had gone"' (Lowndes 1931: 208), which references an issue about inheritance which was a key topic of the Walpolean Gothic. They leave a door unlocked under the orders of Mr Torquil, who believes that one day his son will return. The story focuses on the tensions between Mr and Mrs Torquil and the petty resentments they harbour, in part because, for Mrs Torquil, as 'dearly as he loved her, close as they were to one another, she had always known that John cared most for his inarticulate father' (208). The couple had heard the news of their son's disappearance when Mr Torquil was recuperating at home from his own war wounds, and he has become socially and emotionally withdrawn. The fact that John is missing gives him solace because he 'had gone on not only hoping against hope, but firmly convinced that, from the depths of some German prison, or even from some German mental home, the boy would come back' (210). Mrs Torquil notes how aged her husband has become while she has retained her youthful looks, and such is the nature of their emotional and physical estrangement that 'For the first time in her life, to-night, Anne asked herself, with a touch of unease, if her husband was as unhappy as she was herself' (210), even as she becomes aware of the 'chasm which was yawning wider and wider' between them (211). As the clock nears midnight and the day of the Armistice commemoration approaches, 'There came over her an odd, unexpected impulse. Just to go out and bid him good night. But she restrained that impulse' (214). The couple sleep in separate rooms and lead largely separate lives, a division that is both asserted and erased at the story's end. At the climax of the tale, just after midnight, 'the handle of the unbolted door in the hall below turned in the darkness, and there came an upward rush of cold air' (214). After this, for Mrs Torquil:

> there rang out two words in a voice that she had never thought to hear again, even in another life [...]. And the words uttered in her son's voice pierced her innermost soul, for 'Poor father', was all her beloved had come back to say. (214)

Mr Torquil also heard John speak, and Mrs Torquil runs to meet him, where 'with what had become a way of forgotten tenderness, she took his hand' (215). This coming together of the couple is taken a step further when, for the first time in years, they sleep in the same room. Mr Torquil tells his wife that John '"came back for you, my darling; to comfort you", because what he heard John say was '"Dear mother"' (215), not '"Poor father"'.

The return of the dead son reunites the parents as they both believe that he returned to comfort the other because the other was in need of comfort. In effect, the two conflicting statements are what is required to overcome their grief and bring them together. This sense that John is no longer missing but truly dead, although spectrally alive, reflects the local Vicar's attempt to provide consolation after the original telegram had been received. At that time, he told Mrs Torquil that she should not be concerned about John because 'Who being dead yet liveth' (212), a biblical perspective that Mrs Torquil feels cannot yet apply to them because of her husband's view that John is not physically dead.

'The Unbolted Door' and the other tales discussed here reflect many of the impulses that we find in 'The Uncanny'. Death is not an absolute state in this symbolic world, in which reality has become obscured by the presence of ghostly forms or ghost-like states in which identity has been lost, if only temporarily. However, it is the return to the home and to parental love that overcomes the feelings of unease that the uncanny generates. The ghost is not Thurston's rebellious guest in this instance because, as a returned member of the family, they are an intrinsic aspect of the home and can, however briefly, be accommodated. Love becomes crucial as lovers are reunited in both 'A Case of Lost Memory' and 'The Unbolted Door', where the returning son reunites his parents. These tales and restored relationships are predicated on overcoming the uncanniness generated by the metaphorical presence of death. 'A Case of Lost Memory' and 'The Unbolted Door' are about how to overcome absence through love, a message which is arrived at in different ways as they engage with the Gothic at different levels of explicitness. Lowndes's tale is a ghost story in which the ghost reunites rather than disrupts. Balmer's tale could not be construed as Gothic in any generic way, but is tacitly informed by the uncanny and a symbolic ghostliness which has points of contact with a Gothic tradition. Both tales also centre on how to deal with the returning soldier and the anxieties which are generated by this experience. In 'The Uncanny', Freud cannot find a solution to the presence of cultural expressions of trauma, but these tales do because they assert that, from out of absence or death, a new life is generated, so that those damaged by the war (including parents) can be made well. These tales therefore represent attempts to manage trauma by evoking and moving beyond the uncanny.

Both tales also centre on issues of projection. Corinna's emotional and physical need for Paul brings him back to life and the Torquils' need for contact with their dead son seemingly conjures his voice, and its different messages. This may seem to elude uncanniness because of the consoling narrative resolutions, but echoes Freud's idea in 'The Uncanny' about 'the belief in the omnipotence of thoughts and the technique of magic based on that belief' (Freud 1990b: 363), which had once, for Freud, characterised primitive societies. The idea that Corinna and the Torquils are magical conjurers of their needs represents an uncanny return of desire. Tellingly, Freud sees magical projection as 'the unrestricted narcissism [...] that [...] strove to fend off the manifest prohibitions of reality' (Freud 1990b: 363). As we have seen, post-war reality is associated with a disorientation against which only the return to the home can protect. However, the issue of a narcissistic projection implicates the needs of those in grief, rather than those who have fought. Scrutinising the nature of the uncanny love of those at home becomes inseparable from how the soldier is brought back home (physically and emotionally).

'The Mirror and the Incense' by Gerald Villiers Stuart, published in *The Strand* in 1920, provides a more complex evaluation of the redemptive possibilities of love by questioning whether the affection of those who await the return of the soldier can be relied upon. This tale centres on a love affair between Lawrence Blake and Judith Heaton. Lawrence is a widely travelled adventurer who has worked as a spy: 'he wandered through China disguised as a Burman [...] through Burma disguised as a Chinaman, gathering information in bazaars as a bee gathers honey in a garden' (Stuart 1920: 120). Judith, an accomplished professional actress, has also led a colourful life, informing him of 'the wreckage of her ideals by a bigamous marriage, of her consequent vendetta against men [...] her career as a militant Suffragette' (122). This narrative of personal and political rebellion conceals another story. As part of her wish for revenge on men, Judith had tormented a man named Ellison by making him believe that she shared their love, only to tell him that her involvement was due to a role she was rehearsing for the stage, leading her to reflect that, as a result, she 'ha[d] smashed everything that was good in him as a resentful child smashes a doll' (122). She feels guilty about this, and Ellison appears later in the story, seemingly to threaten Lawrence and Judith's relationship. At the outbreak of World War One, Lawrence is sent to fight in Persia and Afghanistan, but maintains that they can stay in touch through a supernatural device. Lawrence had earlier travelled through Tibet, where he had encountered some monks who had developed an apparently magical form of 'Human wireless' (124), a telepathic ability to communicate which recalls the omnipotence of thoughts that Freud regarded as a 'narcissistic overvaluation of [...] mental processes' (Freud 1990b: 363). This highly advanced form of telepathy has not been properly developed by Westerners, but Lawrence has a solution near at hand, a mirror which he had acquired from an 'old monastery' (124) and which can unite them in a partial way. The mirror represents the possibility of a narcissistic self-reflection but its powers are more complex than that as it enables them not just to see each other, but to see how each of them sees the other at any given moment. The process requires the burning of incense and Lawrence tells Judith that 'When you burn it and look into the mirror through the smoke, you will see yourself exactly as I am thinking of you' (124). For Lawrence, this will be a vision conjured out of wisdom, since it will be 'the *you* God planned, the *you* of the past and the future, the vision wonderful which I have seen through all the dust of the earth' (124, italics in original). The supernatural mirror becomes a device through which perceptions are projected and creates a line of communication that is about their shared feeling for each other. It is the one uncanny device in what is otherwise a conventional romantic story about parted lovers. The mirror projects an idealised version of her but she knows, because of her treatment of Ellison, that it is an unreal vision. She stares into the mirror, losing 'faith in herself, in her personality' (125) as she becomes concerned that Lawrence loves somebody who is not really Judith.

As in the other tales discussed here, the emphasis is on the loss of self during a time of war. Judith may stay at home, but she loses a sense of who she is because of what is projected back to her from the war zone. In keeping with the other tales, there is both an evocation of the uncanny and a movement beyond it. The telepathic communications in the tale are one-way and distorted and, while they may seem different in kind from the uncanny, they capture a sense of misrecognition and the loss of self that Freud, in 'The Uncanny', recalls in this anecdote about a mirror:

> I was sitting alone in my *wagon-lit* compartment when a more than usually violent jerk of the train swung back the door of the adjoining washing-cabinet, and an elderly gentleman in a dressing gown and a travelling cap came in. I assumed that he had been about to leave the washing-cabinet which divides the two compartments, and had taken the wrong direction and come into my compartment by mistake. Jumping up with the intention of putting him right, I at once realized to my dismay that the intruder was nothing but my own reflection in the looking glass of the open door. I can still recollect that I thoroughly disliked his appearance. (Freud 1990b: 371)

For Freud, this moment represents an encounter with a double whom we do not 'recognize', and the dislike constitutes 'a vestigial trace of that older reaction which feels the double to be something uncanny' (Freud 1990b: 371). The image both is and is not us. In Freud's anecdote, the other seems to be another, although one whose disagreeable appearance is related to the 'elderly' image that he sees. Self-knowledge of an abstract kind is generated by the encounter with an unflattering version of the self. Such a reflection might seem to be different in kind to Judith's idealisation, but it is similar because Lawrence sees her in this way as he does not know about Ellison. Judith seeks an antidote to this problem, one which moves beyond the strictly Freudian uncanny, by looking in her own mirror, not Lawrence's, and there sees a face that she knows only all too well:

> The face of a woman men kissed lightly, in a moment of passion. There was a devil behind the eyes, beckoning them towards the soft red lips which curved below. What was the use of trying to live on a summit with a face like that, a devil-haunted face? What was the use of struggling? (Stuart 1920: 125)

In this instance, she sees herself as she imagines most men see her, and yet for her it is a vision with which she identifies. Judith is thus caught between Lawrence's idealism and her own and other men's erotic projection of the *femme fatale*. It is between the pull of these two visions that a new version of selfhood becomes negotiated. Later in the tale, Judith looks into the magic mirror and witnesses a distorted version of what she had seen in her own mirror: she sees 'This beautiful harpy, this subtly-baited trap, this intellect rejoicing in the devastation of spirit, in evil for evil's sake, in the destruction of all good and human impulses. It was a caricature, the opposite pole of idealism' (126).

The mirror at this point is linked to, but also moves beyond, the idea of the double that Freud outlines in 'The Uncanny'. For Freud, the double appears in the subject's early development as it progresses through a stage of 'primary narcissism' in which the subject triumphs over time and mortality, but thereafter 'the "double" reverses this aspect. From having been an assurance of immortality, it becomes the uncanny harbinger of death' (Freud 1990b: 357). We become aware of our finite lives at this point, and so this double has both negative and positive attributes. At one level, the double represents a critically self-aware 'conscience' (Freud 1990b: 357), but this check to Id-like impulses also indicates that it is a potential force of repression. As Freud notes, there is 'death' here, which is echoed in his own self-reflection, in the 'elderly gentleman' that he sees in the mirror. The problem confronted by Freud is how to reach out for what is authentic because such images represent painful moments of self-identification which are concealed within instances of misrecognition. At one level, Judith recognises this version of herself as a *femme fatale*. She is both alluring and destructive, and it would be tempting to align this with Freud's account of *Thanatos* and *Eros* in *Beyond the Pleasure Principle*, were it not for the case that Judith wants to set the record straight: 'She had a pathetic hope that if she prayed very hard at the hospital [...] the mirror would relent, would reveal her as she really was, neither angel nor devil, merely a suffering, struggling woman' (Stuart 1920: 126). The problem of the lost self which runs throughout these tales is shaped by the perceptions of others and by the self confronting itself in self-reflections. The tale suggests that Lawrence's visions of her are extremes, from angel to *femme fatale*, and that neither is true, but Judith needs to know why this uncanny transformation has taken place.

Judith's anxieties precipitate a nervous breakdown, and it is while convalescing that she is reunited with Lawrence, who had been captured but subsequently escaped 'on the prisoners' death march from Kut to Mosul'. Judith witnesses 'the face of a man who has had illusions and lost them' (128). Lawrence had fought alongside Ellison, who died in captivity, but not before telling Lawrence about Judith, which had led Lawrence to believe that his own and Judith's love for each other was not real. She indicates that she knew about the changes because of the mirror. Lawrence, however, has forgotten all about the mirror, and when he does recall it, he confesses he went off it when he found that it was made in Germany. He claims that her visions must have been dreams, but, nevertheless, he concedes that somehow they had telepathically communicated and that this could be possible only if their love was genuine, and so they are reconciled.

'The Mirror and the Incense' centres on the problem of the returning soldier but also on the morality of those left behind. It is a tale about understanding the self in all its emotional complexity and about how to overcome the type of uncanniness envisaged by Freud. Doubleness implies alienation, whereas love brings subjects together in an act of forgiveness, so that, for Lawrence, 'the betrayal of you, your betrayal of Ellison, they have all gone to the creation of this "you" I love, to the bringing of us together' (130). The tale therefore envisages a way of managing post-war anxieties about the changes that have taken place in those who have fought and how those changes have transformed their perceptions of loved ones at home. At work is both a psychology and a form of politics (including a depoliticising of suffragettes) combined with a conscience which reflects on judgement and punishment. The self becomes reconstituted through these competing demands, which argue for a self that is protean and unstable – in good ways – as it adapts to change and context in a journey of self-discovery. In this fashion, these tales provide a safe way of thinking about issues of trauma and morality. Again, we witness how a tale incorporates uncanny elements within it which centre on a Gothic device, here a mirror rather than the figure of the ghost, in order to move beyond them. The trauma of war is thereby undone through safely managed emotional reconciliations in which love regains a form of purity which restores the traumatised soldier back to health – and replenishes the love of those on the home front. Romantic love again provides the antidote to feelings of loss and functions as a rebuttal of the uncanny forces which it had initially entertained (that mirror). A clear cultural script thus emerges in these stories about the need to effect a cure for the type of war-induced ailments that are associated with disorientated, putatively Gothic, uncanny states.

It was noted that Freud's account of the double appears to apply to the motif of the mirror. However, in keeping with the other stories discussed here, it is an aspect of the uncanny which is asserted and then challenged because the model of protean subjectivity that the tale explores is beyond the framework of the double. In 'A Case of Lost Memory' we also saw that Paul cannot be easily conflated with his traumatised other self because the tale more clearly addresses the possibility of a resurrected self. Both stories argue for an authentic self, the appearance of which becomes ratified within a discourse of romantic love. The return home takes us beyond the uncanny; however, how to think about the home, and how to return to it, are often more difficult in tales which centre on the return of the soldier suffering from shell-shock. The protracted presence of an alternative self which appears to be just as authentic as the supposed primary self questions the limitations of the home as the place in which a healthy psychological resurrection can be staged; the double therefore becomes an issue. A representative example of this is provided by F. Britten Austin, a war veteran who had many stories about the war published in *The Strand*.

Austin's 'A Point of Ethics' (1919) is a lost memory story published under the strapline 'What would *you* have done?' The story begins with Evelyn and Jack enjoying a celebratory meal on their first wedding anniversary. Evelyn has been married before, to Harry Tremaine, who was killed in the war and by whom she has a young daughter. As in 'A Case of Lost Memory' and 'The Unbolted Door', this is a story about the missing. Evelyn laments that 'I wish I could have got some news of him – of how he was killed. No one in the regiment seemed to know anything. It is dreadful to go out like that – no one knowing how!' (Austin 1919: 556). This becomes a cue for Harry's return and he lets himself into the flat, prompting Evelyn to see him as '*Harry's ghost!*' (556, italics in original). The tale suggests that Harry is legally dead when Jack, a lawyer, informs him that 'You are dead my friend! [...] Killed in action, October 10th 1918' (558). Jack intends to keep it that way to protect Evelyn from a charge of bigamy: 'I do not propose to make her name a public scandal. Officially you are dead. Well – remain dead' (558). Harry is recognised by his daughter and asserts ownership over the family and the flat, but is unable to account for his absence, given that he has no recollection of where he has been since being reported as killed. A fight breaks out between Jack and Harry and, after being punched, Harry comes round with a different personality, someone with the surname Durham. Harry thinks that he has been involved in a fight, during which Jack has come to his assistance and brought him back to the flat to recover. The 'new' Harry is also married, and they agree to telephone his wife to come and collect him. Meanwhile, Jack tells Evelyn:

> 'It's clear enough what has happened. He was shell-shocked. The hospital authorities found nothing on him by which to identify him. No one happened to recognize him. When he recovered consciousness, he thought he was someone else – was, in fact, someone else. There are half-a-dozen cases on record, to my knowledge – cases that have nothing to do with the war. Dissociation of personality is the technical term for it.' (562)

Harry now has a double life, and Jack's assessment is rooted within the type of psychological explanations which can be found in W. H. R. Rivers's *Instinct and the Unconscious* (1920). There, dissociation is identified as one possible consequence of shell-shock, but it is also a pre-existing condition. Jack asserts that such a dissociation occurs in cases which are unrelated to the war, which demonstrates an awareness of the general understanding of dissociation at the time. Shell-shock provides one specific production of a dissociated state in which a double life is generated, one which moves us (again) both towards and beyond the uncanny. For Freud, the double is related to moments of painful self-recognition and repression. The double is a 'harbinger of death', but also the subject's 'conscience'. It is destructive, repressive and moralising. The dissociated self is of a different order because the two personalities have almost no connection to each other, a position made clear in 'A Point of Ethics' by the difference between Harry's first choice of wife (Evelyn) and his second: 'Harry Tremaine's two wives entered together: the one beautiful, refined, exquisitely dressed; the other commonplace, dowdy, the cheaply-attired product of a cheap city suburb' (Austin 1919: 564). Conveniently, Harry and his second wife are about to emigrate to Argentina, and Jack tells Evelyn that he will send them some money, while Harry's daughter is persuaded that she had dreamt about her father's return. Harry's return to the home and his family thus fails to bring him fully back from the war. The home is not an uncanny place as such, but is beyond the memory of the new subject that Harry has become and so has no emotional effect. However, a form of doubling is presented and, to that degree, other aspects of the uncanny are incorporated even while Harry's return from the dead is regarded as problematic for Jack and Evelyn. This is not a welcomed soldier's return because the home has been transformed due to Jack's presence and there can be no place for Harry in it. Again, aspects of the uncanny are developed even while other elements are excluded. This is not a tale about reconciliation, which has characterised the other stories; rather, it is about a moral dilemma concerning the obligations that those on the home front may still owe those who fought. This is not a love story in any conventional sense and as such it does not undo the uncanny in the same way that the other tales have.

The tale raises an ethical point about whether Harry should be informed about his past. In the end, the tale suggests that he is happy in his new life, and that there would be little to gain in the dissolution of this second marriage. The tale indicates that legally, and ontologically, Harry did die in the war, but only to be reborn as someone else who had recalled his other self, if only momentarily. The divided life of the shell-shock victim is taken for granted. It is not a story about rehabilitation but about how, yet again, to manage the returning soldier. These Gothic contexts, about divided selves, thus shape a theory of psychology centred on the double, which becomes key in the evaluation of shell-shock.

The idea of dissociation (developed by Janet) is cited by Jack in the story and it was a theory of the mind that underpins the double both in the Gothic and in the treatment of shell-shock victims. 'A Point of Ethics', in keeping with the stories we have examined, both evokes a familiar language of doubling that is rooted within a Gothic psychology and revokes it by confirming Harry in his new identity and sending him off to Argentina to embark on a new life – so that, yet again, the war is forgotten and left behind, and a cure of a kind is found.

The tales explored here have elided the difference between physical and metaphysical death. 'The Unbolted Door' centres on a spectral return of a dead soldier's voice, whereas the other tales have addressed soldiers who are psychologically missing. The return of a dead voice into the home in Lowndes's tale is generated out of parental need. The bereaved reach out for the dead and, in doing so, deny their death and projectively bring them back to life. The tale suggests that the ghost is real, but what the ghost says is heard differently, prompting the parents to recover their need to come together over shared feelings of grief and so finally allow their son to die: the ghost thus manages feelings of loss. The other stories are about those who have become ghost-like because they have lost a sense of who they were, albeit temporarily. These tales also manage the return of the soldier to domestic places in which putatively Gothic dramas are undone by romantic narratives. At the same time, these diverse tales all argue for a particular version of the subject which moves beyond the uncanny. The self may be brought to life in the home, but the presence of the substitute self indicates that the picture is more complicated than it initially appears. These 'missing' selves have independence and, in the case of Austin's tale, have acquired a new life. The self is discontinuous and forgetful, and not, as Freud would have it, continuous or repressed. Indeed, 'The Mirror and the Incense' argues for a self that is malleable and susceptible to transformation and reconfiguration. These tales implicate the presence of a new version of the subject, often dissociative or doubled, that is protean and not dependent on earlier versions of the self even while, paradoxically, many of the stories strive for the reassurance of resurrecting the pre-war self. Austin's tale, too, is specifically about the effects of shell-shock, and discussions about shell-shock help to clarify the grounds on which this new version of the subject is generated.

Shell-shock: W. H. R. Rivers

The academic psychologist Charles Myers was the first to use the term 'shell-shock' in print in an article published in February 1915.[5] Tracey Loughran notes that 'shell-shock' was always beset by problems of definition, and, although it became a term quickly appropriated by the army, they 'did not quite know what to do with it' (2017: 11) because it was characterised by a complex panoply of ailments. Loughran concedes that, even from our vantage point, the term is difficult to define with clarity, concluding that 'there are no neat resolutions to the problems raised by a nebulous, disputed, and endlessly elastic diagnostic category' (15). This view is supported by Fiona Reid, who has argued that 'the medical-military profession was unable to assign one clear discrete meaning to the term shell shock, and this confusion was reflected in diagnostic and treatment regimes, as well as in later post-war recollections of shell-shock treatment' (2010: 29). These problems of definition show how much an understanding of trauma is difficult to pin down, especially by specialists such as Rivers, who attempted to adapt Freudian ideas to the specific context of shell-shock.

Rivers's *Instinct and the Unconscious* provides a complex engagement with Freud which attempts to negotiate a position combining ideas from biology and psychoanalysis, but without emphasising the presence of sexual neuroses, which tended to typify the view of Freud at the time.[6] Rivers struggles to define shell-shock as anything other than a mixture of already understood psychological conditions. This epistemological problem about how to 'know' the damage caused by shell-shock is, of course, a feature of 'The Uncanny' and *Beyond the Pleasure Principle*, where Freud wrestles (as we have seen) with the terms of his argument.

Loughran makes the astute observation that all 'that was new about "shell-shock" was refracted through the prism of existing modes of understanding, but this did not alter the fundamental unknowability and awful novelty of war itself' (2017: 55). Rivers's account of shell-shock grapples with this problem even as his patients try to come to terms with and make sense of the seemingly new subject that they have become – in what constitutes an alternative discourse of the double to that found in 'The Uncanny' – but one which, in its divisions and anxieties, still owes much to a Gothic sensibility.

Rivers asserts that shell-shock should be regarded as a predominantly psychological condition because 'the essential causes of the psycho-neuroses of warfare are mental, and not physical' (1922a: 2–3). However, just as Freud would acknowledge the comparative relevance of biological interpretations of trauma, Rivers's *Instinct and the Unconscious* is revealingly subtitled *A Contribution to a Biological Theory of the Psycho-Neuroses*. Distinctions between mind and body are elided in a theoretical attempt to blend a version of the subject and its animal instincts, a composite figure drawn from Charles Darwin, with a modern therapeutic model which asserts that treating the mind can repair the body.

For Rivers, at the start of the war, both medicine and surgery were ill equipped to deal with the mental damage inflicted by warfare (Rivers 1922a: 2). His solution to this problem rests on his account of doubling, which appears in his chapter on dissociation. Rivers's view of the divided and doubled subject is one which also appears in the literature of the time, as in 'A Point of Ethics', where, as previously mentioned, it is employed to try to make sense of psychological conditions which have been exacerbated by the war. Rivers's model of dissociation, though, is an attempt to understand how a *new* personality might come into being due to traumatic experience. As in many of the tales explored here, the self becomes lost and replaced by an alternative version of the subject. The key questions raised relate to authenticity. What is the real self in these circumstances? Is it a suppressed version of the subject that has been stifled by other factors? Rivers attempts to resolve this by asserting the validity of the original, rather than an emerging, self. For him, 'The special feature of dissociation' occurs when 'the suppressed experience does not remain passive, but acquires an independent activity of its own' (1922a: 73). This state is known as the *fugue*, 'in which a person shows behaviour, often of the most complicated kind, and lasting it may be for considerable periods of time, of which he is wholly unaware in the normal state' (73). For Rivers, the issue is whether this alternative self lurks in the unconscious or constitutes an alternative self. He concludes that the unconscious does not come into play in any definitive way:

> We have not all to do with an example of the unconscious, but with consciousness cut off or dissociated from the consciousness of the normal waking life. A person in a fugue usually behaves in a manner somewhat different from his normal state, and shows what is usually described as a difference in personality, but the difference may be very slight. (Rivers 1922a: 74)

The problem confronted by Rivers is how to account for the relationship between these two seemingly independent subjects. He speculates 'that the fugue-consciousness may persist beneath the surface of the normal state, though the two are so completely dissociated that neither becomes accessible to the other'; however, as there is 'no evidence that this is so [...] till we have such evidence it will be more satisfactory to speak of alternate consciousness, the reality of which is now well established' (75). Rivers is concerned with the grounds on which this new self is generated, and this takes him back to an idea of suppression which is linked to trauma. The problem is as much rhetorical as it is ontological, illustrated by his reaching out for a metaphor in order to account for how these two selves might be related:

> To use a metaphor, it is as if the activity of the suppressed body of experience is accompanied by an affective disturbance which boils over on certain occasions, so that some of the steam reaches the conscious level, while the main disturbance continues to be wholly cut off from consciousness. (Rivers 1922a: 78)

In 'A Point of Ethics', Harry is described as a victim of shell-shock and so is the alternate figure of Durham, who recalls that 'They discharged me from hospital – shell-shock it was – and I just started life afresh' (Austin 1919: 563), having forgotten everything about his life before and, crucially, having no memory of the trauma engendered by shell-shock. In Rivers's terms, the new self has been produced in order to take Harry away from the life in which the trauma produced by shell-shock would need to be admitted and revisited.

Austin's tale asserts that Evelyn is wealthier, better dressed and more demonstrably upper middle-class compared to the new wife. However, the story also asks whether it would still be better for Harry to give up on his past life in order to embrace a new one, and a new start, in Buenos Aires. An alternative form of redemption is suggested in this escape, even if Jack's logic about supporting the emigration is flagrantly self-serving. The point of the tale is that, ethically speaking, the choice is a stark one: lingering trauma or happiness? Rivers sees a potential biological explanation for this alternate self, arguing that, in evolutionary development, the animal that becomes the human might learn important skills of compartmentalisation. This separation of tasks becomes psychologically introjected as a way of trying to contain trauma, in which the subject 'has brought it under control and to a large extent graduated it to meet the special needs of the developed mental life' (Rivers 1922a: 82). In this way, the alternate self represents the possibility of self-control rather than some continuation of a trauma-based pathology, so that the fugue state has a positive psychological effect.

Dissociation here solves a problem of the uncanny and its connection to doubling. For Freud, the uncanny is experienced in a problematic moment of projecting a second self, which involves painful, but very partial, self-recognition. This projection is bound up with issues of self-knowledge and understanding in which a conscience socially regulates behaviour but represses the more primal self. Self-insight becomes lost in this process because, for Freud, no epistemology of the self is produced. The uncanny appears as a threshold beyond which analysis struggles to progress, in part because Freud identifies literature and art as representing more fertile examples of uncanniness than that which can be found in life. Yet this model of the authentic self versus its inauthentic projections (literature, art) recrudesces in Rivers's account of dissociation. The authentic self is, for him, the 'normal' or everyday person who, when exposed to trauma, generates an inauthentic, secondary, model of the subject as a way of managing trauma. For Rivers, this supplement creates an epistemologically understood and coherent narrative in which the self becomes known because of what it has cast off. The projected self gains a life of its own as it sheds the damaged life, which has become a type of non-life dogged by feelings of unresolvable trauma. The therapeutic process, for Rivers, thus centres on how to lead the primary self through trauma so that the doubled self is able to reinhabit its old life. The process requires a modification of Freud's theory of abreaction because reliving the memory of a traumatic experience on the battlefield keeps the trauma fresh, rather than dulling it. In the uncanny, feelings of unease appear in reconstructed narratives about the dead and ghosts. Rivers's theory of dissociation addresses the nature of that reconstruction by emphasising that, in the generation of the alternate self, we witness an act of self-preservation. This ironically founded version of the subject, in which, to preserve yourself, it becomes necessary to lose your self, is one that, in the literature that we have looked at so far, is overcome by love. The returning soldier is redeemed by domestic acceptance, which makes the home a safe, *heimlich* place once again. The tales discussed here stop at the moment at which the lost self is restored ('A Point of

Ethics' being a notable exception). The end of the story typically occurs when the soldier is safely returned to the home. The point is to return to a time when the war seems not to have taken place so that the post-war domestic home resembles the pre-war home. Couples are reunited and can proceed with their lives. The tales thus provide a cultural way of managing what would appear to be an experience that is traumatic and hostile to domesticity.

However, these lost memory stories only generalise about the causes of this amnesia: the instance of shell-shock itself is different in kind and requires alternative strategies for managing this specifically damaged version of the subject. These are strategies which are indebted to a Gothic sensibility founded on division, doubling and self-haunting. Many of the tales explored in this book concern how the fantastical images employed in the Gothic are used both to articulate feelings of unreality (uncanniness, dissociation) and to manage feelings of anxiety and trauma. Fictional representations of shell-shock provide some clear examples of that process, and, as we shall see, issues about gender and sexuality play an important role in these Gothic tales which reflect upon identity and forms of identity politics.

Shell-shocked Spectres

Henrietta Dorothy Everett is a now largely forgotten popular novelist whose heyday was between 1890 and 1920 (she died in 1923).[7] Her 1920 collection of ghost stories, *The Death Mask and Other Ghosts*, contains several tales which reflect on the casualties of war, including 'A Perplexing Case'.

'A Perplexing Case' develops a politically inflected narrative about displaced identities which centres on the trauma of shell-shock. The tale features two soldiers, a French *sous-lieutenant* named Henri Latour and an English lance-corporal, Richard Adams, who are in hospital after being wounded by the same shell. The shock of this shell has resulted in them exchanging identities, so that Latour, who is described as middle-class, slender and 'somewhat effeminate-looking' (Everett 2006: 169), finds himself in the body of Adams, who is described as 'a herculean young fellow of the Saxon type' (171); meanwhile, Adams finds himself in Latour's body. The story thus entertains ideas about a fugue-like state, but in this instance the two subjects are granted authenticity, although in a clearly displaced (swapped) way. This is a tale about doubling, only to the degree that it addresses the contrasts between the two soldiers. The fugue is a state that needs to be overcome in order to eradicate the traumatic shock that has enabled Adams and Latour to exchange bodies. The solution to this crisis turns out to be a blood transfusion, which swaps the two men back, suggesting that national identity and forms of masculinity are to be found within the blood. Adams is described as working-class and 'rough-toned English', and his chief worry is that his wife, Liz, will be unhappy with his now strangely effeminate form. Once restored to his own body, he is happy to accept the diagnosis that he had been suffering from shell-shock. The physical cure is at odds with the type of therapeutic cure proposed by Rivers and others, but makes sense because of the specific requirement of returning bodies to their rightful owners. In this instance, fugue-like figures do not represent alternative selves that displace feelings of anxious trauma, but rather pre-existing, othered, forms of subjectivity. Everett's focus is more political than psychological and she symbolically exploits the trope of the fugue to articulate that.

This seemingly bizarre body-swap story conceptually addresses the idea of post-war reconstruction, in which national alliances forged during the war are now redundant. The closing images of the tale focus on Adams's return to England, which suggests that the war, at least for him, is now over. His type of working-class English masculinity has seemingly done its bit and can now be sent home. Written in 1920, the story also endorses English masculinity against an effeminate, perhaps because occupied, France. The tale ends with Adams looking at his hand, which, he approvingly notes, 'was broad and muscular again, not the slim olive member' (176) that belonged to Latour. The implied phallic diminutive of Latour's hand is the mark of his femininity; earlier, when Adams had found it belonging to him, 'he had thrust the slender olive hand [...] away under the bed-coverings: he could not bear the sight of it' (169). Such men are also defined by the women who love them. Liz, Adams's wife, is described by him as a 'good old girl', who 'takes in fine sewing' and looks after their eight-month-old son, whereas Latour is visited by his fiancée, Julie, and his sister, Ottilie. The tale is more concerned with Ottilie's relationship to her brother than with his relationship with Julie, again de-sexing Latour. Captain Senhouse, who is treating the case, notes that Ottilie looks like her brother and he sees her as 'beautiful' and as 'of the very type of womanhood that [he] admired' (169), which again unmans Latour by associating him with her femininity. The tale is thus not only about national crossings but also about a form of linked cross-dressing which ultimately needs to be properly demarcated.

The gender aspects of Everett's story are indeed explicit and unusual, and are out of keeping with how gender was often elided in accounts of shell-shock. Loughran has noted that the apparent hysteria of shell-shock victims did not feminise them but did make them child-like, so that 'doctors were forced to assume a strict maternal stance towards their charges' (2017: 144). In the evolutionary schema which underpinned ideologies about shell-shock the child was aligned with the animal due to shared primitive instincts. Everett's story, however, reads shell-shock through a narrative about gender that doctors at the time were keen to evade. This was because, as Loughran notes, the treatment of shell-shock was one centred on the 'restoration of self-control, the critical signifier of "civilized" British manhood', so that the seemingly radically disorientating potential of shell-shock was 'constrained' by 'existing cultural discourses around will and nervous breakdown', designed to ensure that 'The war did not force a fundamental reimagining of human nature' (Loughran 2017: 151). Everett's story is in keeping with the type of redemption Gothic that has been explored here. Identities are restored and subjects returned to their homes. However, what is the obviously noteworthy aspect of the story is how it employs the fugue to blur the boundaries between national and gendered identities. The fugue becomes the figure through which troubling identities are asserted – troubling because they are in the wrong place. For Rivers, the fugue is generated out of trauma and the split self that it articulates is indebted to older Gothic tropes centring on the double. Everett's story, as in all the tales discussed here, is in search of a cure and asserts the idea of home as the key destination to which the restored soldier will be returned. He is not made better in the home, but it is clear that a domestic context, with fiancées, sisters, wives and children, is what is really important here. Bringing the soldier back home means correcting the disorientation of the fugue, overcoming a split self, restoring a pre-war manliness and so revoking any troubling Gothic context even while the tale entertains the possibility of transgressive gender identities – if only to correct them.

However, some other literary examples of shell-shock explore radical, transgressive freedoms from social and sexual convention: a core feature of a particularly interrogative strand of the Gothic. 'Dispossession' (1929), by C. H. B. (Clifford Henry Benn) Kitchin, explores shell-shock within a homosexual paradigm that is implicit in Everett's representation of Latour in 'A Perplexing Case'. Kitchin was famous for writing detective novels, and novels which have gay themes, including *The Sensitive One* (1931) and *The Birthday Party* (1938). In 'Dispossession', a fugue-like state is used to explore the sexual politics of taking erotic ownership over a male body. A form of uncanny is generated in which the self appears to be doubled as one traumatised war veteran finds himself controlled by another. 'Dispossession' begins with the seemingly dead body of Harry Duke, who lies as 'still as a corpse' on his bed but who slowly comes back to life: 'Suddenly a muscle twitched beneath the sheets. The body grew warmer. A leg stirred, then a hand. The spine and loins shuddered. Drops of sweat crept through the skin. The mouth opened and gasped' (Kitchin 1931: 157). This uncanny coming back to life is followed by a moment of erotic self-regard in which he:

> looked with hesitant pride at his naked body, felt one hand with another, caressed with a lover's fingers his lips, moustache and eyes, and turning himself this way and that, as if the glass had never before reflected such an image, stroked trunk and arms and legs. (158)

The narcissism evokes Freud's idea, discussed earlier, that narcissism 'strove to fend off the manifest prohibitions of reality'. In this instance, the emphasis is on 'prohibitions' as the self is defined by a transgressive self-reflection in which the subject is effectively erased. Harry is not Harry at this point but has become inhabited by another, who objectifies Harry into an erotic spectacle. The moment quickly passes so that, whilst delighting in 'his strength, a dizziness came over him' and he collapses on the bed so that 'His senses ebbed away,' leaving his body 'as it had been before, quiet and untormented and almost dead' (158). Harry's death-like state provides the prelude for a discussion about the extent to which Harry has been displaced by the life of another and the degree to which he is aware of that. As in the fugue, the second self is unaware of the activities of the primary self from which it has departed.

Harry is due to go to France to visit friends in Wimereux. He oversleeps by a day and is concerned that this lapse means that he is unwell, that it represents a recurring 'crisis' to which he has been subject over the previous months. In order to keep track of immediate past events, he had kept a diary which consists of a record of partial blackouts and nightmares, which doctors attribute to heavy drinking. However, despite his becoming sober for a period, his journal entry for 2 December notes that 'All the energy seemed sucked out of me, and there was a kind of whirling at the back of my head, as if I was a corkscrew being drawn backwards through putty' (Kitchin 1931: 162). A later entry recalls that, at a house party on Christmas Eve, the guests take turns telling ghost stories. Harry has another blackout and the following day is quizzed about his war service by one of the guests, Joan Averil, a 'devotee of psychical research' (179). Harry had served in France at Loos, Vimy, Arras, Fauqissart, Ypres and Cambrai, but she asks whether he had been attached to the Third Middlesex Rangers who served at Miraumont because his story from the night before had been about that. Harry has no recollection of the story, which he attributes to drinking too much punch, and confirms that he was not in that regiment or in that part of the line. The context of the war provides the space in which a fugue is generated: an alternative self which has war stories of its own. It is also clear that these recollections of the war are traumatic and implicate the fugue that Rivers associates predominantly with shell-shock. Joan writes down Harry's earlier story, the story told by the fugue, and sends it to him.

The story is told from the point of view of a junior officer in the Third Middlesex Rangers serving between Miraumont and Grandcourt in January 1917. His sergeant is killed and his dead body left under a tarpaulin in the narrator's dug-out. He recalls the sergeant's fine build, 'not without a sense of jealous inferiority' as 'I thought of my own poor body, stunted and thin, never free from some ache or uneasiness'; he desires to fall asleep and 'wake up as a new creature with a body equal in vigour to my mind' as he strokes the 'splendid muscles' of the dead soldier (166). He lies on top of the dead body, 'my mouth on his mouth, my legs along his legs', and when he awakes finds that he has swapped places and inhabits the muscular body of the sergeant, whereupon, 'gazing with hatred at the prostrate body that had been mine, I kicked it heavily in the ribs'. The transformation is only temporary, however, as an hour later his servant discovers him 'bruised and numb' (166) and back in his old body. The tale thus centres on a fugue-like condition that afflicts Harry, in which the figure in the fugue is also subject to a fugue of their own. Identity is repeatedly displaced around death, and dead bodies are temporarily brought back to life but only because they are vacant and available for possession. Rivers's idea of dissociation is implicit here, in which the fugue functions as 'an occasional escape into another life' (Rivers 1922a: 139), as a means of avoiding emotional conflict. Read in this way, Harry's fugue represents an unresolved conflict which is otherwise hinted at in his alcohol abuse. The alternative possibility is that Harry is periodically possessed supernaturally by the spirit of another, in which Harry becomes that other's fugue. All of these displacements point back to the war as the generator of these anxious stories, which emphasise the desire to be someone else – if only physically.

Harry is touched by the story but he also knows that it cannot refer to him, since he was serving in a different zone and regiment at this time. After reading the text, he turns to the newspapers, which are running a continuing item about a missing architect by the name of de Milas, who had been in the army during the war and whose health 'has given cause for anxiety' (169) – what seems at this point like a separate story. Harry's periodic crises persist and include a dream in which he seems to be spoken to by the person who had narrated the body-swap story. He consults a 'nerve-specialist' but his journal notes only that 'Talked a lot about dual personalities and psycho-analysis. Don't trust him' (171), which appears to be a knowing reference to a certain type of therapy. Later, when he meets Joan again, he asks her 'Do you think I have a double personality?'(171). She thinks that is possible but wants to discuss it further, which he agrees to after recalling Stevenson's original 'Jekyll and Hyde, which frightened me' (172). Yet, in trying to telephone Joan, he instead calls the house of de Milas, claims that he is de Milas and announces he will soon be home. After making the call, he lies down and again feels a force 'entering him, in spiral fashion like a corkscrew'. He feels his normal will draining away and an inner voice taking over, telling him 'to give all you can freely. I have great need of you' (175). Later, the voice tells him to 'Leave this body free for me' (175) and he becomes increasingly frantic, the more it becomes clear that this body is dying (176). Harry telephones de Milas's doctor, who, with the housekeeper, discovers an old trunk that contains the dead body of de Milas 'covered in part by a waterproof sheet as was used extensively by soldiers during the war' (178). And so the story ends.

De Milas has been able to inhabit, if only temporarily, the bodies of others and these bodies are casualties of war: the dead sergeant and the nervous Harry. His is a restless, traumatised spirit, in desperate search for a new body to inhabit. The unconscious way in which the fugue is generated is here granted a suspicious agency in which Harry's reference to *Jekyll and Hyde* is apposite. Harry seems to be turning into de Milas until the body is found and de Milas's wandering spirit is finally laid to rest. Harry exhibits a number of symptoms that are familiar from shell-shock, with amnesia and dissociation being the most overt. His cure is affected by reinhabiting the body which truly belongs to him, and the restoration of that link echoes what we find in Everett's tale. Nevertheless, the story also entertains the notion that new and othered identities may become lodged within the self, and it is this alternative self (a type of ghost that parasitically feeds on others) that the story both evokes and attempts to overcome. De Milas is also a war veteran in poor health, the suggestion being that this can also be attributed to war-induced trauma. His desire for young (he is forty-five years old) and muscular male bodies represents a queer narrative about the penetration of male bodies, with the 'corkscrewing' motion symbolising a penetrative act. At one level, de Milas functions as a Gothic villain, but he is also an object of sympathy who tells his tale of shock and trauma through Harry. Dissociation in this instance functions as a form of liberation in which the anxious de Milas gains an erotic pleasure in the freedom to live a life in a body that he desires. The coded reference to leading a hidden homosexual life is clear, and Kitchin uses the idea of shell-shock to indicate that the model of dissociation which was connected with it could be used for radical ends.

Kitchin's tale has much in keeping with the lost memory stories discussed earlier. These tales of shock and trauma are also about the problem of the returning soldier and how to restore his identity. Again, we see how the tale draws upon ideas about the uncanny, dissociated selves, and a Gothic horror of fear and loss of agency, in order to move beyond them and affect a cure of a kind. 'Dispossession' is recognisably a Gothic tale about a struggle for identity, in which the principal victims of the war are Harry and de Milas. Both struggle with war-induced trauma but do not find their resolutions in romantic love. The tale explores the relationships between soldiers (rather than wives, fiancées, mothers and fathers), which implicates a narrative about masculinity. These are not about ghost-like figures who are restored to life in the home; instead, they are employed to suggest that other spectral identities, such as homosexual ones, are invested with a cultural liminality that cannot be clearly articulated. While many of these stories are explicitly Gothic, as in Everett and Kitchin, this is an impulse which can also be found within works which are not centred on body-swapping. As we have seen, the issue of dissociation is politically nuanced by Everett and Kitchin to address national and gendered contexts, as well as issues of sexuality. Such tales not only help to enrich the context in which shell-shock was culturally explored but also suggest points of contact between explicitly Gothic tales and other narratives, such as 'A Case of Lost Memory', which are defined by Gothic preoccupations. Stories about lost selves and possessed selves are aligned as they are both shaped by a Gothic sensibility which is working within the post-war culture to represent the legacies of war, before the tales cast off these Gothic moments as a way of moving beyond war-induced trauma.

A key convergence between these stories relates to descriptions of states of mind. Many of the tales discussed here explore how it feels to inhabit the damaged mind and the emotional consequences of that. Emphasis is also placed on the importance of culturally containing the psychological and social disorientation induced by the war, which is central to the conclusion of the tales by Everett and Kitchin. The process of embedding the shell-shocked soldier back into the home provides another way of negotiating this plight, as illustrated by the following tales which reveal common ground with the more generalised lost memory stories, discussed earlier.

'MacKurd: A Tale of the Aftermath', by the crime and science fiction writer Bertram Atkey, published in *The Strand* in 1919, centres on Major John MacKurd, VC, who is physically damaged – he has lost an eye and has a wooden foot – and is emotionally erratic due to shell-shock, which leaves him with what he refers to as 'the Buzz', making it difficult for him to think straight (Atkey 1919: 429). After the war, he writes to a banker, Sir David Glende, about working in his bank, a role he is singularly unsuited for; MacKurd admits that, when he has the Buzz, he may 'take a few notes home at night to fool about with – making 'em rustle, don't you know' (430). MacKurd is unreliable and emotionally unstable, but Sir David has a son, Davie, posted as missing in action, who wrote a letter to his father relating how, on the eve of battle, he had nearly lost his nerve in front of his men until an unfamiliar officer calmed him down, enabling Davie to command his troops. Davie writes that the officer's name was Claskind, and Sir David wonders if Davie had meant MacKurd, as the names sound similar. Sir David therefore agrees to look after MacKurd and to take him into his home.

In their initial encounter MacKurd tells Sir David what the Buzz feels like:

> 'It's a soft, thick, cobwebby sort of a Buzz in my head. Nothing much – it comes and goes, you know. You know those very soft woolly shawls that one's mother used to wear – that sort of thing – sky-blue. Well, if you wrapped your brain up in one of those and it had a bumble-bee entangled in it buzzing very softly – that's about the idea. Nothing much – but awkward for thinking sometimes, that's all.' (Atkey 1919: 429)

MacKurd's description of his shell-shock is a strangely comforting one, evoking images of domesticity and motherhood. It functions as a soothing image of emotional containment but also, paradoxically, seems to stifle thought. Strictly speaking, this 'cobweb' is not an example of uncanny ambivalence, but the reference to the home employs a language of a disrupted domestic world which is occasioned in the story by the missing Davie. MacKurd is clearly subject to a nervous disorder which is manifested by the Buzz, and in the tale this progresses to the point where a fugue-like figure appears, who is different in kind to the pre-traumatised MacKurd. MacKurd, who has forgotten all about applying for the job in the bank, receives a letter from Sir David, who is unaware of the transformations taking place in MacKurd, asking him to become his private secretary. This time the Buzz is 'rather pronounced' and 'his brain seemed queer – shaky – quivering steadily, like heat-waves' (432). We also discover that MacKurd seemingly lives the life of a champagne-fuelled *bon viveur* in a way that, for a time, conceals his darker tragedy:

> He was a little pale, but one watching him would never have dreamed that MacKurd V.C., was a nervous train wreck, flying at a fearful speed upon a swift, golden stream of champagne to the rapids of insanity and the deep falls of death. (433)

His hedonism is self-destructive (and anticipates Harry's problems with alcohol in 'Dispossession'), and he nearly bankrupts Sir David, who is warned by a friend that he should not persist in supporting the irresponsible MacKurd. Sir David's response is informed by cultural guilt, so he defends MacKurd as:

> 'a man who has fought so – for us, who sat snugly at home and took the profits that were literally thrown at us! A man who was torn apart with hot metal – as he has – as so many have! Aren't there any proper places for such cases in the England they paid flesh and blood and sanity and souls to guard?' (435)

Later, Sir David receives a telephone call that indicates that Davie may have been found, having been in a German prisoner of war camp. The authorities are not sure who he is because he has lost his memory: 'He has never spoken of his life previous to his capture,' when the Germans found him 'dazed, shell-shocked, in the rags of what was once an officer's uniform, at Passchendaele' (437). Just recently, however, he has mentioned Sir David's name and so is brought to the house to see if a positive identification can be made. Davie is introduced to his father and his sister, Madeline, but fails to recognise either, although they are able to confirm his identity to the army doctor. It transpires that Sir David was right in thinking that MacKurd was Claskind, and the two veterans greet each other, albeit in a scene which reconjures the war: 'They looked horribly ill. That their tortured brains had tricked them into believing that they were meeting again after some "do," which was perhaps Davie's first battle, was self-evident. MacKurd was swaying on the edge of collapse' (440). Ultimately, as it happens, the encounter proves mutually beneficial. The fact that it is staged within Davie's home brings him into the present '"*I know this billet!* I – why. I'm hanged if it isn't my home! *My home!*"' (440, italics in original). Meanwhile, MacKurd, who has been injured in a car crash due to his reckless driving, is also restored: 'The culminating excitement of Davie's arrival, following the shock of the motor accident, had straightened out that odd little twist in the mind of the V.C.' (440), and the final lines proclaim that 'even as Davie had come back to his own home and his own memory again, so MacKurd V.C., had come back to his own manhood. And the Buzz was utterly gone' (440).

Atkey's tale cannot be construed as a Gothic one in any formal sense, but its focus on lost selves being restored so that they can be made fit for the home is in keeping with the other Gothic narratives discussed here, which also implicitly evoke the uncanny in order to move beyond it by emphasising the restorative possibilities of the home. The evocation of the uncanny as a state of liminality makes the returning soldiers appear ghost-like as alternative versions of them traumatically appear, but only so that they can be banished in moments of redemptive epiphany which are so often staged within the home. MacKurd's Buzz has taken him on a journey in which he has become quite different to the heroic soldier that he once was. His transformation into a drunk overwrites this older self. It represents a gradual move into a fugue-like state from which he can be redeemed by briefly revisiting the trauma of war evoked by post-battle fatigue. Davie also overcomes a fugue-like state by reconnecting with MacKurd and the experience of war. However, it is important that this is also staged in the *heimlich* place of the trauma-free home. Atkey's story, like Everett's and Kitchin's, forges links between trauma and masculinity. Broken men are able to fix themselves without any intervention by medicine.[8] Mentally going back to the battlefield and then being restored to the home becomes a therapeutic journey which requires a casting off of the Gothic uncanny and the psychological, war-induced anxieties with which it is associated. Making men well is what lies at the heart of so many of these narratives and, although dissociation is not explicitly addressed in this tale, it is clear that MacKurd has temporarily become someone he is not – undisciplined, selfish and irresponsible. He needs to reconnect with the manliness that earned him the VC, to 'come back to his own manhood'. Davie and MacKurd thus become the type of men that the post-war world needs and, in order for all that to happen, these 'othered' identities need to be cast off. Davie, when first introduced into the home, is described as 'a boy, but with blank eyes and an old man's face' (439). This aged emptiness represents war weariness, before he is restored to his youthful energy. The war is thus temporarily remembered but then quickly forgotten. This movement between recollection and forgetting reflects, indeed, a type of therapeutic cure; however, it also illustrates British culture's ambivalent impulses to honour those who fought, but also to forget about its traumas so that a new post-war world can be embraced. Such plots represent persistent attempts to manage plights and overcome the apparent psychological fragmentation engendered by the war.

The divided self, in other words, is made whole again in these narratives in the Gothic-indebted way that they foreground the haunting presence of the 'other' in order to expel it. These tales come to this conclusion from very different positions, as in Balmer's 'A Case of Lost Memory', which shores up conventional gender and class narratives, and Kitchin's 'Dispossession', which furtively explores the transgressive possibilities of queer freedoms and identities. But these are nearly always tales in which the recollection of authentic selves exorcises the disruptive Gothic self that has temporarily appeared, thereby reasserting the therapeutic possibilities of home.

Lost in Time: *The Return of the Soldier*

The tales discussed so far in this chapter have focused on soldiers returning to the home, or otherwise dealing with war-induced trauma, in the post-war period. How a Gothic uncanny is developed *during* the war provides a counterpoint to some of these stories, as a pre-war self cannot be returned to until the war is over. The following discussion of *The Return of the Soldier* (1918) demonstrates how a Gothic sensibility is retained in a war-era text.

The home appears to be the place which offers salvation, but the home, of course, might not always function in this way, which is the situation depicted by Rebecca West in *The Return of the Soldier*. This novel has more in common with the Freudian uncanny, since it suggests that the home might not provide a redemptive counterpoint to battlefield trauma and so provides a challenge to the type of redemption narratives explored so far. The novel is described here as a counterpoint to those tales and to give an example to what happens with issues associated with the uncanny during the war, when the uncanny cannot be so easily rejected during a period of ongoing conflict. However, we will see that the novel extends the debate about the uncanny, by moving beyond a fugue-like state, but with potentially tragic consequences.

The Return of the Soldier has been subject to considerable critical scrutiny, certainly much more so than many of the stories published in the popular periodical press discussed in this chapter, in part because West's novel is more intellectually complex and literary than many of these tales. At the same time, it is also a novel which, in its focus on the difficulty of managing trauma, anticipates some of the narratives which will be discussed in Chapter 2. The tales discussed so far, while exploring shell-shock, have not placed trauma at the centre of their concerns because they have, at a plot level, been more concerned with affecting a cure in order to enable the soldier to re-enter the home, or otherwise be fit to take a place in the post-war world. These are tales which focus on the construction of a coherent narrative which makes this transition possible. West's novel, initially, also seems to be about this moment, seeing as it reflects on the return of Chris Baldry to his ancestral home, which is presided over by his wife, Kitty, and her cousin, Jenny, the narrator. Yet, as Kate McLoughlin has noted, Chris has no 'capacity for storytelling' (McLoughlin 2018: 222) and so is 'unable to pass on experience', making him a representative 'figure of a collapsing epistemology' (223). No knowledge is produced about the war because the war cannot be expressed in a coherent narrative form. Kitty and Jenny become aware that Chris has been wounded when Margaret, an old love from fifteen years earlier, arrives on the Baldry estate to inform them that she has had a letter from Chris. It transpires that shell-shock has meant that Chris has lost fifteen years of his memory; when he is reintroduced to the home, he does not know who Kitty and Jenny are and has no recollection that he and Kitty had lost their two-year-old son, Oliver, some five years before. This returning Chris is not in a fugue-like state as such because he has not become transformed into someone else. However, his personal relations are dramatically altered in what is mentally a return to the pre-war world, so that he both is and is not himself – even while his return seemingly overcomes this ghostliness, in which his return from the front is likened to a return from the dead. When he is first reintroduced to the home, Jenny records, 'I hear, amazed, his step ring strong upon the stone, for I had felt his absence as a kind of death from which he would emerge ghostlike' (West 1987: 213). Even on his return, he is both there and not there at the same time, a material presence with his heavy step and yet like a ghost, 'impalpable' (213). Wyatt Bonikowski has advanced a Freudian reading of this novel in which 'The soldier who returns does not bring death home, since he is very much alive [...] Instead the soldier brings home the death drive' (2005: 518). This death drive is reflected in the other characters, who, to a degree, are all in mourning: Kitty for her lost son; Margaret, who has also lost a son; and Jenny, who wrestles with unrequited feelings for Chris. Trauma is therefore absent from the story to the degree that Chris has no memory of the shell-shock event, but it is manifested through those who populate the home front. Much of the self-reflection in the novel is worked through by Jenny because Chris has no self which can be developed until the end.

Jenny is struck by, among other things, Chris's choice of Margaret over Kitty. Kitty is shallow and selfish, whereas the lower-class Margaret is generous and giving so that Chris's 'determined dwelling in the time of his first love [...] showed him so much saner than the rest of us, who take life as it comes, loaded with the inessential and the irritating' (West 1987: 255). Margaret lives in some 'dreary poverty' (258), which contrasts with the opulence of Baldry Court, but this seems preferable to the fragile version of civilisation that the Court represents. As Bonikowski notes, Chris is the one non-traumatised person within what otherwise appears to be a world of trauma (2005: 515). Cristina Pividori has argued that the novel is about being able to bear testimony so that

'West needs to make Chris remember so that he can forget' (2010: 96). However, it is not clear what testimony that would produce because, although Chris regains his memory at the end, we are not taken back to the battlefield, even while the story understands that his recovery could likely send him there:

> When we had lifted the yoke of our embraces from his shoulders he would go back to that flooded trench in Flanders under that sky more full of flying death than clouds, to that No Man's Land where bullets fall like rain on the rotting faces of the dead. (280–1)

To be cured in such a context of ongoing conflict is highly ambivalent, and West's focus on that is clear from the final words of the tale, which are uttered by Kitty – 'He's cured!' (281) – which she says after getting her husband back, only to lose him again to the army. The nature of his cure acquires a psychological slant when a medical expert, Dr Anderson, suggests strategies that could restore Chris to himself. It is eventually agreed that Margaret should tell Chris about the loss of his son because the emotional connection to Oliver should be enough to bring him round. Chris is told exactly that, but this now re-established self has negative consequences. Chris is restored to a type of military manliness that he had lost: he walks towards the house 'not loose limbed like a boy, as he had done that very afternoon, but with the soldier's hard tread upon the heel' (280). This reversal might suggest the restored manliness that we have witnessed elsewhere but it is a soldier's manliness, which can only take him back to the front where he was traumatised.

Jenny watches this departure from a window, accompanied by Kitty, who cannot bear to look as Margaret tells Chris about Oliver, all of which makes the final scenes effectively muted and the change effected by the cure highly ambivalent. Jenny notes that, as Chris heads back towards her, 'He was looking up under his brows at the over-arching house as though it were a hated place to which, against all his hopes, business had forced him to return' (280). This turn towards the domestic is undeniably negative, with Jenny noting that 'He wore a dreadful decent smile' (280), as his return is motivated more by feelings of duty and responsibility than by love.

The Return of the Soldier, then, is about death, but it is about death at home, the deaths of children and relationships. The returning soldier appears to complete the family but the family is already fractured by these earlier deaths. The management of death is one of the drivers of the narrative but loss is so integral to the characters' lives that the soldier simply represents another way of thinking about death at this time. The home is thus an uncanny place, which cannot unproblematically restore

Chris to his current self. This changes the direction of the tales that we have looked at so far. Stories set in the immediate post-war period restore the soldiers by eradicating the war and by retuning them back to their pre-war selves. In West's novel, to return Chris to the present means moving beyond his pre-war self and placing him back within the trauma of the war which had generated his amnesia in the first place. Chris's turning back of the clock by fifteen years enables him to find a place which precedes the deaths of his father and son, and his feelings for Kitty. To bring him back into the present is to confront him with the multiple bereavements which he has evaded by his retreat into the past. To restore this Chris is to lose him again as he becomes associated with public service rather than private domestic ties. Kitty, unable to watch, asks Jenny 'How does he look?', to which she replies, '"Oh …" How could I say it? "Every inch a soldier"' (281). That qualifying 'How could I say it?' indicates that his return is to the army and not to them, but also that the deeper, ominous threats in that return now have to go unmentioned.

Bonikowski argues that 'Chris's shell shock presents itself as a blank space that demands interpretation' because 'the word "shell-shock" enters Baldry Court's world of surfaces to challenge the distinction between physical and mental, what can be seen and what remains invisible' (2005: 534) – and, one might also add, between what can and cannot be said. Mara Scanlon has argued that, while Jenny initially seems to take the side of Kitty against Margaret, that choice, based on class affiliation, does not last. Later, Jenny switches allegiance to Margaret once she sees her as a more soulful partner for Chris than Kitty has been. Scanlon also argues that Jenny's final 'powerful identification' with Chris 'illuminates a crucial, gendered tension between battlefront and home front that preoccupied writers during the Great War' (2017: 67). These series of identifications and the movements between them require Jenny to interpret the actions of the principal characters, and by doing so she attempts an interpretation of the effects of the war. Scanlon sees Jenny's dream about Chris's frontline experience as indicative of her desire to inhabit the masculine world of war. In her dream, Jenny witnesses 'Chris running across the brown rottenness of No Man's Land', in a landscape populated by body parts in which life was 'packed full of horror' (West 1987: 195). Scanlon notes of this dream that 'Jenny's identification with battle effectively connects it to […] the soldiers' tremendous anger at those on the home front, whom they felt to be incapable of understanding the trauma of combat' (2017: 76). However, ultimately, Jenny 'cannot fully bridge the divide between home front and battlefront', leading Scanlon to conclude that she relies upon a 'delusional and inappropriate reading practice' (77). McLoughlin also notes that Jenny's narrative 'is an attenuated, derivative version of First World War veterancy' (2018: 222), which fills, but cannot understand, the vacuum of the veteran's silence. Chris's silence about the war remains the absent presence which is at the heart of *The Return of the Soldier*. The complex love triangle between Kitty, Margaret and Jenny demonstrates the effects of the war on those closest to a traumatised combatant, and the resulting triangle of women is complicated by the fact that these characters are also dealing with specific traumas around the death of children. In the end, battlefield experience is only present as affect, not as an interpretable reality. This conclusion, as I have noted, is different from the endings of the other tales discussed in this chapter, most of which effectively banish the possibilities of trauma in order to embrace a post-war world. West's novel represents ambivalence about the war, which is in part due to it being written during the war. The novel challenges the idea of the home as a place of therapeutic cure, and, while not heavily Gothic *per se*, *The Return of the Soldier* repeatedly emphasises that the shell-shocked Chris is like a ghost.

West's novel helps to nuance the discussion of the uncanny and ideas about the fugue by demonstrating how a return to an *unheimlich* version of the home has consequences for the returning traumatised soldier. Chris may be brought back to the present, but his future is highly uncertain and his restored military bearing indicates that the home is to be left behind once more. The psychological drama posed by uncanny states and shell-shocked states is thus granted a different type of authority from that of tales which attempt to undo the uncanny and restore the soldier to health.

The stories discussed here have emphasised the role that plots centred on romantic love and the home play in trying to manage the trauma of the homecoming veteran. The uncanny appears in these encounters with symbolically dead soldiers. However, the uncanny, as Freud defines it, is swerved away from by the assertion of two incompatible conclusions. The first is that the self lacks the continuity that Freud claims, and that the new self, as it appears in the fugue state or through dissociation, represents a new model of the subject. These subjects are neither doubled nor repressed, but are autonomous in not being strongly tied to past states of being. Rivers accords primacy to the historically earlier self but, despite this, these new subjects appear as having lives of their own. The second position, which undoes the uncanny and supports Rivers's position, is that the home is not, after all, the locus of uncanny encounters. The home becomes the place where the new, ghostly, self is cast off and the pre-war subject resurrected, largely in post-war stories which are eager to move beyond the upheaval of the war in order to engage with a peace that resembles the pre-war world. Such tales try both to manage trauma and to deny its ongoing presence. These briefly glimpsed alternate selves have to be expelled and this dismissal is achieved by moving beyond the Gothic towards narratives of family love, although in the case of West's *The Return of the Soldier* this view is given more challenging critical scrutiny. A rather different cultural impulse can be observed in narratives about ghosts who cannot be cured in any way. The presence of traumatised ghosts who exist beyond coherent narrative domestic plots is discussed in the following chapter. In these tales the Gothic cannot be so easily evoked and denied.

Notes

1. Ellis Ashmead-Bartlett, 'Life on a Battleship', *The Strand*, June–December 1917, pp. 563–71 and Anon., 'What is the Greatest Deed of Valour?', *The Strand*, June–December 1917, pp. 582–7.
2. A similar point is made by W. Scott Poole in *Wasteland: The Great War and the Origins of Modern Horror* (Berkeley: Counterpoint, 2018), p. 112.
3. Sassoon, in *Sherston's Progress* (1936), also recalls an incident in hospital in which he claims to have seen the ghost of Ormand, a soldier who had been killed six months previously; see p. 32.
4. Lowndes's novel *The Lodger* (1913) was based on Jack the Ripper and was turned into a film by Alfred Hitchcock in 1927. She was also the author of *Good Old Anna* (1915), about a German-born long-term resident of Britain and her life as a servant in a British home during the conflict.
5. Charles Myers, 'A Contribution to the Study of Shell-shock: Being an Account of Three Cases of Loss of Memory, Vision, Smell, and Taste, Admitted into the Duchess of Westminster's War Hospital, Le Touquet', *The Lancet*, 13 February 1915, pp. 316–20. See also Ben Shephard's *A War of Nerves: Soldiers and Psychiatrists, 1914–1994* (London, Cape: 2000), in which there is extensive discussion of the wartime debates surrounding the term's use and of how it 'caught the public imagination' (p. 73). Shephard also provides important material on the networks and connections between the various psychologists, psychiatrists and military doctors.
6. Loughran (2017) notes that J. T. MacCurdy's study – *War Neurosis* (Cambridge: Cambridge University Press, 1918) – is a direct Freudian account of shell-shock in *Shell-Shock and Medical Culture in First World War Britain*, p. 79.
7. Under the name of Theo Douglas she wrote novels of mystery and suspense, including *Iras: A Mystery* (1896), *Behind a Mask* (1898), *A Legacy of Hate* (1899), *Three Mysteries* (1904) and *The Grey Countess* (1913).
8. See Fiona Reid's *Broken Men: Shell Shock, Treatment and Recovery in Britain 1914–1930*, (London: Continuum, 2010).

Chapter 2

The Ghosts of War: Writing Trauma

The previous chapter focused on how various tales of World War One attempt to manage and contain anxieties stemming from war-induced trauma. There, the returning soldiers were often restored to their pre-war selves in the home. This chapter explores representations of ghosts who cannot be so easily plotted within structures that attempt to manage trauma. These are ghosts without homes and so without the domestic ties which restore the soldiers to a semblance of their pre-war lives. Trauma is not eradicated in these narratives, all of which indicate a problem with how to articulate war-induced anxieties. Familial structures and conventional narrative forms respectively fail to cure the soldier or to represent their plight coherently. These are ghosts who retain a disorientating Gothic presence as they wrestle with fears and anxieties which cannot be cast off or lived with.

These tales engage with representations of trauma which are clearly influenced by a Gothic sensibility, centred on divided selves and damaged emotional states. The subjects take on Gothic characteristics as they wrestle with fear and anxiety and struggle to find any narrative form which can express their emotional state. We can read the Gothic as a form that is founded within trauma, which often addresses specific historical concerns. The late eighteenth-century Gothic frequently addresses issues about social and political change generated by the French Revolution, just as the *fin-de-siècle* Gothic reflects concerns about degeneration, invasion and sexuality. That World War One, as a moment of crisis, would also produce a new formation of the Gothic condition is therefore unsurprising. It is a Gothic which inherits much from the earlier Gothic tradition, but which has a particular focus on figures of depersonalisation, such as ghosts and animals. How to represent this new Gothic sensibility is also closely aligned with forms of narrative expression which foreground the problem of representation.

Samuel Hynes has argued that realism is difficult to apply to soldiers' accounts of war and suggests '*battlefield gothic*' as a more appropriate term to make sense of 'when we observe the dead, or, more precisely, when we observe soldiers observing the dead' (Hynes 1995: 403 italics in original). For Hynes, what we witness is the often callous way in which soldiers observe the dead of their enemies, but we need to understand that their testimony is Gothic in character due to the very uncanny unreality of the war zone itself.

Characters within these tales are frequently haunted by the war, to the extent that they themselves become ghost-like. In these tales there is no possibility of reconciliation and redemption, although the home does not thereby appear as an *unheimlich* place for the simple fact that it rarely appears at all. Damaged and divided selves who are forced to confront their potential for subhuman, animal-like, behaviour evoke a tacitly formed narrative about degeneration, which played such a key role in shaping the late nineteenth-century Gothic. The *fin de siècle* appeared to many conservative commentators, such as Max Nordau, to indicate that civilisation was under threat by barbaric forces and it is an argument that reappears during the war. The war seems to turn soldiers into animals and trauma appears to measure the depths of that possible descent. Freud, in his essay 'On Transience' (1916), writes of the war that 'it revealed our instincts in all their nakedness and let loose the evil spirits within us which we thought had been tamed by centuries of continuous education by the noblest minds' (Freud 1990a: 289). This cultural plight echoes *fin-de-siècle* concerns that civilisation may just be a prelude to a deeper barbaric decline. A new, if culturally familiar, type of the Gothic emerges at this point, one centred on the slippery relationship between ghosts and animals as both come to register this newly liminal, barbaric, combatant.

This chapter begins with a discussion of the relationship between ghosts and animals in narratives centred on the trauma of war. The animal strand is indebted to a form of the Gothic in which the divided self takes on animal-like qualities. *Jekyll and Hyde* is an obvious precursor text here, and how one wrestles with this inner animal becomes progressively supplanted by ideas of haunting. These may feel like different types of the Gothic, but both are centred on ideas about what it means to be a person (a key issue, given the psychological and emotional turmoil of the war) and what it is that the subject inherits (a biological trait that atavistically lurks, or the persistent haunting by the war). A new type of Gothic hybrid is manifested along the way – one which appears in tales, dreams and memoirs.

Ghosts and Dreams of Animals

That war is the antithesis of civilisation was addressed by Freud in 'Thoughts for the Times on War and Death' (1915), where he argues that war creates an obstacle to human progress, one which may not be overcome because 'it may well happen that a later and higher stage of development, once abandoned, cannot be reached again' (Freud 1991c: 73). This fear is manifested in a troubling inward turn by the subject, which can be accessed only via dreams because 'It is only dreams that can tell us about the regression of our emotional life to one of the earliest stages of development' (73). W. H. R. Rivers explores the significance of dreams in depth in *Conflict and Dream* (1923), which develops his view of regression in *Instinct and the Unconscious* (1920) where he claims that 'War calls into activity processes and tendencies which in its absence would have lain wholly dormant' (Rivers 1922a: 5). This engagement with the inner animal is due to the 'affective responses' (80), which predominate on the battlefield, allowing unconscious factors to come into play. Psychoanalysis is able to access these instinctive, animal responses because of its interpretative authority over the unconscious. Descents into animality are especially evident in traumatic states which do not present as clear physical wounds (even when trauma might be accompanied by the physical wounds of war). Freud, in his 'Memorandum on the Electrical Treatment of War Neurotics' (1920), his written testimony to the Austrian War Ministry, submitted as part of its enquiry into how shell-shocked soldiers had been treated, argues that, during the war, doctors concluded that conventional ideas about 'functional change' had been replaced by a model of 'mental change'; Freud attributes this in part to the advances made in psychoanalysis (alongside doctors' acceptance that new non-physical ailments had been generated by the war) (Freud 1955: 212). He is critical of the electric shock treatment of traumatised soldiers because 'It did not aim at the patient's recovery' but rather at 'restoring his fitness for service' (214). His final proof that war neuroses are psychological in origin is this: 'with the end of the war the war neurotics, too, disappeared – a final proof of the psychical causation of their illness' (215). The animal responses finally disappear as the returning soldier reconnects with civilisation, but this presence of the animal lingers on and reappears in symbolic form.

In the previous chapter, we saw how Moberly's 'Inexplicable' employed animals as a source of the uncanny. The domestic space of the home is occupied by something which is incongruous to it, a wild, untameable animal associated with the swamp. Such writings might seem different in kind to the figure of the ghost, but they are linked to the spectre via a shared impulse which claims that the human is not quite human. Such non-human figures represent, symbolically, the seemingly subhuman soldier who appears as non-domestic and violent. Managing the return of the soldier is at the heart of Freud's 'The Uncanny', which is why Moberly's tale struck a chord with him. Rivers, meanwhile, notes that animals frequently appear in the dreams of the traumatised as a way of managing fear, so that 'The original fear is objectified in the snake or the rat through a process of symbolisation similar to that by which fears are in the dream' (Rivers 1922a: 140). Rivers published a paper titled 'A Case of Claustrophobia' in *The Lancet* in 1917 in which he explored the intense anxieties of a thirty-one-year-old army medic, who had suffered from claustrophobia throughout his life and found the condition exacerbated by his experience of living in cramped dugouts on the Western front. The account provides an example of the presence of a new form of the Gothic sensibility that is mapped in this book. The subject is haunted by a past populated by previous encounters with animals, in which they have themselves behaved like an animal. A form of depersonalisation appears, in which the subject is both lost and confronted with painful acts of self-recognition – producing a peculiar blend of sadism and masochism. Rivers records that an attempt had been made to cure the patient of his fears by using psychoanalytical techniques, to which he had been unusually receptive, due to his interest in Freud. After taking over this patient's treatment, Rivers emphasised that, although he was focused on analysing the patient's dreams, he did not subscribe to Freud's theory about an underlying sexual neurosis to dreams. Animals recur repeatedly in this brief case history, beginning with a dream the patient had about being in France, in which he is pursued by a man who kills a rabbit, instead of him, and throws the rabbit into a scum-covered pond. The rabbit then comes to life and a girl tries to kill it, egged on by the patient, but she only wounds it. Rivers records that 'In the dream the rabbit was regarded as a ferocious animal which the patient feared would get away, and this fear continued for some time after he awoke' (Rivers 1922b: 174). The dream evokes a litany of childhood recollections of animal cruelty, including knocking unconscious a pet rabbit belonging to his brother, watching three boys drowning a dog in a pond, and attempting with two other boys to drown a cat in a bucket. The cat was strong; they struggled to keep it submerged and 'The patient experienced definite fear at the thought that the animal would escape' (175). Rivers relates these scenes to an experience the patient had when he was three or four years old, when he had received a halfpenny from a rag-and-bone merchant. On trying to leave the premises, the patient found himself trapped in a narrow alleyway by a growling spaniel. This sense of being trapped, and its links to animals, were thus the apparent cause of the claustrophobia. Rivers is emphatic on this point, since it demonstrates how psychoanalytical techniques can be applied without recourse to an analysis which incriminates a sexual motive. The patient is cured of his claustrophobia, but is still troubled by dreams about the war. There is, ultimately, no obvious plot generated for the patient, merely a series of memories and plights in which there is a recurring narrative about animals. The result is a quasi-narrative which is not obviously connected to war trauma and so fails to explain anything about the war, even while it provides some explanation for the causes of the claustrophobia. Nightmares like this permeate the Gothic from the eighteenth century onwards, and how to interpret them is often key to decoding the wider psychological dynamics of the text (Victor Frankenstein's dream of giving his fiancée, Elizabeth, the kiss of death being just one example in which a character incriminates their unacknowledged hostilities). In this instance, what Rivers's analysis overlooks is therefore telling.

Rivers at no point connects the acts of childhood animal cruelty to the suggestion that the patient had himself behaved in an animal-like way, which is why the patient dreams about a vengeful rabbit and recalls an instance in which a dog threatens to be aggressive. The patient recounts the incident in which he had knocked his brother's rabbit unconscious and is then nearly beaten similarly unconscious by his enraged brother, with the patient recalling that at this point 'the rabbit came to life again' (174). The war calls up animal-like instincts, which are echoed in the dream of an undead battlefield rabbit who seeks revenge and is subjected to sustained violence. This is a story which appears plotless, even though it is an event in which claustrophobia is managed through a decoding of dream associations. A continuity of the self is asserted here, but the war, and its attendant anxieties, do not go away. Animality and war are closely aligned, and although the patient is cured of his anxiety about his animal-like life in a near-frontline dugout, he is still haunted by the war itself. Interpreted in this way, the dream can be read as an attempt to make sense of feelings of dread. Such fears appear in animal symbolism and reflect anxieties of being killed and of killing. A Gothic sensibility is manifested here, not solely because of the horror of the situation but because no clear explanation of the dream appears which links it to the war: the narrative of the dream both articulates fear and produces an analysis which makes that fear, but not the war, explicable. The anxieties generated by war itself are not fully contained or managed in this moment, which means that the war-induced Gothic anxiety of persecution, as manifested in the nightmare, is not resolved.

For Rivers, war taps emotions which exist below the level of consciousness – emotions which align the subject with the animal. *Sapper Martin: The Secret Great War Diary of Jack Martin* (2009), an account of serving as a Sapper in the Royal Engineers in France and Italy which was written during the war but not published until 2009, describes how war generates an animal reversion, in which 'the thin veneer of civilisation has been washed away leaving revealed primitive human instincts that at one time we would scarcely have acknowledged' (Martin 2010: 228). For Jack Martin, in fact, there are two versions of him: 'Sapper Martin is not the respectable law-abiding Mr Martin of pre-war days. They are quite distinct personalities and are apt to eye each other rather insolently at times' (228). This referencing of a *Jekyll and Hyde* narrative feels more explicitly knowing than it does in Rivers's account of his nightmare-inflicted medic. This doubled and divided self is reflected on with some humour, rather than horror, by Martin. However, despite the wry tone at this point, Martin hints at the type of dissociation that Rivers elsewhere explores in relation to shell-shock. Here is a pre-war self and a soldier at odds with each other. A peacetime world of 'law-abiding' citizenship is replaced by the uncivilised experience of the battlefield. However, this divided Gothic subject overcomes division by becoming immersed in a herd mentality which creates ties that bind, leading Martin to assert that 'Even the most materialistic cannot deny the existence of a definite spirit permeating groups or bodies of men' (229). Soldiers thus support each other in shared moments of fear. Rivers supports the view that war creates a herd instinct, albeit one inflected by class, in which the war reinscribes existing class hierarchies because NCOs, such as Martin, are trained to suppress their individuality while officers were trained to develop 'initiative and independence' (Rivers 1922a: 132) and so lead at a time of crisis. Despite this apparent division of emotional and psychological labour, provisional group membership is foregrounded as a way of trying to manage war-induced anxieties. The divided subject now, paradoxically, gains unity by losing a sense of individuality within the group.

These images of the inner animal are conceptually linked to the ghost since both assert the essential non-civilised qualities of the soldier. A novel which forges links between animality and ghosts is Frederic Manning's *Her Privates We* (1930) (originally published as *The Middle Parts of Fortune* [1929]), which caused a stir at the time, in part due to its frank use of expletives which later editions, such as that of 1930, omitted. Notable in Manning's novel is the elision between animals and ghosts. The novel centres on the Somme-based experiences of a Private Bourne, with the focus as much on Bourne's encounters behind the line as on his battlefield confrontations, thereby offering a broad picture of wartime service. While in the trenches, 'Only the instincts of the beast survived in him' and he likens himself to 'a stoat or weasel' (Manning 1999: 8) as he navigates the turns in a trench while coming under fire. It is a quality he shares with the men in his regiment, who 'had lapsed a little lower than savages, into the mere brute' (12), so much so that they 'had reverted to a more primitive stage in their development, and had become nocturnal beasts of prey' (40). The descent into animality is a condition which occurs repeatedly in accounts of the war. The presence of a type of uncivilised Hyde is not construed as a problem, however; rather, this descent demonstrates the soldier's capacity to adapt to the environment. It is clear that there is not much call for civilisation on the frontline, even if its values are what is ostensibly being fought for – surviving is all that matters. Manning's novel also comments on the type of herd instinct that Rivers viewed as a form of regression and that Martin saw as supporting necessary ties of group loyalty. The individual is lost in this moment as they become both animal-like (engaging with instincts) and spectral (there but not there, losing their sense of self). For Manning, violence is brought out under war conditions as 'a blind and irrational movement of the collective will' (109). This assertion of a biological identity is paralleled by a discourse of spectrality, which hints at a possible death that already lurks, as a potential plight, within the subject. The biological narrative reflects a desire for self-preservation which is rooted within the instincts, whereas the ghost represents a death instinct of the kind that Freud outlines in *Beyond the Pleasure Principle*. There can be no resolution to this paradox, which reflects an idea that life is finite so that the ghost (as a figure of death) configures a fear of death. It is noteworthy that the roaming battlefield ghost cannot be accommodated within any meaningful structure and Bourne thinks of himself and the men around him 'as so many unhoused ghosts', whose 'hands [...] reached [...] out of their emptiness, to seek some hope' (Manning 1999: 117). This reference to spirits that are 'unhouseled' (spirits who have not received the Eucharist before death) recalls the lines from *Hamlet* where Hamlet's father's ghost says that in his death he was:

> Cut off even in the blossoms of my sin,
> Unhouseled, disappointed, unaneled (I, v, 76–7)

These 'Unhouseled' and 'unaneled' (unanointed) spirits are lost souls condemned to a spiritual wilderness. The horror of a purgatorial living death (explored further in Chapter 3) is reflected in the beseeching way that the hands of the lost reach out for the living. In *Her Privates We*, the dead are imagined as resentful of survivors, so much so that 'Bourne wondered why the dead should be a reproach to the living: they seemed so still, and so indifferent, the dead' (233). The dead do not quite die, and the living are not fully alive as they await their deaths. The novel argues that trauma is generated by the claims of the dead on the living. There is bitterness here – that one cannot escape the clutches of the dead – which also appears in Bourne's dream of coming under shell-fire when 'terrible hands, terrible dead hands came out of that living mud and fastened on to him, dragging him down inexorably' (224). These hands stretching out of the mud represent a return of the dead as they reach out of the mass grave of the battlefield. Tellingly, these dead soldiers become alive in the 'living mud' of the inanimate battlefield. Within a dead place there is a Gothic presence which cannot be eluded as the hands try to grasp the living and to pull them into a shared mass grave. These specific Gothic images of the dead reaching out of their graves for the living are closely linked in the novel to ideas of recollection, so that these become hands that haunt. This is world of Gothic terrors in which the battlefield becomes alive with the dead, and death appears unavoidable in the novel, which concludes with Bourne's death, when he is killed on a raiding party shortly before he would have reached the comparative safety provided by an officer training course. Bourne's dreams are uncanny, as Freud would have it, and offer a continuing sense of horror rather than solace.

Ghosts cannot be accommodated because of their inherent out-of-placeness. The men can belong only to themselves insofar as they are members of a regiment, and this conundrum makes them both animal-like and spectral. Like Sapper Martin, they lose a sense of who they once were. The nature of this new self is shaped by a Gothic uncanny, in which the subject loses their sense of their pre-war self, becomes animal-like and is transformed into the spectral presence of a living-dead soldier. In effect, the combatant becomes haunted by the ghost that they may become, which represents a fear of violent death on the frontline. Repeatedly in these narratives, the ghost is the outcast but also represents what the subject might, or has, become.

What constitutes reality is consistently compromised, Bourne losing his 'own identity' as it merges 'with those objects of sense which he did actually perceive', all of which dissolves 'their objective reality into something incredible and fantastic' (Manning 1999: 225). Subject and object distinctions are erased, and this intermixture generates a fantastical notion of belonging. Earlier, it is noted that, while under fire, 'One's sensibility seemed to grow finer, more acute, while at the same time it became somewhat distorted' (160), so that the landscape reflects human anxieties by way of morbid personification when Bourne notes the presence of 'the shattered trunks and boughs of trees, lunatic arms uplifted in imprecation' and 'the ruins of a shattered farm, an empty corpse of a building' (160). He also records that 'one seemed to be travelling through some soulless region on the shadowy confines of hell' (160). The unreality is a manifestly Gothic world of death, from which there can be no escape because the subject has imaginatively fused with this dying world. The subject thus finds their plight reflected back in a series of inescapable Gothic images which centre on death, trauma and depersonalisation.

Trauma, as identified by Freud and as we have seen, reappears retrospectively and often in dreams. Early in this novel, Bourne is woken from a nightmare in which 'The darkness seemed to him to be filled with the shudderings of tormented flesh, as though something diabolically evil probed curiously to find a quick sensitive nerve and wring from it a reluctant cry of pain'; in this liminal state of mind, 'The formless terrors haunting their sleep took shape for him. His mind reached back into the past day, groping among obscure and broken memories' (Manning 1999: 6). The reaching out for memory occurs because, during the attack which provoked these nightmare visions, 'One had lived instantaneously' within 'the perilous instant' in order to master the situation psychologically, without which Bourne would have '[fallen] back among the grotesque terrors and creatures of his own mind' (3). The horror of the moment takes precedence over the horror of the mind, but the experience of trauma is made sense of only retrospectively.

Ultimately, trauma cannot be made explicable and the symbolic employment of ghosts and animals, and the elisions between these symbols, captures the combatant's feelings of metaphysical disorientation. The world of the battlefield is simultaneously unreal, populated by living-dead soldiers and horrifyingly real in its awakening of base instincts. Ghosts and animals might seem to be different entities but they symbolically represent a shared view of the dehumanised subject. The soldier's animal instincts are seemingly activated by the war and this troubling model of the self is reflected in the disembodied figure of the plotless spectre. How to read the animal symbolically, as in Rivers's account of the medic's dream of a rabbit, and how to decode the wandering ghost pose problems for analysis and interpretation. Narrative structures and plots do not make trauma explicable, so that anxieties generated by the war are not contained or managed because that level of psychological consolation is never reached. Even Rivers's reading of the significance of the rabbit does not directly reflect on specifically war-induced anxieties, but merely on a particularly intense form of claustrophobia.

The narratives discussed so far are not about homecomings, as they emphasise what is generated by the battlefield rather than what can be ameliorated by the home. The issue of the lack of emotional and psychological containment is key here. Symbolic animal forms and spectres retain a Gothic presence because they fail to generate a world which is beyond the trauma induced by the war. They indicate the presence of trauma but they do not make sense of it. A notably Gothic model of symbolism appears in which the traumatised subject is unable to move beyond their feelings of fear because those feelings cannot be contained, merely projected. Failed acts of psychological and emotional containment can be helpfully exemplified by an examination of the work of the psychoanalyst and World War One tank commander Wilfred Bion.

Containing Trauma

Many of the stories discussed in the previous chapter centred on how to restore peace by managing the psychological restoration of the returning traumatised soldier. Those narratives frequently strike an optimistic note, which reflects the desire for reassurance on the part of the readership of the popular magazine press in the post-war era. Such tales are different in degree, although not always in kind, to what we find in the psychoanalytical writings on war. In Rivers's account of claustrophobia, the subhumanity of the animal is reflected in fugue-like states in which the soldiers lose their 'true' self, due to war-induced trauma. Such soldiers have become spectres of themselves who need to be brought back to life, rather like the brother's rabbit noted above. These fugue-like states also indicate the presence of a discontinuous self and, although Rivers acknowledges this, he seeks to assert a psychological continuity with an earlier, supposedly more 'authentic' self which exorcises the discontinuity – a strategy adopted by many of the stories explored in the previous chapter. As we saw, the tales in the magazine press articulate some strongly held social anxieties but in a socially acceptable way that provides reassuring conclusions not found in the more complex writing of Rebecca West. Fears about depersonalisation and ways of containing such fears are also to be found in the war-inflected theory of the self developed by the psychoanalyst Wilfred Bion, which emphasises the idea of containment as a key stage in the child's psychological development. It is a theory of the subject which breaks down when the rebellious tendencies of a Gothic sensibility cannot be contained because sense cannot be made of them. The tales in the previous chapter demonstrate a variety of ways in which this uncanny Gothic subjectivity can be eradicated, but the narratives in this chapter address what happens when these interventions fail.

Bion's idea of containment was developed in *Learning from Experience* (1962), where he argues that the child becomes fearful if the mother is unable to contain the child's general sense of anxiety, an anxiety which, from the child's point of view, feels unfocused and is impossible to articulate fully. The reaching out for the mother is also a reaching out for the home as a *heimlich* place of domestic security. The model thus has much in keeping with the strategies employed in the stories discussed in the previous chapter. Michael Roper argues that wartime tensions permeate Bion's model of containment. If the mother cannot soothe the child, then Roper notes that the child is subject to a sense of horror because the baby understands 'that its anxieties are not only intolerable, but cannot be made sense of', so that 'Its anxieties fragment within the psyche, and are then felt to attack it' (Roper 2009: 250). Roper argues that this shattering replicates how soldiers thought about the home as an idealised safe place which could make sense of their fears, but if it failed to do so, the combatant would remain psychologically damaged. Not being able to represent safely, and so contain, memories of war trauma means that the traumatised subject remains haunted by them. As noted at the beginning, the Gothic as a form often appears during moments of social crisis and it is therefore understandable that the Gothic becomes employed in accounts of the war as a way of accounting for an emerging sensibility shaped by earlier Gothic trauma narratives. This disoriented Gothic state of mind appears in the impressionistic temporal lapses of Bion's autobiography, *The Long Week-End 1897–1919: Part of a Life*. Writing from the vantage point of 1982, he recalls the opening days of the war and his enlistment in this way:

> There breaks a yet more glorious day. And this – dark, sodden, sulphurous Liverpool Street – was *it*. Surely it *must* be a pool whose stench-borne waters close over one for ever. So like the shell-hole – no, no; not yet. That was later; or long ago; take your choice. (Bion 1985: 104, italics in original)

These temporal shifts reflect an anxiety that is inherent to the process of recollection. That experience becomes slippery when confronted by trauma is also articulated in his memory of a nightmare that he has just before going into battle:

> The dream was grey, shapeless; horror and dread gripped me. I could not cry out, just as now, many years later, I can find no words. Then I had no words to find; I was awake to the relatively benign terrors of real war. Yet for a moment I wished it was only a dream. In the dream I must have wished it was only a war. (237)

He takes this dream with him into the fighting too: 'I was off and hurried, hurried with the dread of the dream chasing me, sometimes walking by my side in the way figures at Ypres hurried along the duckboards beyond the canal' (238). Bion is haunted by a dream which is about the untreated 'grey, shapeless' form of fear that cannot be psychologically contained. Even then, 'as now', the words cannot be found with which to capture and so make sense of this experience. The fear is reassembled as a feeling of dread in which the dream chases after him or, otherwise, horrifyingly keeps him company. It is the failure to 'find no words' which is key to this experience.

Containment functions as a way of making safe, articulated by words and through story-telling, and what is interesting is Bion's refusal to impose a narrative arc that seems to explain the meaning of the trauma generated by the war. His impressionistic temporal confusions plus the presence of strange oneiric hauntings capture a flavour of what it is like to be still dogged by these anxieties about war. It all corresponds to Kate McLoughlin's idea that what subsists in accounts of the returning soldier is a radical otherness, predicated on the failure of analysis in which 'deep critical listening does not convert the not-said into knowledge' (McLoughlin 2018: 240). Instead, what emerges is a form of Keatsian negative capability 'when man is capable of being in uncertainties, mysteries, doubts, without any irritable reaching after fact and reason' (Keats 2018: 1017), which produces 'an act of attention, not explication; a hermeneutics of acceptance, not suspicion. It cares without comprehending, plumbs without fathoming' (McLoughlin 2018: 240). Not being able to contain acknowledges the emotional complexity of the moment. Temporality is a key issue here.

For Freud, trauma is always belated; the importance of the traumatic moment cannot be understood at the time, which is why it is subject to a repetition which echoes the child's game of *fort-da* discussed by Freud in *Beyond the Pleasure Principle*.[1] Narrative use can make retrospective sense of trauma by providing the type of structural containment that helps to manage the traumatic moment culturally, and this is where the Gothic plays an important role. As we saw in the previous chapter, Gothic narratives often became subsumed by romantic ones in tales about homecoming soldiers, but there is a strand of Gothic writing which appears at the time and is much more ambiguous in its contribution to the possibility of a post-Gothic narrative of containment. It is a form which has its roots in the type of Gothic sensibility that has been outlined here.

Roper makes brief reference to a narrative written by Alan F. Hyder and published in a compilation of war recollections in 1930, arguing that it represents a typical account of how veterans were haunted by their war experiences (Roper 2009: 17–18). What is telling about this recollection is its narrative structure, which is clearly indebted to the Gothic. Hyder's narrative is titled 'A Nightmare' and it centres on a real-world experience in a captured German fortification known as a pillbox, which involved himself and another soldier known as 'Sparrer' (as in Cockney Sparrow). They are detailed to knock some holes in the pillbox so that it could be accessed from the British side and fired out of from the wall facing the entrance, effectively repointing it towards the German line. The narrator notes how the commonplace noises of the night-time battlefield resolve themselves into Gothic images in which 'the thin chinkle of an empty beef tin carelessly tossed into barbed wire, the faint squelch of stench rising in slow bubbles from the noisome pool in the old shell hole, were magnified into weird whisperings and stifled sighs' (Hyder 1999: 153). When they arrive at the pillbox they realise that they do not have the appropriate tools, and Sparrer is sent back to get them. Left on his own in the pillbox, the narrator becomes conscious of a noise outside, which gets progressively nearer. He recalls with horror that 'Closer and closer he, it, or whatever the thing was, came silently crawling.' He is trapped in the pillbox because there is only one entrance, a small, tunnel-like aperture that he cannot get out of in time. His response is fearful but also evocative of a discourse of terror familiar from the Gothic:

> Little icy-cold drops of sweat ran down my spine, as, with rather a shaky hand, fumbling in the darkness, I silently slid back the safety catch of my rifle and, drawing the bolt, saw to it that a cartridge was in the breach. (156)

At this point he is unclear about the nature of the danger but entertains the possibility that it might not be human. This possible 'it' or 'thing' is what provokes the fear. The narrator thus positions themselves within a Gothic narrative in which an unseen monster cannot be evaded. The anxiety builds as he hears this form crawling down the entrance tunnel, so that 'With beating heart and dry lips, I listened' (157). The horror culminates with the arrival of what is an apparently wounded German soldier whose face is lit up by a Verey light, which reveals 'a white face, the top portion black under the shadow of the grim German steel helmet' (157). The German seems non-human here, facially reduced to bold contrasting colours and without expression, as if he were some type of Gothic creature. The narrator then shoots the soldier twice in the head, and on Sparrer's return they remove the body. The final lines of the narrative record that all this took place 'Twelve years ago, and still at night sometimes comes a sweat that wakes me by its deathly chill to hear again that creeping, creeping' (158).

As a memoir of the war, 'A Nightmare' is unusual. While fear is recollected and the continuing sense of a traumatic memory hinted at, the narrative structure does not ring true. The tale is structured like a horror story with a conventional beginning (a sense of nameless terror), a middle (the preparation for defence) and an end (the defeat of the monster and the triumph of order). The persistence of memory differs from the type of trauma explored in 'A Case of Claustrophobia', which presents trauma in a symbolic form. Freud, in *Beyond the Pleasure Principle*, argues that while dreams about traumatic experiences are frequent, he is struck by the oddity that they occur at all because 'I am not aware [...] that patients suffering from traumatic neurosis are much occupied in their waking lives with memories of the accident' (Freud 1991a: 282). The memory may come back as a dream but, because the horror of it would awaken the subject, it destroys the restorative function of sleep, and it is thus too difficult, for Freud, to ascribe any evolutionary purpose to it. 'A Nightmare', as the title suggests, claims that the experience was like a horrifying dream but the only genuinely frightening elements in it for the narrator relate to the sound of the creeping, which recalls the moment when the metaphysical status of the anticipated assailant is unknown. Hyder's assessment of the man he has shot is devoid of emotion: 'I switch the torch on him. One bullet hole through his temple and another through his jaw under the ear' (Hyder 1999: 157). Sparrer also pragmatically complains that now they have to drag this body outside, noting that it would have been better to have shot him before he had tried to enter the pillbox. The drama of the recollection is thus not about the killing, which is simply narrated as 'I had shot him' (158), but about the horror that he might have been something other than a German, that he might have been a real Gothic monster stealthily creeping towards him. The narrative of the Gothic, and the feeling that it provokes, are thus at odds with the dispassionate recollection of killing the soldier. The literary narrative of containment that we witnessed in Chapter 1 breaks down at this point as the Gothic form seemingly captures feelings of terror which significantly overwrite the ostensible memory of a killing. It is tempting to read this as an act of displacement, in which the horror of the shooting has been projected on to the narrative form itself, as if the narrative cannot provide a way of negating trauma but rather keeps it alive precisely because what is chilling in the tale, although seemingly not for Hyder, is the ease with which the shooting is recounted. The haunting nature of the memory, in which Hyder must know how it ends, suggests that it is the memory of the encounter with the German soldier which has not been properly resolved and which subsists as a traumatic moment that is displaced on to the creeping sounds. In this instance, a Gothic image keeps alive an unacknowledged traumatic memory about the war.

In 'A Nightmare', the horror of war is overwritten by a Gothic narrative which places the horror of the scene somewhere beyond the moment of shooting. The war does not present as a Gothic trauma, but the Gothic structure of the narrative can only provisionally contain, or manage, the horror of war by displacing it elsewhere, much as West's *The Return of the Soldier* projects trauma away from the soldier and on to the grieving female protagonists. Trauma is, in Freud's terms, understood only after the event, and it is a ghostly figure (the 'creeping' German) which reconfigures that very belatedness. Strategies of containment thus break down as trauma becomes re-presented in symbolic forms which keep alive the experience of the traumatic moment, a feature of both Hyder's narrative and Bion's memoir as it too recounts his nightmare in which 'I could not cry out, just as now, many years later, I can find no words.' These ghostly presences represent a trace of the past that cannot quite be cast off. Richard's Aldington's short story 'The Case of Lieutenant Hall' (1930), set in the immediate post-war period, provides another example.

Aldington: Narrating Trauma

Aldington's 'The Case of Lieutenant Hall' is told in diary extracts by one Henry William Hall between 12 November 1918 and 21 March 1919, all of which centre on Hall's haunting by the memory of a dead German soldier. The tale explores the plight of those who fought in the war and makes visible, to those who did not, the terrors confronted by the soldiers. The story is thus intended to communicate what the war was like for those combatants who have been unable to overcome their traumatic experiences.

Hall is a figure with whom we are meant to sympathise. We witness his joy at having survived the war, which is closely followed by apprehension about what type of peace he will be returning to as he waits to return to civilian life. His time in the immediate post-war army camps proves difficult for him, however, as he is morose, and prone to drinking heavily and arguing with his fellow officers. His post-war camp life is a type of limbo in which he is caught between the end of the war and a homecoming. In keeping with the nightmares of Rivers's medic, Bion and Hyder, Hall sleeps badly and his Boxing Day diary entry reads:

> I'm getting very worried about myself. I sleep very little, and pass the hours in a constant apprehension of some undefined horror or calamity. I can't settle

to anything. It is all complicated with almost nightly dreams – horrible – of those Boches. (Aldington 1930a: 234)

As Hall heads towards peace, the war will not let him go. On 15 January, he notes a moment in which the moon resolves itself into the face of a dead German soldier whom he had killed. The moon:

> looked like a face, a yellow dead man's face swollen with corruption […] The most awful feeling of sick terror and apprehension went through me – infinitely worse than waiting to go over the top. I felt all the hairs creep on my skull, and I almost screamed aloud. I broke out in a cold perspiration, which was also a horrible experience in itself. (236)

This was not a dream, but a vision of horror associated with four unarmed German soldiers that he had killed on the Somme in 1916, which haunts him whether he is asleep or awake. The incident occurred while Hall helped clear out a German trench and shot three Germans who were trying to surrender, bayoneting a fourth as the soldier attempted to run away. He recalls that 'He screamed as he fell, rolled over, and looked at me with an awful expression of loathing, hatred and reproach. I gazed at him in horror, shaking all over' (237). It is an action that he cannot account for and deeply regrets. The feelings of guilt and the memory of the man's face become increasingly insistent as the tale develops. Unlike in 'A Nightmare', horror is not displaced beyond the moment of killing, but rather the killing is projected on to the physical world so that it becomes inescapable. Hall's plight is similar to that of Bourne in *Her Privates We*, discussed earlier, when he sees his anxieties reflected back by the war-torn landscape. In Aldington's tale the moon retains the man's features – 'It had just that same look of hatred and loathing' (238) – so that 'For a moment I was frozen quite motionless, with my hair rising on my head, and that filthy cold sweat on my face' (238–9), before he turns and runs.

While Hall's killing of the four men is inexplicable, even to himself ('O God, why did I do it?' [237]), we are not meant to judge him, largely because he is already punishing himself through self-recrimination. It is also clear that the focus is not on the horror of the killings themselves but on the aftermath in which the guilt is manifested. The German's hatred of him continues post mortem when Hall notes that, in stepping over the corpse, 'The face of the bayoneted man still glared horror and hatred at me' (238). This ghost is all too real for Hall. Caruth has stated that 'for those who undergo trauma, it is not only the moment of the event, but of the passing out of it that is traumatic; that *survival itself*, in other words, *can be a crisis*' (Caruth 1995: 9 italics in original). Hall may suffer from a form of survivor guilt but it is also clear that at some level he feels the justice of his ghostly persecution. The type of symbolism that characterises the uncanny does not apply here because the moon does not represent anything other than the inescapability of the presence of the dead soldier. Hall's sense that he is haunted is taken for granted by him so that

> When I do fall asleep, I immediately wake up in horror, with a vision of that face of loathing and hatred threatening me. I believe that man meant to haunt me when he died. I feel his presence, his dreadful, decayed, loathsome presence in the room. Last night I had a feeling he was standing there, invisible, watching me suffer with a dreadful revengeful glee. (Aldington 1930a: 243)

This is a type of haunting that is different to Hyder's because there the focus was on the sounds which led up to the killing. Also, Hyder's killing is not gratuitous and so not tinged with the same explicit feelings of guilt. Aldington's ghost story queries the presence of the ghost as it is clear that this ghost has no independent reality, since only Hall can see it, even while the tale acknowledges the psychological truth that the ghost represents, concerning ongoing feelings of guilt, fear and war-induced trauma. This spectral entity is part ghost and part rotting corpse, not the figure of the recently killed man that he had obsessed about at the beginning. The figure represents a battlefield death and, although Hall's horror is generated by this specific memory, there is a more general sense that the drama of the tale is about surviving soldiers who cannot forget what they have seen: how to communicate that liminal condition is part of the narrative. The diary format suggests that we are witnessing a progressive mental decline of the kind we have seen before in Kitchin's 'Dispossession'. For Hall, the ghost has a reality to it because it refers directly to an act that he has committed and reflects his feelings of guilt over and responsibility for it. Moreover, post-war reality looks unreal to Hall, compared to his war experiences. He notes on his return that 'All this existence in London seems most unreal. What gave a false appearance of reality to our life in the line was that we were not – at least directly – merely slaves of the economic idea' (Aldington 1930a: 248). Life in the trench thus has an alternative reality to it which is beyond the cash nexus. There is acknowledgement here that this war reality might be provisional and 'false', but it is a reality that Hall cannot cast off and which Aldington wants to communicate. The reflection on different types of reality generates the type of disorientated Gothic sensibility which we have explored throughout this chapter. Subjects feel disconnected to the world because they feel that psychologically they no longer belong to it. These are not soldiers who can be symbolically brought back to life in the home. Their memories of war cannot be made sense of and consequently cannot be escaped. Rivers's medic and Hyder's narrative both evoke feelings of claustrophobia, which represent this sense of being psychologically entrapped. In Aldington's tale there is no escaping the ghost, and even religion grants no solace. Prior to his move to London, Hall enters a cathedral in Belgium as 'a reminder that there might be something else in the world beside blood, death, horror, mud, greed, money, money, money'. However, although Hall understands the importance of a spiritual message, he notes that 'Unfortunately, I thought that the head of Christ looked like the bayonetted man' (246), so that for Hall there is no possible redemption; this means that, unlike in those stories which evoked the uncanny, his homecoming cannot be one in which a pre-war self is restored. It is, as Caruth has noted, the fact that he has survived which paradoxically destroys him.

In the previous chapter, we witnessed how the Gothic was employed to reflect on the issue of returning soldiers. The world that they inhabit is often a traumatic one, and that state of irrationality is associated with a level of disorientation which is a central characteristic of the Gothic text. What we consider abnormal mental states are managed via this Gothic idiom in order to make visible what otherwise appears to be beyond representation. In those tales the uncanny was employed to manage a return into the home, a return which would neutralise uncanny affect. However, the stories discussed in this chapter are of a different order because they articulate a cultural concern that this return to the home, or some version of civilisation (in Aldington's tale, London), is much more problematic. The Gothic in this instance makes visible feelings about trauma rather than enabling an overcoming of uncanniness by a return to the home. The resulting fictions have implications for the type of Gothic that we are witnessing in this instance. In Hyder's 'A Nightmare', the Gothic appears as a mood, one which articulates a horror about the war, but which is ostensibly detached from it, since the German soldier is not a Gothic monster and his killing is dealt with pragmatically. 'The Case of Lieutenant Hall' entertains a different form of the Gothic because the haunting is not displaced, but this raises questions about responsibility and culpability. The ghost might be a reminder from the past, but is it the Gothic monster of the text, or is it Hall who is demonised due to his unnecessary killing of the soldiers? There is ambivalence here about whether Hall is a victim of the war or a villain. The tale ultimately suggests that Hall is both a specific perpetrator and a general victim, and what he is ghosted by is also both specific (the ghost of the dead German) and general: it is about being haunted by the horror of war.

Aldington's tale thus plays a double game as the reader is meant both to be appalled by Hall's actions and to sympathise with him for his remorse and for the horrors that he has committed and to which he has been subject. To reconcile these positions is conceptually difficult, and Hall's eventual suicide appears as an inevitable conclusion. No coherent narrative emerges which could therapeutically manage Hall's anxieties. As in Bion, containment breaks down because the world looks dangerous. Self-murder is used to emphasise symbolically that the self-destruction of the war has made good people, such as Hall, do bad things. Hall, in effect, is always already as ghostly as the projected figure which haunts him. He is also conscious that the ghost eludes him even while it will not leave him alone, so that 'If I walk up to it, the damn thing disappears; I turn around, and there it is on the other side of the room. When I read or write I can feel it behind *me*' (Aldington 1930a: 251, italics in original).[2] The tale echoes Wilfred Owen's 'Strange Meeting' (composed in 1918), in which the killer and the killed are bonded forever; the closing lines reflect this blurring of identities:

'I am the enemy you killed, my friend.
I knew you in this dark: for so you frowned
Yesterday through me as you jabbed and killed.
I parried; but my hands were loath and cold.
Let us sleep now … .' (ll. 40–4)

The experience is a shared one, although Owen's protagonists find peace only in a version of hell. Hall's final diary entry recalls 'I've had no sleep for three nights now. Every time I fall into a doze the German comes and presses his decaying face against mine. God in hell, it's horrible! I can't stand it' (Aldington 1930a: 252). The final part of the story is a news item that carries an account of the Coroner's inquest into Hall's suicide. An especially chilling part of the story is to be found in the Coroner's summary. The Coroner holds Hall responsible for his death and regards his unsound mind as reflecting a refusal to adapt to civilian life, which constitutes a moral failing on the part of returning soldiers who do not appreciate the sacrifices made on their behalf by the civilian population during the war. The Coroner's report notes that such veterans 'must also realise that they had no right to expect that they should drop into easy jobs, or that they could all keep up the standard of extravagant living they had been accustomed to in the Army' (Aldington 1930a: 253). His final comments are 'that it was about time these young men came to their senses, realised that life is not all sky-larking, and settled down to do a little honest work' (253). Aldington thus leaves the final voice to a peacetime culture that not only cannot understand the experiences of those who had fought in the war, but actively condemns them based on a view that the inability to adjust to civilian life is due to 'sky-larking' rather than the kind of trauma that had occasioned Hall's suicide. Hall's plight does not generate a story that makes sense to a peacetime world, whereas stories about the missing or those with shell-shock do. Hall's case is one of generalised trauma which invites no specific form of therapeutic intervention. It is trauma without a plot, or a cure, or any form of containment and so lacks any possible narrative closure.

There is a concluding bitterness in this tale about how combatants were perceived by non-combatants. Aldington addressed similar themes about the disjunction between home life and the war in his novel *Death of a Hero* (1929), which includes references to Gothic writers such as Horace Walpole and Ann Radcliffe. Here, he sees the Allies as united with the Germans in death. His principal protagonist, George Winterbourne, while in a French village, notes that it is seemingly covered in crosses that mark the graves of the dead; he sees 'The dead men's caps, mouldering and falling to pieces [...] hooked on to the tops of the crosses – the grey German round cap, the French blue-and-red kepi, the English khaki' (Aldington 1929: 309). He also notes that 'There were also two large British cemeteries in sight – rectangular plantations of wooden crosses. It was like living in the graveyard of the world – dead trees, dead houses, dead mines, dead villages' (309). In the end, the British combatants appears to have more in common with their enemies than with the civilians. Death is construed as an ever-present aspect of this Gothic sensibility, in which the traumatised ghosts of the dead projectively inhabit the trauma of those who have killed them. As in Owen's poem, enemies become reunited in death. The Gothic, in this instance, erases distinctions between self and other (reflected in Hall's projected ghost) as the subject becomes, again, trapped by feelings of loss and trauma. The graveyard captures these feelings, which are reflected in the pathos of the 'mouldering' caps, which evoke the mouldering bodies in the grave. That thoughts about violent death haunt the culture is also demonstrated by graves, which, like the ghost, are in pursuit.

Mobile Graves

This chapter has explored how the war dead do not, culturally speaking, stay in place and this problem is addressed with distinctive force in L. P. Hartley's 'The Travelling Grave' (1929). Hartley had been conscripted into the army during the war but, due to ill health, did not serve overseas. He was friends with C. H. B. Kitchin, and 'The Travelling

Grave' includes queer undertones which can also be found in some of Hartley's novels. The tale reads like a notably dark, single-sex rendering of a country-house crime story, made popular at the time by Agatha Christie, and centres on a country house owned by Dick Munt, an eccentric collector of curiosities. He is joined by his friends Tony Bettisher, who works at the British Museum, and Valentine Ostrop, who has invited his friend Hugh Curtis to join the party, although Hugh is unknown to the others. Hugh is initially sceptical about attending an all-male house party because he liked to spend his leisure 'time in the society of agreeable women' (Hartley 1929: 9). Valentine's attempts to persuade Hugh to join the party seem unpromising, given Hugh's antipathy to all-male gatherings. Valentine's language is thinly coded as homosexual; he describes Dick as '"original and – and queer, if you like"' and says that Hugh is '"just the type he likes"' (10). Hugh is persuaded to go but has doubts about Valentine because, although enjoying his company when they are together, he notes that 'directly Valentine fell in with kindred spirits he developed a kind of foppishness of manners that Hugh instinctively disliked' (10), which is suggested in the story by Valentine's seemingly affected, camp intonation when he is with Dick and Tony. This queer context to the story emphasises that the ties between the men are, despite Hugh's misgivings, putatively personal and at one level Hugh is construed as a type of plaything for the other men. Hugh, although apprehensive about the weekend, reassures himself that whatever ordeal the house party might pose, it will not kill him. However, 'With the war, this saving reservation had to be dropped: they could kill him, that was what they were there for', although he attempts to reassure himself with the consoling idea (construed as a type of lucky charm) that 'now Peace was here, the little mental amulet once more diffused its healing properties' (11). Unbeknown to Hugh, he is heading into a situation in which Dick intends to murder him with one of his new curiosities.

Hugh is scheduled to arrive late at the house while the other three meet and discuss Dick's new acquisition. The conversation has a somewhat surreal air to it, with Valentine thinking that Dick has been collecting perambulators. This seems a discreet, if knowing, joke about the homosocial bonds which exist between the men, implying that they are not family men. Valentine's misunderstanding thus functions as a protracted joke in which he demonstrates an aversion to babies because '"I do not care to contemplate lumps of human flesh lacking the spirit that makes flesh tolerable"' (15). The joke is that Dick collects coffins, not perambulators, but Valentine's revulsion towards babies is also a revulsion towards the dead, present in the reference to mangled remains as 'lumps of human flesh'.

Dick's most recent addition to his collection, which he has acquired from abroad, is a type of motorised coffin which can seek out and kill a person that it makes its occupant. This coming to life of a death machine evokes Freud's idea that the uncanny is characterised by inanimate forms coming to life. The coffin seems to have a life of its own, so that 'You couldn't quite tell where it was coming; it seemed to have no settled direction, and to move all ways at once, like a crab' (18). The coffin also represents the presence of *Thanatos*, which is associated with the war, despite Hugh's confidence that peace might be finally present. As in the sudden and seemingly random killings on the battlefield, the coffin has the attribute of being able to conceal itself and to pounce on its victim. Dick explains '"It just doubles the man up [...] directly it catches him – backwards to break the spine. The top of the head fits in just below the heels. The soles of the feet come uppermost"' (18). The death machine appears to be oddly sentient because it can be hidden within most surfaces, except a stone floor where '"it screams in agony and blunts the blades"' (18). This roving Gothic coffin represents an apparently unstoppable force, and although intended for the outside, it can be brought into the home, with its knives concealed under a parquet covering; it can also be made to resemble a chest. The coffin thus ghosts the house in uncanny ways as the home now becomes associated with death and danger within the context of a sinister country house game which playfully employs the coffin as a form of entertainment.

Dick proposes that they play a game of Hide and Seek in the dark, with Hugh to be given instructions on arrival that he has to be the one to find them. Valentine regards this as a game of 'mimic warfare', and it is one in which the coffin is intended to play a central role. Valentine accidentally hides in a chest he finds in the bathroom, which turns out to be the deactivated coffin. From there, he hears Dick telling Tony that they should test the coffin on Hugh, who is unknown to them, and who has no relations and would not be missed. The tale indicates that it is Dick who is the Gothic monster of the text, although one who has unleashed forces that he cannot control. Tony tries to talk him out of this plan and simply to test whether the device can bury itself in the way that it has been designed. When they leave the room, Valentine takes the coffin and hides it in a cupboard inside a room, which he then locks. Valentine intends to escape when Hugh arrives but finds the house quiet, with Hugh waiting in the Library. Hugh tells him that he has discovered something odd in his room: a pair of shoes, with the soles uppermost and seemingly nailed to the floor. An investigation reveals that the shoes contain feet and that below them, within the floor, lie the 'crushed' (37) remains of Dick.

This seemingly bizarre tale of mechanical graves and a country house set makes sense within the context of the war. The idea that graves seek you out and that our understanding of death has been fundamentally changed by the war was also acknowledged by Freud when he noted in 'Thoughts for the Times on War and Death' that people are now confronted by 'the altered attitude towards death which this – like every other war – forces upon us' (Freud 1991c: 62). In 'The Travelling Grave' death is portable, seemingly robotic and impossible to resist. The coffin is a death machine but Dick is the Gothic agent in this, one who mistakenly believes that he is able to control the coffin and its role within the game of Hide and Seek. Dick might get his comeuppance at the end but his body is a representationally mangled manifestation of the war dead, one which evokes the '"lumps of human flesh"' that Valentine had cited earlier. Dick's death also seems accidental rather than providential. His sadistic mentality, in which killing constitutes a form of amusement, captures the horror of battlefield death. He articulates a variation of the type of Gothic sensibility that we have explored here, to the degree that he is defined by the violent impulses of war that cannot be moved beyond, and he is definitively not associated with the peace for which Hugh optimistically reaches out. In this post-war world, death has become inescapable as it now enters into the home in a notably traumatic rendering of the uncanny which indicates that the war permeates the post-war culture.

'The Case of Lieutenant Hall' addresses a ghostly revenge from the past and civilian contempt in the present. 'The Travelling Grave' is also about how violent death seems to stalk you in a symbolic articulation of the continuing effects of war. Both tales are complex revenge narratives in which death, rather than peace, triumphs in the end. The new Gothic sensibility, defined by a feeling of being trapped by war-induced horror, is also manifested in the impossibility of finding a narrative form which can coherently explain trauma, precisely because a post-traumatic world never appears. Psychological disorientation and narrative confusion bear testimony to the disturbing lingering emotional legacies of the war. Ghosts who are not easy to contain within a reassuring plot reflect directly on the problem of how to narrate the war. Ghosts who roam outside of plots illustrate another way in which this new Gothic sensibility appears – such ghosts defy meaning and so fail to provide the type of closure, or psychological containment, which is needed in order to move beyond the war. The memoirs of Edward Blunden repeatedly refer to plotless ghosts which are used to reflect on the persistence, and the new psychological reality, of the war experience and help to develop further our understanding of the new Gothic sensibility explored here.

Blunden's Ghosts: Narratives of War

Blunden's poem 'The Aftermath' (1923) includes the lines:

> Who goes there? come, ghost or man,
>   You were with us, you will know;
> Let us commune, there's no ban
>   On speech for us if we speak low
>
> Time has healed the wound, they say,
>   Gone's the weeping and the rain;
> Yet you and I suspect, the day
>   Will never be the same again. (Blunden 2015c: ll. 5–12)

Blunden's poetry and his memoir, *Undertones of War* (1928), repeatedly employ ghosts to reflect on the experience of World War One. The sentiment expressed in the above lines recalls the message of Aldington's 'The Case of Lieutenant Hall' and Owen's 'Strange Meeting'. There is a connection here between the living and the dead that only they can comprehend. As the title and date of the poem indicate, this is a post-war reflection and exposes a gulf in understanding between the combatant and non-combatant. In memoirs of the war, this problem of representation recurs when a narrative tries to capture a sense of the unreality of frontline experience, which, as we have seen with trauma generally, requires new representational forms to express it. In September 1916, while based in Auchonvillers, Blunden notes that 'The sector began to look extremely neat – except the front line, which remained impressionist, and bulged and silted at its own sweet will' (Blunden 2015a: 84). This view of an 'impressionist' frontline reflects a view of the war-torn landscape which was often recycled in the narrative forms adopted to represent World War One. Aldington's dedication to *Death of a Hero* (to the playwright Halcott Glover) acknowledges this issue about representation in a statement which both refutes an artistic influence and acknowledges, if very grudgingly, its possible presence: 'I am all for disregarding artistic rules of thumb. I dislike standardised art as much as standardised life. Whether I have been guilty of Expressionism or Super-realism or not, I don't know and don't care' (Aldington 1929: ix). He prefers to see the book as 'a jazz novel', indebted to the free-form, improvisational poetry that he had developed before the war (x). Here, Aldington is like the ghost story writer A. M. Burrage, who notes in his war memoir, *War is War* (1930), that the abrupt shift in its tonal registers was due to 'trying to recapture the mood of the moment. Out there

Comedy and Tragedy tumbled over each other's heels as in one of the old-fashioned melodramas' (Burrage 2009: 6). How to accommodate the ghost poses problems for narrative coherence when the narrative is obviously not influenced, as is Hyder's 'A Nightmare', by the conventions of the ghost story. In Blunden, ghosts seem to roam freely and their meaning is unclear precisely because they cannot be incorporated within a narrative structure which would make sense of them. These newly formed Gothic ghosts defy the expectations of the conventional ghost story.

On 3 September 1916, while waiting to go into battle at Hamel and putting out buckets of grenades for use in the forthcoming attack, Blunden notes the presence of 'a stranger in a soft cap and trench coat' who asks him the way to the German lines. He recalls that 'This visitor was white-faced as a ghost' (Blunden 2015a: 77) as Blunden directs him towards the communications trench. Blunden is unsure if the man is British or a possible spy and is unclear why he is in the trench at all. His suggestion about the deathly pallor of the man is not intended to imply that he is symbolic of death, or that he might be the ghost of an old combatant, but emphasises his being out of place, given the context of the battlefield preparations which are structured and planned. A language of the spectral employed to emphasise that a person does not belong is a feature of battlefield ghosts, who also do not seem to relate to any coherent, pre-existing, reality. We have noted how this new Gothic sensibility is characterised by feelings of psychological and metaphysical disorientation, which generate spectral forms that are closely related to it. On 13 November 1916, Blunden recalls coming under heavy bombardment at Thiepval, during which he becomes disorientated by 'the furious dance of high explosive' which surrounds him and his men, but then notes that 'At this minute, a man, or a ghost went by, and I tried to follow him' (Blunden 2015a: 109). The ghost might be a helpful guide but its ontological status is unclear. As in the first anecdote about the pale-faced 'ghost', the figure is out of place because he has no obvious function other than as a possible guide, but it is not clear where to, given the chaotic condition of the frontline. In these instances, ghosts appear without stories, as roaming entities, and that is because the frontline is a disorientating ghostly place which generates these unaccountable spectres.

No-man's-land is a living dead place, inhabited by invisible armies (dug into their trenches), who are seemingly awaiting death. Siegfried Sassoon recalls this possibility of death on the eve of an offensive when he reflects upon 'the soldiers who slept around us in their hundreds – were they not like the dead, among who in some dim region where time survived in ghostly remembrances[?]' (Sassoon 1997: 72). They are both alive and dead, trapped in a limbo world topographically suggested by no-man's-land itself, which, for Sassoon, is left in a state of radical uncertainty because the soldier 'can find no meaning in the immense destruction which he blindly accepts as part of some hidden purpose' (73). It is this lack of narrative and definite substance which makes the experience devoid of meaning (unless one 'blindly accepts [...] some hidden purpose'), so that, for Blunden, 'It was all a ghost story' (Blunden 2015a: 42). These new Gothic ghosts are specific entities which haunt, in a conventional way, the geographical place with which they are associated (as *genius loci*), even while, unconventionally, no meaning is ascribed to their presence. Later, Blunden recalls a bombardment of trench mortar shells (minnies) on the German line and references his exuberance at being able 'To throw minnies into that ghost of a front line!' (57). Ford Madox Ford, in his essay 'War and the Mind' (1917), similarly recalls that 'No Man's land always remains in my mind as blue – a blue grey mist; a blue grey muddle of little hills – but fabulous and supernatural' (Ford 2004: 42). The liminality of the place is also repeatedly used to reflect on the ghost-like feeling of trying to live in a world of death, which Manning had also addressed in *Her Privates We*.

Identity can also be erased in other ways through the sheer scale of casualties. In October 1917, Blunden recounts meeting with two officers from the Royal Fusiliers. Over drinks in the new half-built dugout, the Colonel tells Blunden that '"We no longer exist"' (Blunden 2015a: 182), explaining that as their casualties were now over 400, they were no longer a viable fighting unit. He instructs Blunden about what needs to be repaired in the trench system of what was known as the Hedge Street Tunnels and reiterates that his men cannot undertake the work because '"*We no longer exist*"' (Blunden 2015a: 183 italics in original). While the Colonel's comment is intended to provide a pragmatic explanation for why his unit has been forced to pull out, Blunden tacitly reads the words as having more metaphysical connotations when, in the following lines, he recalls this damaged trench system as a 'dirty but precious underworld' (183). It is both physically present but utterly unreal, a place in which people do not exist in any obviously human form. Just prior to this encounter with the officers, he states that he has been reading Edward Young's *Night Thoughts* (1742–5), a key Gothic precursor text, 'At every spare moment' because Young's reflections on life and death are 'applicable to our crisis' (178); the Graveyard School of poetry speaks directly to his concerns, echoed in that line about a 'precious underworld'. Blunden's encounter with the Royal Fusiliers also appears in Guy Chapman's memoir *A Passionate Prodigality: Fragments of Autobiography* (1933). Chapman recalls that his Colonel had said '"We no longer exist"' (Chapman 1965: 205) because they had sustained 80 per cent casualties. Chapman refers to Blunden as 'a very young, very fair and very shy subaltern' (207), who gave him a copy of his poetry collection *The Harbingers* before Chapman left the frontline.

Chapman, in turn, was married to Storm Jameson, whose *Company Parade* (1934) includes many post-war ghosts (some of which are discussed later in this chapter). Chapman repeatedly refers to ghosts when writing about the landscape which has effectively been destroyed by the war. These ghosts represent the spirit of the place and pre-date the war. Chapman notes:

> While you wander through the corrupted overgrown orchard, there is always someone at your back. You turn. It is nothing but the creak of a branch, broken with the same wanton merriment with which a shell breaks a human limb and leaves it hanging by the frail tension of the skin. In all these destroyed places at the fringe of the line [...] there is always the apprehension of ghosts; not those of the men who have died there, but of something older, something less perishable, the spirit of the place itself which watches the inquisitive idler with eyes half fearful, as if to ask, 'Will you too profane me?' (Chapman 1965: 43)

The landscape is possessed by a *genius loci*, or guardian spirit, which has a longstanding presence in the tradition of the ghost story in the guise of protective or vengeful ghosts, which appear repeatedly in the tales of M. R. James, discussed in Chapter 4. This violation of the landscape, and the sadness of its *genius loci*, acknowledge that it too is a casualty of war. Chapman's projected animation of the dead landscape glosses typical references to no-man's-land as a liminal ghostly place, but it also represents it as a victim which cannot be adequately protected from the ravages of high explosives. The guardian spirit of the place cannot make sense of the war but it can provide a context, and a type of witnessing, for the seemingly mindless nature of the conflict.

If literature provides one way of rationalising battlefield experience, the specific figure of the ghost is troubling because, at least in these instances, it cannot be contained within any narrative structure that would help to generate the type of meaning for which Blunden and Sassoon are looking. To be a ghost is to become an interloper, and Blunden finds this status confirmed when he semi-humorously suggests that he and some other officers have ousted, and so made ghostly, the French occupants of a large, well-appointed and undamaged manor house. He notes of the main room, with its expensive furnishings and piano, that 'The room was unreal and supernatural, nor did I feel easy about the spirits' attitude towards my drinking my whisky by that incredible piano. Surely strange music would begin in tones of protest and prophecy' (Blunden 2015a: 87). The *genii locorum* of the house are acknowledged but wryly handled, and consequently do not function as a formal uncanny element within an occupied home. If there is a Gothic element here, it is in the reflection that Blunden is the figure of war who has ousted the peaceful occupants, and how much he represents a possible source of destruction is indicated when he contrasts this pleasurable hiatus with the reality of war; he wonders how long it would be 'before the spell was snapped and the day gaped impudently through irreparable shell-holes on these exorcised haunters?' (87). It is not clear at this point who these ghosts are: the original occupants or the current ones? Is the house ghosted by its pre-war inhabitants (and their projected annoyance) or the occupying officers (and their illegitimate temporary ownership)? The point is that Blunden sees this version of civilisation as a fragile one because it can be so easily supplanted by images of the war while the vestiges of the immediate past continue to reside there quite spectrally.

In this new Gothic sensibility, ghosts can appear as a trick of the imagination but such tricks have symbolic import. In May 1916 at Festubert, Blunden proceeds down a road which has been riddled by machine gun fire, and he later recalls:

> Giving such things their full value, I took my road with no little pride and fear; one morning I feared very sharply, as I saw what looked like a rising shroud over a wooden cross in the clustering mist. Horror! But on closer study I realized that the apparition was only a flannel gas helmet spread out over the memorial. (22)

A supernatural anticipation of death, in which a dead soldier arises from the grave, is displaced by a synecdoche whose presence is due to the gas attacks which so many of the soldiers feared. This is a classic act of Gothic displacement, in which one terror conceals another. What is Gothically present – the ghost, the monster – conceals the fear which it symbolically articulates (a fear of a notably terrifying death). The dead do not come alive again but the fear of death is made present, despite Blunden's use of 'only'.

As we have seen, this Gothic sensibility sees death as inescapable, which is why Blunden's reading of *Night Thoughts* represents an attempt to find meaning in death, or at least in some version of spiritual transcendence. Signs and portents are thus eagerly looked for and decoded. Shortly after this encounter with the cross and the gas helmet, Blunden records how some men in his battalion see shapes in the mist, so that 'when one evening a wisp of vapour was seen by my working party to glide from west to east', it became construed as forming the shape of either a cross or a sword, and 'then there was a subdued conversation about it, which spread from man to man' (23).[3] Blunden notes that his batman, Shearing, reads the image as a sword and interprets it as indicating a pending disaster. This superstitious reading of a questionable image in a cloud formation was not unusual during World War One. Arthur Machen's 'The Bowmen' (1914), about the Angel of Mons, was born out of such superstition. The decoding of these 'visions' represents an attempt to make sense of the war by identifying structure, meaning and purpose – and so the type of psychological containment, albeit here non-maternal, identified by Bion. In this instance, Blunden's soldiers are stimulated by some discussion from the night before about what the lights used by the Germans to communicate with each other might mean, because to the British soldiers it all looks like 'wild incoherence' (23). In Blunden's memoir, the roaming ghost repeatedly figures this incoherence.

Blunden's reflection on ghosts long after the war is different from his evocations of wartime spectres. In his Introduction to the 1964 edition of *Undertones of War*, for example, he emphasises that the book was intended to introduce the war to a 'new generation', so much so that 'I wish for no phantoms to disturb such as may pass through the Old Western Front' (Blunden 2015c: 328). In his poem 'Mont de Cassel' (composed 1917, published 1920), Blunden reaches out for a more immediate possible post-war moment:

> To us, let the war be a leering ghost now shriven,
> And as though it had never been;
> A tragedy mask discarded.
> A lamp in a tomb. (Blunden 2015d: ll. 9–12)

The message is to let death stay dead (because 'shriven' and so in receipt of absolution, unlike Manning's 'unhouseled ghosts'), and yet death also illuminates (as a 'lamp') and gives reasons for why the war dead lie in a 'tomb'. Ghosts mean many different things in Blunden's writings; that he was self-conscious about such matters is indicated by the title of his 1932 pamphlet, *Fall In, Ghosts*. The figure of the ghost is just beyond meaning in Blunden and functions as a liminal figure who is both absent and present. Such encounters with ghosts, after all, indicate a hesitant pursuit of certainty and coherence in what otherwise appears as the irrational and chaotic circumstances of a notably Gothic no-man's-land.

Blunden's inter-war writings were also shaped by his experiences of the war. Desmond Graham has noted that Blunden's essay on *King*

Lear, published in 1936, addresses issues of 'madness' that Blunden had encountered in the trenches.[4] John Greening has noted that much of that essay can be related to *The Undertones of War*, since Blunden remarks of *King Lear* that 'I do not know that it can be called a study of insanity. It is rather a revelation of the sanity, or inevitable sequence, underlying and co-ordinating what superficially seems incoherence' (Blunden 1936: 328), an apparent incoherence represented by the roaming ghost in his memoirs. How to think about the new realities of the war, and their relationship to such Gothic tropes, is also tacitly explored in Vera Brittain's *Testament of Youth* (1933).

Brittain's Ghosts

Testament of Youth is a work of mourning, not just for the death of Brittain's fiancé, Roland, her brother Edward and her close friends, Victor Richardson and Geoffrey Thurlow, but for a way of life. Brittain states that she found it impossible to connect with the lives of those who had not been through the conflict, which she saw at first hand in her experiences as a nurse in the Voluntary Aid Detachment (VAD), both in Britain and in Malta. For her, the war fundamentally changed the nature of reality and so the anticipated future of her quite privileged social world. She notes, as mentioned in the previous chapter, that, with the war, 'now the universe had become irrational, and nothing was turning out as it once seemed to have been ordained' (Brittain 2014: 259). Her night-time encounters with ghosts appear to confirm this metaphysical shift: 'Once, in the midst of trying to read a Strindberg play, I felt ghostly fingers gently stirring my hair, and twice mysterious footsteps walked slowly up the ward, stopped opposite my table and never returned' (203). These are, like Blunden's ghosts, spectres without a narrative and her memoir illustrates how this war-induced Gothic sensibility permeated the experience of those beyond the frontline. Her memoir may not focus on battlefield encounters, but Brittain's day-to-day dealing with death on the hospital ward leads her to view the world, by way of a psychological projection that is highly Gothic, as possessing a deathly immanence which disrupts her pre-war notions of an ordered reality. She notes, for example, when recalling a night-time walk in Camberwell: 'In front of me on the frozen pavement a long red worm wriggles slimily. I remember that, after our death, worms destroy this body – however lovely, however beloved – and I run from the obscene thing in horror' (215). Brittain is clearly in mourning for Roland at this stage but it is not just grief which tempers this sense of a new world governed by death. Rather, it suggests a fundamental shift in how to think about the world and ultimately, as her memoir progresses, how to change the nature of that world politically; it is an impulse which, typically in such memoirs, is reflected in the problems Brittain has with narrative composition.

Brittain notes in her Foreword that she had originally planned to translate her war experiences into the form of a long novel but found the subjects too close to her to exercise the necessary imaginative detachment. The attempt to create the narrative out of her edited journal with the names changed also did not work, since 'the fictitious names created a false atmosphere and made the whole thing seem spurious' (xxvi). In the end, she settles on a textual structure which draws upon her journal, letters and poems to create a composite narrative of overlapping forms. While it would be difficult to claim her memoir as indebted to Modernist bricolage, it is telling that a new form of writing about the war is needed in order to make coherent sense of war experiences so that the very diversity of material generates an 'honest' (xxvi) account. The effect is to make Brittain appear as an editor, reflecting upon the documents written during the war. These reflections are often coloured by the importance accorded to signs and symbols, frequently in ways that recall the Gothic. On the first anniversary of Roland's death, she notes that she was kneeling by her bed thinking about him when, 'at the very hour of his death, the whole sky was lighted up and everything outside became queerly and startlingly visible' (290) – reminiscent of Nathaniel Hawthorne's *The Scarlet Letter* (1850). She had assumed that this was lightning but, as the light lingers, 'I felt quite uncanny and afraid and hid my face in my hands for two or three minutes' (290). She later learns that it was a shooting star, and although she attributes the timing to 'coincidence', finds it 'strange from my point of view' (290). It is a moment which recalls Blunden's account of soldiers reading cloud formations for signs and portents. The implication is that the world has become a Gothic space which tries to communicate with us, although not in a reassuring, quasi-Christian way. Shortly after this, she recalls a moment in Malta when, clambering over some rocks on her journey back to base, 'I never felt quite at ease among those rocks; a strange silence pervaded them and a sense of being observed, as though age-old presences were watching [...] with hostile, inhuman eyes.' The world is freighted with a Gothic malevolence – *genii locorum* of a more hostile kind than that found in Chapman and Blunden. She also records that 'among the rocks a deep scarlet vetch grew from so shallow a soil that it seemed to spring from the very face of the stone, and created, quite startlingly, an illusion of spilt blood' (293). This is a landscape that, in its danger, reworks the conceit of the haunted wilderness that we find recurring so often in the Gothic tradition of the weird, such as that of Algernon Blackwood and Arthur Machen.⁵ It is entirely apt that a Gothic version of a bloody landscape is evoked here, as it suggests the battlefield but also grants it a hostile supernatural agency.

Death is seemingly never very far way in these moments, and frequently, too, the figure of the ghost has a role to play in them. These ghosts are not always malevolent Gothic entities, as they have more in common with the culture of spiritualism, which is discussed in depth in the following chapter. Brittain, for example, recalls an instance in her hospital when a number of soldiers discuss encounters with ghosts on the battlefield. One recounts how a much-admired dead officer reappeared in the midst of a battle to help spur his men on, while another affirms that some dead stretcher bearers were recently seen 'carrying the wounded down the communication trench' (379). Another mentions giving a biscuit to a pale-looking soldier that he then remembers having helped to bury a week before. Brittain quizzes the Sergeant about this recollection, and he insists '"Aye, Sister, they're dead right enough. They're our mates as was knocked out on the Somme in '16. And it's our belief they're fightin' with us still"' (380). These ghosts are not the chance encounters that are found in Blunden. The continuing combatants serve a purpose because they are bound by ties of loyalty to their comrades, and this structure provides coherence to what is otherwise metaphysically confusing. This narrative of male bonding makes sense of the ghost as a friend and saviour. Brittain, however, dismisses the idea of battlefield ghosts as suggesting 'Angels of Mons still roaming about, I thought. Well, let them roam, if it cheers the men to believe in them!' (Brittain 2014: 380). However, these are not ghosts who roam; they fulfil a precise purpose in supporting their comrades. Brittain's response to the discussion of ghosts is rooted within her experience of nursing, in which the dead do not come back, so much so that 'I recognised my world for the kingdom of death, in which the poor ghosts of the victims had no power to help their comrades by breaking nature's laws' (Brittain 2014: 380). This pragmatic dismissal of the soldiers' superstition is also because their ghosts are quite different from hers. Ghosts for Brittain are about memory and mourning, and how that has changed her version of the world, as she sees it as a Gothic place inhabited by malign forces – which is a psychological *and* a political assessment of the effect of the war. For her, other ghosts are simply forms of optimistic emotional or psychological projection, which makes her memoir a knowing exercise in psychological self-reflection. Different communities reach out for different ghosts.

Brittain recalls that, after the death of her brother, killed on the Italian front in June 1918, 'I remember walking down the shimmering Sunday emptiness of Kensington High Street on the hot summer morning after the telegram came, intoxicated, strangely *exaltée*, lifted into incongruous ecstasy by a sense that Edward's invisible presence was walking beside me' (407, italics in original). The sense of loss has clearly not yet fully registered, and after this one moment 'everything lapsed into paralysis. I did not want to speak or even to think much about him' (407). Ghosts for Brittain do not keep the past alive, but constitute an absent presence in which loss is felt only through mourning. She is unable to find solace in the popular spiritualist practices recommended by friends. After the armistice, she notes that 'The War was over; a new age was beginning; but the dead were dead and would never return' (424). She recalls that, on returning to Oxford after the war, she initially threw herself into tennis parties, 'for I was sick beyond description of death and loss' (442), and yet these distractions provide only temporary relief from a Gothic sensibility; as she notes in a later letter to her Oxford contemporary, Winifred Holtby, 'I am bogy-ridden by ghosts' (Brittain 2014: 550) because she cannot yet cast off the past. For Brittain, these ghosts do not make sense because they reflect the meaninglessness of the war itself. Again, it is this inability to make sense of the war which constitutes a central element of this new Gothic sensibility, which is haunted by the past and unable to envisage the future because, on a psychological level, peace seems impossible.

Brittain's account of the war illustrates how trauma is not confined simply to those on the battlefield. Her memoir is motivated by a question which she states in the closing pages: 'If the dead could come back, I wondered what would they say to me?' (603). The war cannot be cast off because 'The surge and swell of its movements, its changes, its tendencies, still mould me and the surviving remnant of my generation whether we wish it or not', since those still alive have become ghosted 'by the universal breakdown of reason' (603) initiated by the war. The plotless, roaming ghost thus becomes a representative figure of unreason and is produced out of war-induced anxieties. This is a new form of the Gothic which registers feelings of loss and alienation. We will see in Chapter 4, in the work of E. F. Benson, how his post-war ghost stories, in contrast to his pre-war ghost stories, are populated by seemingly randomly malevolent spectres, which develops further Brittain's sense of occupying a hostile world.

This chapter has explored the repeated difficulty with narrative form in accounts of the war. How to narrate the war is part of the story of how to plot experiences of a war which often felt random or subject to the type of irrationality that so many memoirs record. Blunden and Brittain's accounts are canonical, but this feature also appears in more recently published memoirs which often draw upon previously unpublished journals and diaries deposited with the Imperial War Museum. *The Reluctant Tommy* (2010) by Ronald Skirth is based on an account of his experience of the war begun in 1971 and subsequently bequeathed to the museum.[6] Even from his 1970s vantage point, the war is still a difficult topic for narration. Skirth notes that his account is 'a scrapbook, a hotch-potch, a medley. It doesn't follow any pattern at all' (Skirth 2010: 5) and has required editorial intervention finally to develop it into a publishable form. Part of the fear is related to having to recollect painful memories that may take on a life of their own, which prompts Skirth to state at the start of his account of arriving in France that 'I shall get on with my story. I have just one fear: that before long the story will take over from me' (33). The problem for Skirth is that he narrates different contexts which relate to the war *and* to his home life (the memoir is, in part, a love story about his wife). He acknowledges the difficulty in relating, and so narrating, the connections between these different worlds, which is 'as if a child had thrown the pieces of several different jig-saw puzzles on the floor and had to find not only <u>which</u> pieces belong to <u>which</u> puzzle, but how each individual puzzle fits together' (104, emphasis in original). These concerns cannot be attributed to the difficulties confronted by a non-professional writer because they are also a feature of Blunden and Brittain's memoirs. They also reflect an anxiety about textual fragmentation which implicitly reflects on bodily fragmentation. One of the more harrowing experiences related by Skirth concerns his discovery of the dismembered bodies of two of his friends. As he heads back towards the British frontline, he records that 'It was my loneliness as much as my fear that made me see those ghastly swollen parts of bodies somehow assembling themselves into horrific evil beings' (74). This fear of the dead has depersonalised these bodies. This conversion implicitly addresses the concerns of Freud and Rivers that, during the war, the subject becomes associated with a reawakened subhumanity. The dead become reassembled as Gothic monsters who are potentially (as 'evil beings') out for revenge. Many of the writings discussed here are retrospective accounts of the war, although often situated within its timeframe. Painful recollections help to shape an emerging Gothic sensibility which employs ghosts in order to make sense of the past. Texts set in the immediate post-war period provide an alternative context for the Gothic, one which suggests, as does Brittain, that the peacetime world is haunted by the ghosts of the war.

Time and Ghosts: Storm Jameson

Storm Jameson's writing was, like her friend Vera Brittain's, defined by the war. She was a social realist writer whose work was shaped by socialist ideals and tempered by progressive gender concerns. Two of her novels, *The Three Kingdoms* (1926) and *That Was Yesterday* (1932), focus on the wartime struggles of those on the home front. Her use of ghosts seems incongruous, given her adherence to social realism, but her employment of them tellingly reflects on ideas about time – specifically, about whether a pre-war world exists that can be viably revived or whether that world merely retains a spectral cultural presence. The question is addressed most forcefully in Jameson's *Company Parade*, the first part of her *Mirror in Darkness* trilogy (1934–6), which focuses on the life of one Hervey Russell. It is a narrative about those who have returned home after fighting in the war; however, unlike the stories discussed in the previous chapter, the return home does not exorcise the war. The novel centres on Hervey's decision to move to London from Yorkshire after the armistice in 1918, in order to make a living and to be near her feckless husband, Vane, who has served in a non-combatant role with the RAF during the war and has yet to leave the service. Hervey is a novelist working on her second novel, and when she moves to London she meets up with old friends T. S., married to an influential magazine editor, and Philip, who has ambitions to establish a radical newspaper, and who is able to secure a place for Hervey as a copywriter working in advertising. The process of writing and editing unites a number of the principal characters, who are all struggling to find their post-war voices through either politics or literature. Hervey is conscious that advertising is a type of lying that requires skills of manipulation that she is not fully comfortable with, despite the view of the company's director that, although 'advertising still lacks its Shakespeare', nevertheless 'Great advertising is the expression of deep emotional sincerity' (Jameson 1982: 15). Finding truth in such an artificial world is the problem confronted by Hervey as she tries to reconnect with her deceiving husband. Advertising articulates a truth about a commercial culture which generates a specific rhetoric that stands in contrast to the political and aesthetic ambitions found elsewhere in the novel. The book is not a Gothic novel in any explicit way, but it is ghost-ridden and an analysis of it helps to advance our understanding of how the Gothic shaped certain ways of thinking about the war.

David and the aforementioned Philip are former soldiers whose lives are haunted by the war. Philip has withdrawn from London and lives on the outskirts in the country, but a 'spectre followed him day and night' and he is pursued by the haunting feeling that 'In the last War the flower of England died *uselessly*' (Jameson 1982: 172, italics in original). He is haunted by feelings and ideas of failure and, on occasion, by specific individuals. As in the texts discussed throughout this chapter, reality has become Gothic because it harbours within it images of ghosts which reflect psychological and metaphysical disorientation. Philip discusses the war with David, a poet who has given up on poetry and who is attempting to write an account of a wartime retreat that they had been involved in, only to find that '"I can't find any words hard enough. They ought to be as sharp and hard as flints. I've given up"' (173), which is in keeping with the narrative difficulties that we have witnessed in Brittain, Skirth and others. Part of the problem with representing reality is associated with the culture of advertising. Philip, for example, is conscious of the injustice of the war, which leads him to contemplate wider social divisions and the sense that his generation was 'born to be defrauded' (172), all of which implicitly reflects the dominant world of advertising that the novel construes as economic and cultural propaganda. Philip may live in isolation but he is conscious of the war dead that surround him, to such an extent that 'there was always a ghost or two to step up and keep him company' (43). The war is ever-present for Philip, who sees these ghosts, not as objects of terror, but as lost comrades, so that 'He liked to feel them about when they came, but he never encouraged them' (43). Their presence enables a sense of a righteous bonding, in which the war dead retain a transcendence in which they all remain 'very young' (43). These are ghosts which are different to the malevolent entities associated with the conventional ghost story; instead, they emphasise Philip's difficulty with engaging with the post-war world. They help to nuance our critical understanding of the Gothic ghost because they demonstrate that a Gothic sensibility has been internalised as a way of thinking about a relationship to the war itself – one in which tensions between the present and the past form the temporal terrain traversed by these newly formed spectres. This sense that the ghost enables you to step out of the present suggests the presence of the type of duality that recurs so repeatedly in the Gothic tradition of Stevenson and Wilde. Philip becomes conscious that 'He had two bodies, one which sweated and rebelled, and another which remained apart and could think clearly concerning everything except time' (172). This second self is free from time, so that 'he was often surprised to find night falling on a day no longer than the single thought that had occupied him since waking' (172). This new self is not the shock-induced fugue that Rivers discussed in *Instinct and the Unconscious* and yet, to the degree that it is produced in reaction to the war, it bears a symbolic association with it. The double is, of course, a key Gothic figure and here we see an instance in which a Gothic trope becomes incorporated within a text to exemplify how a new form of self-reflection becomes generated. This transcendent self bears witness to the damaged bodies of those who, like Philip and David, have fought in the war. It represents the optimistic possibility of a new agency, because of which Philip 'still believed that he could help the world' (43). This second self functions as an inner spirit and is the ghost within the body, but by virtue of being a ghost it is beyond death because it appears to stand outside of time. It represents a new level of self-awareness that enables the subject to stand outside of the traumatised self. Here, the Gothic double does not hold you back, as it would in Stevenson and Wilde, and in Freud's account of the double in 'The Uncanny', but represents the possibility of envisioning a new world and the subject's relationship to it. However, there is another aspect of the double trapped within time which inherits something of a more conventional Gothic form because it occupies a place within finite time. Although one version of the self appears to be transcendent, the other version exists within time and is susceptible to change. The temporally conditioned self threatens to alienate the potentially positive transcendent inner spectre. The subject is thus trapped between the pull of the past and ambitions for the future. This stands as a notably Gothic rendering of a peacetime world eager to embrace the future but constrained by memories of the war. These issues about time and the capacity for reflection are linked to ideas about social and cultural belonging that relate to the pre-war world.

Company Parade is self-conscious about whether a post-war culture can reconnect with a pre-war world. Hervey's friend, T. S., tells her about a trip that he and Philip made to a place in Surrey in 1913 and then their more recent visit to it:

> 'The place was torn to pieces. The field of the chestnut tree is a street of new houses, ending nowhere, so ugly you never saw, the grey manor house is a tea-shop, the hedges have been cut down, houses everywhere, like a disease, and the air reeks of petrol. We couldn't find our way and were as lost as ghosts.' (150)

T. S.'s assumption is that ghosts roam and this view reflects those of the unaccommodated ghost which so often appears as the site of trauma in war memoirs and is used here to emphasise T. S.'s and Philip's alienation. The use of 'we' in this passage is also telling; while it refers to Philip and T. S.'s experience, it is also intended to suggest that they are representative figures of a type of post-war community that does not recognise this post-war world. They are 'lost as ghosts' because this is a new world which does not culturally accommodate them. T. S.'s account of their visit registers the view that a pre-war world has been lost due to the development of a post-war suburban sprawl which implicates the presence of a lower-middle-class culture (tea-shops replacing manor houses) that upsets the old order. T. S. relates Philip's response: '"I'm glad we didn't go over to look at the battlefields. I shouldn't be surprised if some brute has gone and built houses on them"' (150). This scene represents the erasure of the pre-war world and a concern that the war will itself become forgotten, overwritten by social and economic developments. There is no way back and no way to proceed, so the future looks uncertain. As with Philip's dualism, the body ties you into the past, and the spirit seems to connect you to the present, but there is no identifiable way forward. For Philip and T. S., these erased worlds do not eradicate the Gothic horrors of the war; rather, they constitute a different order of horror because of their failure to deal honestly with the past. That is why the ghosts that T. S. refers to cannot be accommodated, except in Philip's sense of being haunted in the present by the war dead, whose experiences cannot be articulated. The past cannot be returned to and the future does a kind of violence to the past by overwriting its traumatic reality, which comes back in spectral form. These ghosts are familiar from a Walpolean Gothic tradition which asserts that the past haunts the present because there is unfinished business.

Testimony and bearing witness are narrowed down in these moments, since the world that one might bear witness to is one that might well become forgotten, if it were not for those who, like Philip, wish to preserve it as a shared experience for those who had participated in it because 'He [...] took care not to speak of the War except with soldiers' (43). Ghostliness, however, does not relate just to combatants. Hervey, walking the London streets in the dark, becomes aware that other pedestrians seem 'smaller and spectral' and that 'To walk [...] alone is to fancy oneself a ghost' (318). This moment suggests her alienation but it is not one of mental emptiness: 'This ghost of Hervey went on, thinking of her husband' (318). As in Philip's dualism, contemplation happens in a ghostly moment, represented in the novel as an ambivalent model of freedom which combines physical mobility with feelings of estrangement (especially since, at this moment, Hervey is pondering her husband's latest affair).

How to remember the war dead is central to *Company Parade*. Philip is comforted by the ghosts of 'Thin young men in shabby khaki' (43), who seem more like memories than spirits. However, Hervey's mother, whose son, Jake, has been killed in the war, is confronted by more painfully personal memories for which ghosts provide only temporary relief. Hervey's mother has a dream in which she encounters the type of undeveloped countryside that T. S. and Philip have gone looking for in Surrey: 'It was the kind of country she liked, with tall trees, meadows, and in the distance a range of hills' (331). In the dream, Jake says '"they're your trees, and this is our own house. We're going to live here together. You see I'm quite well and safe and I shan't want to go away again"'; hence 'Mrs Russell was filled with joy. Her son, whom she had thought dead, was alive. And this house was what she had always wanted' (331). She proceeds to look for him in the house, but is unable to find him and wakes up. Her dream represents a desire to speak with the dead, but it also engages with the restoration of a pre-war world imaged as the type of arcadia that has been displaced by new suburban developments. The dream also represents a familiar Gothic narrative founded on the tensions between the past and the present, and echoes the visions of Philip and the disappointments of T. S. The question is whether a form of remembrance is possible in a world which seems to want to forget both the war and the world that existed before it.

In *Company Parade* there is ultimately no transcendence or solace. The pre-war world has been erased and the war itself now forgotten in the pursuit of new forms of progress. In particular, religion is identified as part of the problem. Hervey, on a visit to a church on Armistice Day, 1921, which houses the memorial tablet to her brother, notes of the officiating priest that

> This stiff and believing old man stood to her for all those priests who accept, no, who excuse war. Their words, with the words used at the unveiling of war memorials, are the pus oozing over a wound. I could never forgive you, she thought. (262)

The church she sits in, however, 'was part of her life; she could not deny it', since it includes within it memorials and memories of many members of her family – and yet is now so empty that 'All now waited – but for what? Nothing came' (264). Ghosts are finally traumatic echoes of a world which has ceased to exist.

In 1935, Storm Jameson edited *Challenge to Death*, which included essays about a reconstructed peacetime written by J. B. Priestley, Julian Huxley, Rebecca West, Vera Brittain and Edmund Blunden. How to think about peace was, for her, shaped by how we think about the war. Trying to bear testimony in a rapidly changing environment is the challenge confronted by her ghosts. All of them are figures in limbo, caught between the circumstances that gave rise to them and an emerging world to which they can never belong. This attempt to reach out to the past, via the figure of the ghost, is also addressed in Ford Maddox Ford's tetralogy *Parade's End* (1924–8).

Ghosts of War: Eighteenth-Century Pastoralism

Ford's tetralogy powerfully shows how writing on the war engaged with the cultural form of the pastoral. The novels exemplify how an idea of a cultural and national narrative, centred on place (and home), fails to generate the type of solace and containment of trauma explored throughout this chapter. Homes do not function as places which exorcise the war because they are infiltrated by a Gothic presence which keeps alive, rather than eradicates, war-induced trauma.

It is repeatedly noted in *Parade's End* that Christopher Tietjens is a product of the eighteenth century. His love of his country estate and his political and cultural leanings all emphasise his eighteenth-century affiliations. The cutting down of the Great Tree of Goby on his estate by American tenants – prompted by Tietjens's estranged and vindictive wife, Sylvia, towards the end of the tetralogy – indicates that this older world cannot, in the end, be maintained. The emphasis on estate management references an old-style world of the landed gentry and a pastoral world with which it has some associations. Early parts of the narrative emphasise the importance of the countryside that surrounds the estate, and this pastoralism has links to a form of class-bound homesick nostalgia that is found in First World War writings. Paul Fussell has noted how officer-class memoirs and poems (Blunden, Owen, Sassoon and Guy Chapman, among others) describe battlefields as affronts to an eighteenth-century pastoral tradition. Fussell argues that 'Sometimes a pastoral oasis can be found without leaving the line' (Fussell 2009: 298), as when writers recall how the light touches a wood, or forms of birdsong, or types of flower such as roses and poppies. Fussell summarises:

> Recourse to the pastoral is an English mode of both fully gauging the calamities of the Great War and imaginatively protecting oneself against them. Pastoral reference, whether to literature or to actual rural localities and objects, is a way of invoking a code to hint by antithesis at the indescribable; at the same time, it is a comfort in itself, like rum, a deep dugout, or a woolly vest. (296)

It is also a version of 'comfort' which is associated with the home and constitutes a fabrication of Britain that is reassuringly distanced (culturally, emotionally and temporally) from the war. Pastoralism functions as another possible form of containment which superficially provides an antidote to the traumas of battle. Such a pastoral tradition recalls exemplars from the English Renaissance and earlier, but Fussell notes that it is the later Classical and Romantic traditions which shape war writing. Tietjens's eighteenth-century associations evoke these cultural milieus, but the damage done to his estate by his American tenants indicates that the home is not immune to acts of violence (which is how Tietjens see the cutting down of the Great Tree of Goby). The home is not a safe haven after all, as it is subject to a hostility that implicates a Gothic malevolence eager to overthrow ideas of ancestral authority – a theme central to the eighteenth-century Gothic of Walpole's *The Castle of Otranto*. Within the context of these historical engagements, Sara Haslam has noted the significance of Ford's obituary for Thomas Hardy (Sassoon's favourite author), which was published in the *New York Herald Tribune* on 22 January 1928. For Haslam, the obituary 'manages [...] to crystallize some of Ford's eighteenth-century concerns, especially those related to notions of Englishness' (Haslam 2014: 45). The obituary refers to a ghost story that Hardy once told Ford, which referenced the type of eighteenth-century ethos that appealed to Ford and which appears throughout *Parade's End*. Tietjens is the spectral presence in these novels because he represents a world that has historically ceased to exist but which he insists on trying to maintain, despite the novels' suggestion that the way back cannot be the way forward. Like the other characters from texts considered in this chapter, he can find no place or time to which he can belong, and, like them, becomes a type of roaming ghost. He now haunts a world which has fallen away from him. Haslam notes, 'A tone of loss and mourning suffuses Ford's post-war writing' (Haslam 2014: 45); *Parade's End* is about the loss of the eighteenth century but also about Tietjens's marriage, and raises questions about his faith, his Tory politics and the war itself. He is a subject in mourning for a lost world which has become spectral to him as he has become ghost-like to the modern world which replaces it. His war experiences generate this overdetermined spectrality.

While in the trenches, Tietjens sees a corpse caught in barbed wire: 'One arm raised in the attitude of, say, a Walter Scott Highland officer waving his men on. Waving a sword that wasn't there' (Ford 1982b: 552). This imaginative placement of a Highland officer provides a stark counterpoint to modern warfare. The officer had been killed the day before; on the eve of that skirmish, Tietjens had contemplated all of the officers who had gathered for a final meeting and 'had speculated on which of them would be killed. Ghostly! Well, they had all been killed' (552). The introjection of 'Ghostly!' in part reflects the chill felt by Tietjens at such heavy losses, but it also echoes his own sense that he possesses supernatural capabilities. In the final novel, Tietjens is described as 'clumsy, apparently slow-witted, but actually gifted with the insight of the supernatural' (Ford 1982a: 697). His clumsiness suggests that he is not physically adapted to the world and his supernatural 'insight' indicates that he is not part of it mentally. It is these tensions between the past and the present that, in Jameson's *Company Parade*, generate the new Gothic sensibility founded upon an emerging discourse of spectrality. Tietjens's world is also a Gothic world, full of strange occulted presences both on the home front and on the battlefield. Tietjens in the trenches can hear at night the sound of miners below his trench as they dig tunnels beneath no-man's-land to deposit explosives underneath the German frontline. He notes of the noises 'at night you hear the sound, and always it appears supernatural. You know it is the miners [...] But just because it was familiar, it was familiarly rather dreadful. Haunting' (Ford 1982b: 556). The battlefield becomes an unreal, uncanny place populated by familiar sights and sounds, which become defamiliarised by being placed within the context of modern warfare.

Parade's End is a narrative about the anxiety of being politically, historically and metaphysically displaced. The attempt to maintain some sense of an eighteenth-century identity which might alleviate war-induced trauma is progressively eroded, but it is noteworthy that this apparent high Toryism conceals within it a potentially radical edge. Tietjens discusses with a minister how the rights of workmen should be financially protected and manufacturers punished if they attempt to exploit contracts and workers, so much so that 'the High Toryism of Tietjens' actually reflects 'the extreme Radicalism of the extreme Left of the Left' (Ford 1982c: 79). As Haslam notes, 'An extinct Tory is one whose party was supported by the poor, and the landowners, as well as schoolmasters, parsons, and so on' (Haslam 2014: 42). She also cites Eric Hobsbawm's claim that 1789 was a key year in which economies were still largely rural rather than industrial.[7] This attempt to hold on to a disappearing ruralism was also, as we have seen, a theme in Jameson's *Company Parade*. In Aldington's *Death of a Hero*, the build-up to the war is discussed in some detail. Especially prominent is Talleyrand's view, in which he 'used to say that those who had not known Europe before 1789 had never known the real pleasure of living' (Aldington 1929: 225). This lost arcadia is a recurring theme in war writing by soldiers contemplating the ravages of the battlefield in which industry, in the form of artillery, has destroyed the rural world. Eighteenth-century pastoralism also represents a projected utopian version of Britain as a cultural home that many officer-class writers regarded with affectionate affinity. Fussell notes this archaic strand in Blunden's *Undertones of War*, where 'his attention is constantly on pre-Industrial England, the only repository of criteria for measuring fully the otherwise unspeakable grossness of the war' (Fussell 2009: 336). This archaism is also apparent in Blunden's style of writing; there, 'every rhythm, allusion, and droll personification, can be recognized as an assault on the war and on the world which chose to conduct and continue it. Blunden's style is his critique' (Fussell 2009: 336–7). This engagement with the eighteenth century not only is a reaction against the modernity of the war; it also represents an attempt to find a form of containment which would provide respite from the war. The problem is, as in all the texts and examples discussed here, that these forms of containment do not work. An eighteenth-century pastoral tradition cannot, by definition, be returned to but is reached out for as a comparatively safe space. However, it too is freighted by a Gothic sensibility which undoes this pastoral culture by associating it with a lost world that cannot be psychologically reinhabited.

The ghosts that appear in Blunden and Ford, however, sit outside of any projected eighteenth-century pastoralism. As with the ghosts in Brittain and Jameson, they seem like occasional entities, or as simple tricks of rhetoric in which the ghostly represents a generalised feeling of unease or of loss. Even so, these are not commonplace associations. The ghost represents a type of rupture in texts which otherwise have no obvious Gothic dimension to them. This rupture, in fact, brings the analysis of the war back to the issue of literary form.

Not all war writers celebrated the pastoralism of an eighteenth-century literary tradition. One writer who did not look upon the eighteenth century with such fondness was Robert Graves. In *Goodbye to All That* (1929), he reflects on the poetry curriculum he studied after the war at Oxford, noting that 'I found the English Literature course tedious, especially the insistence on eighteenth-century poets' (Graves 1967: 239). Graves was drawn to Anglo-Saxon poetry, and especially *Beowulf*, because its scenes of violence symbolically resonate with the war, so that 'this came far closer to most of us than the drawing-room and deer-park atmosphere of the eighteenth century' (239). In *Goodbye to All That*, Graves even refers to haunted houses and to encountering the dead faces of his comrades on peacetime civilians, an experience that he also recalled in his poem 'Haunted' (1920):

> I meet you suddenly down the street,
> Strangers assume your phantom faces,
> You grin at me from daylight places,
> Dead, long dead, I'm ashamed to greet
> Dead men down the morning street. (Graves 2003b: ll. 6–10)

The war is inescapable (there is a play here on morning/mourning), evoked by Anglo-Saxon poetry or met in everyday places. Ghosts are not retrospective figures in Graves but represent moments of projection in which, while at Oxford with Blunden, 'The war still continued for both of us, and we translated everything into trench-warfare terms' (Graves 1967: 239). Ghosts are of the here and now, so that in 'The Haunted House' the closing lines dismiss the idea that ancestral ghosts exist because:

> .... What laughter or what song
>   Can this house remember?
> Do flowers and butterflies belong
>   To a blind December? (Graves 2003c: ll. 21–4)

There is no nostalgia for home in Graves (who would find his arcadia in Majorca), but there does appear a cynical awareness of the narrative form of the war memoir. In his essay 'Postscript to "Goodbye to All That"' (1930), he indicates that he included references to drink and food, love affairs and battles because that was what a reader of war memoirs expected. These included

> Ghosts of course. There must, in every book of this sort, be at least one ghost story with a possible explanation, and one without any explanation, except that it was a ghost. I put in three or four ghosts that I remembered. (Graves 1930: 13–14)

Graves does not suggest that he is making up his ghosts but that a principle of selection governs their inclusion. Ghosts might not necessarily be human, and he records that, while he was staying with his in-laws, 'The visible ghost [of] a little yellow dog [...] would appear on the lawn in the early morning to announce deaths' (Graves 1967: 227), which is seen by his wife shortly before her mother dies of influenza. Signs and portents are thus granted the type of credence found among Blunden's soldiers but, underlying Graves's comments on the expectations of the war narrative, there is a sense that ghosts have to fulfil a function: to represent trauma, to anticipate a death, all of which takes us back to the importance of the ghost story as a literary form. Graves's account of the war memoir suggests that the roaming ghost now becomes housed within a new form of narrative expectation in which the inexplicable is accepted because it is anticipated. The ghost, however, is not such an exhausted trope and, as we shall see in Chapter 4, it is ultimately granted a new type of malevolent agency which moves it beyond images of trauma and mourning.

The previous chapter examined how the literary form of the ghost story provided both a way of looking at the war and an attempt at making sense of trauma. How to read the ghost plays an important part in those tales. The plotless ghosts explored in this chapter, however, are of a different order: they fail to generate meaning and so retain a traumatic Gothic presence. At the start of this chapter, we saw how the figure of the restless spectre was reflected in animal symbolism, which also emphasised the depersonalisation of the combatant. Such symbols invite interpretation but this invitation does not make the war explicable. Rivers's attempt to decode dreams about a psychotic rabbit may have helped to contextualise his patient's claustrophobia but they did little to alleviate their war-induced anxieties. Other forms of analysis are also resisted by these wandering liminal figures. Bion's formulation of containment as a way of overcoming fear has its roots in his war experiences, but even here containment breaks down as it cannot properly give voice to traumatic moments. Trauma becomes a wound that needs to be lived with. It is not repressed or forgotten, but rather strategically displaced into symbolic forms, of ghosts, animals, dreams, which are sublimated via a Gothic sensibility. Models of homecoming no longer work in this Gothic imaginary, as the example of a haunted pastoralism demonstrates. The ghost is unaccommodated and this purgatorial roaming ghost articulates a new out-of-placeness – a figure that defies analysis and poses a challenge to conventional narrative forms that would otherwise contain, emplot and explain the spectre. These ghosts are largely characterised by their silence, as in Aldington's Lieutenant Hall, who is silently, but powerfully, admonished by the face of a man that he has killed.

The following chapter examines how ghosts of soldiers operate within a model of a modernist and spiritualist purgatory. An exploration of these ghosts helps to complicate our view of the spectral soldier and reveals how and why the dead finally find a voice.

Notes

1. This game about an absent, or present, mother is also reflected in Bion's model of containment, which emphasises the importance of the maternal.
2. This encounter is strikingly reminiscent of Charles Dickens's account in the *American Notes* (1842) of the experience of solitary confinement at Eastern Penitentiary in Philadelphia, where he notes of a self-haunted prisoner that 'When night comes, there stands the phantom in the corner. If he have the courage to stand in its place, and drive it out (he had once: being desperate), it broods upon his bed.' See Dickens, *American Notes for General Circulation*, ed. John S. Whitely and Arnold Goldman (Harmondsworth: Penguin, 1985), p. 155.

3. For an overview of these type of images see Owen Davies, *A Supernatural War: Magic, Divination, and Faith During the First World War* (Oxford: Oxford University Press, 2018), pp. 70–5.
4. Desmond Graham, *The Truth of War: Owen, Blunden and Rosenberg* (Manchester: Carcanet, 1984), pp. 93–6.
5. See Blackwood's 'The Willows' and 'The Transfer'; for Machen see *The Hill of Dreams* and *The Great God Pan*, where nature becomes freighted with horrifying immanent forms.
6. The veracity of Skirth's memoir has been challenged and, in some instances, his account does not reflect official documents relating to troop movement and levels of artillery ordinance.
7. See Eric Hobsbawm, *The Age of Revolution* (London: Weidenfeld and Nicolson, 1995), cited in Haslam, p. 41.

Chapter 3

Spiritualism, War and the Modernist Gothic

Jay Winter has noted that the growth of spiritualism during the war 'was one of the most disturbing and powerful means by which the living "saw" the dead of the Great War, and used their "return" to help survivors cope with their loss and their trauma' (Winter 1995: 54). As this book has demonstrated, ghosts and trauma are closely aligned because the ghost both references the passing of a life and, by indicating the continuing presence of the spirit, provides an antidote to grief. The previous chapter explored links between trauma and the plotless ghost, and how that related to an emerging Gothic sensibility at the time. The spiritualist context is different because it softens the horror of trauma by refusing to accept that death is the end. But this does not mean that images of the spirit world are free from a Gothic influence. As we shall see, spirit texts dictated by dead soldiers often assert the presence of malevolent spirits which attempt to hold back a soldier's spiritual development on the astral plane. These malevolent forms are shaped by a Gothic impulse that contrasts with the benign spirits of dead soldiers. More broadly, the Gothic has a muted but nevertheless important presence within spiritualism at this time, especially in the spiritualist view of the war as a battle between good and evil.

Previous chapters have explored how the uncanny is reworked in tales about dead soldiers, or how trauma generates new formations of a Gothic sensibility. This chapter argues for the continuing influence of often quite specific familiar Gothic impulses. The three principal Gothic influences identified here relate to how the battle between good and evil is orchestrated, the unique way in which wartime spirits may be subject to corruption, and the difficulties involved in interpreting spirit messages which echo issues about analysis, fragmentation and forms of knowing which characterise Gothic texts such as *Frankenstein* (1818) and *Dracula* (1897). As we shall see, spiritualism does not just transmit the lost voices of dead soldiers; it also channels an earlier Gothic tradition. The Gothic has a tacit presence within the spiritualist context, often helping to shape models of 'evil' associated with the German forces. In addition, spiritualist writings conjure soldier-ghosts who are often the bearers of secrets (a familiar figure of the literary ghost) and the spiritualist text frequently highlights issues about the need for symbolic analysis, echoing the textual complexities of the Gothic novel which also focus on acts of interpretation (as in how the vampire hunters mine each other's texts for clues about the Count in *Dracula*, for example). This Gothic context subtly influences the ghosts conjured by spiritualism and these entities can be helpfully compared and contrasted with the soldier-ghosts explored elsewhere in this study in order to give a broader view of how ghosts were represented at this time.

How much the spiritualist and modernist ghost inherits from the Gothic tradition, and where it departs from it, is the main focus here. Spiritualist writings might seem to be different in kind to the Gothic but, as we shall see, soldier-ghosts frequently find themselves stuck in a quasi-Catholic purgatorial realm in which they are subject to temptations from malevolent spirits, highly sexualised vampires and other forms of monstrosity which are familiar from the Gothic. Nevertheless, it is clear that modernism owes a more explicit debt to the Gothic tradition than spiritualist texts. John Paul Riquelme, for example, has noted that Gothic and modernist texts share an anti-realist impulse and argues that modernism was shaped by an earlier Gothic tradition (most notably associated with the fragmented narratives of *Frankenstein* and *Dracula*). For Riquelme:

> The Gothic [...] is deeply involved in the transition from Victorian to modernist writing, primarily because the juxtaposition of opposites characteristic of the Gothic also helps manifest the world views, aesthetic attitudes, and cultural conflicts that brought modernism into being. It even suggests the violence of modern history, which reveals itself increasingly to be a Gothic narrative of visible and hidden violence, most obviously with World War I and its aftermath. (Riquelme 2014: 20)

Such a view also corresponds to Jonathan Dent's claim that *The Castle of Otranto*'s concealed history of violence disrupts Enlightenment historiographies which looked for coherence and progression (Dent 2016: 59). War, in this instance, provides the ultimate form of disturbance for the Gothic imagination.

A central issue which this chapter addresses relates to how to interpret the significance and function of purgatory in spiritualist and modernist texts. A critical focus on purgatory helps to identify the different types of Gothic which both influence, and emerge from, these contexts.

For spiritualists, purgatory represents a liminal state from which spirits may ascend if they morally improve; modernist texts, however, construct purgatory as a state of persistent mourning from which the subject cannot ascend, or indeed otherwise escape. Matt Foley's *Haunting Modernisms* (2017) provides an illuminating analysis of purgatorial states in modernist texts which can be helpfully contrasted with the representation of the war dead in spiritualist writings. Although Foley argues for a modernism that is not shaped by the ghosts of the Gothic (but by modernist-specific formations of haunting), it can be observed that the tensions between different models of purgatory constitute a cultural struggle over where the ghosts of the war dead go. It is in the conflict between these two cultures that a Gothic influence can be discerned, one which gives shape to a modernist account of persistent mourning *and* populates the astral plane with malevolent spirits.[1]

Before exploring the channelled spirits of the war dead, we need to examine how spiritualist attitudes towards the war developed. These views are shaped by an implicit Gothic discourse which centres on the battle between good and evil. Spiritualism also advances a view of the spectre who speaks directly to us about their war experiences in consoling ways, which is a counterpoint to the more explicitly Gothic-inflected, traumatised spirits that we find in modernism. An overview of how the war was represented in the popular spiritualist journal *The Occult Review* (published between 1905 and 1951) provides an invaluable insight into developments into spiritualist attitudes towards the war. There were other popular publications, most notably the weekly spiritualist newspaper *The Light*, founded in 1881, but *The Occult Review*'s monthly format provided a more in-depth, considered forum for spiritualist debates during World War One.[2]

The Occult Review: The Spirits of War

At the beginning of the war, *The Occult Review* assessed whether the conflict could have been predicted by horoscopes. The Kaiser's birth horoscope revealed a troubling conjunction of Mars with Neptune, which, in combination with the position of Uranus, suggested that the Kaiser was 'faithless' (Anon. 1914a: 128) and false to his friends. By the November 1914 issue, this emotionally unstable and politically capricious Kaiser was transformed into the Antichrist. It was noted that 'The dominant characteristics of [the] Antichrist are […] shameless hypocrisy and blasphemy, and it must be admitted that in the person of the Kaiser the world has seen them exemplified to a quite unparalleled extent' (Anon. 1914c: 251). The literal demonisation of the Kaiser helped enforce the view that God was on the side of the Allies, leading the journal to assert confidently, in the earlier October issue, that 'The unanimity with which all predictions foretell the defeat of Germany is a striking point' (Anon. 1914b: 196).[3] These early prophecies replace the political narrative, found in *The Strand* and elsewhere in the popular press, which tended to see the war as a consequence of unresolved tensions from the Franco-Prussia War of 1870–1. That the Kaiser is a type of Gothic villain responsible for the war prompts *The Occult Review* to explore predictions in prophetic writings drawn from a range of periods and national contexts, all of which appear to confirm his uniquely evil status. After the Battle of Mons in August 1914, however, and in the subsequent retreat, during which Britain sustained heavy losses, the presence of the spirits of the war dead came into greater focus and became appropriated as part of a moral justification for the war.

Riquelme's idea that the Gothic is characterised by the 'juxtaposition of opposites' as a way of managing forms of cultural conflict runs through many of these spiritualist accounts, which focus on the tensions between good and evil. The theosophist A. P. Sinnett, in 'Super-Physical Aspects of the War' from the December issue of *The Occult Review*, reasserted the belief that the war represented a battle between good and evil, and that those killed in this ethical conflict would continue to express their moral identities on the spiritual plane. According to Sinnett, a war death contributes to the righteous cause of the war because the soldier participates 'with a conviction [...] that they are fighting for the right', meaning that 'The effect on the other side of a life sacrificed under these conditions is beautiful in the extreme' (Sinnett 1914: 347).[4] However, he acknowledges that there is a temporary sense of disorientation in which the dead 'go through a period of some mental confusion' because 'Death on the battle-field is attended with a wild excitement which persists in the consciousness for a time, during which the entity, passing on, does not actually realize the nature of the change he has gone through' (347). However, after this brief turmoil, 'even while their names are being printed here in lists of the killed', they 'flit happily to regions beyond, where they enter on a new life which very few of them would be willing to exchange for the one abandoned' (348). The grounds for Sinnett's optimism did not reflect the reality of those caught up in the fighting; rather, they represent an attempt to claim that God is on the side of the Allies in what is a morally just war. Sinnett tacitly draws upon the work of F. W. H. Myers, the spiritualist and co-founder of the Society for Psychical Research, who argued in the posthumously published *Human Personality and Its Survival of Bodily Death* (1903) that the spirit world represents a new form of evolution in which the subject becomes increasingly morally refined, although, for Sinnett, this transition can occur only if 'the entity' has embraced a set of religious principles prior to their demise. According to Sinnett,

> For millions of years in the past, the noblest and best representatives of the human race have been ascending to higher conditions of knowledge and power, until they have become agencies through which the divine purposes of human evolution have been fulfilled. (348)

However, battling against all this is the pursuit of evil, with malign spirits proving a check to progress: 'at this stage of human evolution – we of the most advanced races having passed the mid-way point' are confronted by 'the development of those choosing evil to be their good', resulting in a troubling state of near 'equilibrium' between these factions (349). The evocation of Milton's Satan, 'Evil, be thou my Good', from Book IV of *Paradise Lost* (1674), indicates that a moral (or immoral) choice has been made and that it is one which ultimately construes the Germans as ambitious for a notably Gothic form of domination. This view of Germany was shaped by invasion narratives, which were popular in the 1890s, including William Le Queux's *The Invasion of 1910* (1906), in which Britain becomes invaded by the Germans, who are challenged by the formation of a new secret army. H. G. Wells's *The War of the Worlds* (1898) represents invasion as a cosmic battle, which is also reflected in how the conflict was represented in *The Occult Review*. For Sinnett, the war is a manifestation of a cosmic spiritual conflict and, because the Kaiser represents the forces of darkness, he will be defeated 'in the triumph of Good over Evil' (346), which Sinnett sees reflected in the ultimate 'success of the Allied Forces'. Crucially for Sinnett, the war will be won through a battle of wills in which the physical fighting is psychically determined by those mentally strong enough to defeat evil, which leads him to conclude:

> It is a literal truth that if [...] everyone in London devoted ten minutes a day to earnest concentrated desire to drive back from the territories they have invaded, the aggressive hordes unconsciously guided by the unseen powers of evil, the aggregate value of such thought, as it would affect first of all the battles above, and through them the battles below, would be worth many army corps in the field. (Sinnett 1914: 352)

The view that an exertion of a collective will could defeat the Germans is a theme that *The Occult Review* returned to throughout the war by asserting that the inner spirit could combine with other spirits, both bodied and disembodied, to defeat the enemy patriotically. Such ghosts do not present as traumatised Gothic figures; rather, they represent the continuation of the type of optimism that characterised spiritualist practice in the late nineteenth century. This spiritualist discourse appeared as a counterpoint to popular theories of degeneration which had claimed that the modern subject was, under certain circumstances, capable of slipping down an evolutionary ladder.[5] The spiritualists assert an alternative idea of evolution, in which the reviled body that so frequently appears in accounts of degeneration is cast off and displaced by the moral development of the spirit. That is not to say that there is no Gothic influence here. Clearly, it is the Germans who are cast as Gothic entities – they are malevolent spiritual and physical invaders, which turns the war into a battle between good and evil spirits that can only, at this stage, have one outcome. This is a Gothic world in which satanic forces will be inevitably defeated by the virtuous. The monster becomes defeated by spiritual purity and reason. This is a battle which is beyond the degenerate bodies that we find in *Jekyll and Hyde* and *Dracula*, for example, because Sinnett's view of the British war dead is that they have acquired a spiritual purity due to their very disembodiment. However, ideas of corruption do not go away. The corrupt, degenerate body might be cast off but there is potential for spiritual corruption, which might render the British ghost soldier weak and unable to participate in the ongoing battle against the demonstrably malign German spirits. Theories of degeneration, which assert that the presence of the emotionally and physically enfeebled will herald the end of civilisation, a view outlined by Max Nordau in *Degeneration* (1892) and reworked by Stoker in *Dracula*, become repositioned within the spirit world during the war, although not prior to it. Such a move is designed to explain why spiritual forms of degeneration might, if we are not careful, be as catching as any other type of disease and the Gothic plays a clear role in shaping this reformed view of the spirit world – as witnessed in full-length texts dictated by soldier-ghosts, by Wellesley Tudor Pole and J. S. M. Ward, discussed below.

Messages from the dead are required to help shore up the view of the virtuous soldier-ghost. The June 1915 issue of *The Occult Review* included just such a message. In 'What Happens in the Spirit-World over a Battlefield', by 'H. C.', a dead soldier recounts that in battle 'keen pains shot through my limbs' (H. C. 1915: 352) before he collapsed and was trapped under a fallen body. His final earth-bound memory suggests that he was crushed under the wheels of his own artillery: 'the dreadful wheels approached! I saw them coming; one was directly over my eyes. That was the last I remember' (353). His is not a heroic death. When he awakens from this horror, however, 'I was well, peaceful, happy', with his now dead compatriot John standing nearby: "'You here?' I cried in astonishment; 'I thought you were dead!' 'So I am,' he replied; 'so are you!'" (353). The soldier feels peace because he is now 'free from the horrors of war' (353) but also because he possessed a purity of spirit which he took into the war. All are greeted by friends or guardian spirits who look after them, but the war has an effect on the spirit bodies. The soldier notes that:

> Just as our physical bodies are built up here by slow, painful effort, so the spirit body, which normally is perfect at death, must be rebuilt slowly and carefully after death, in those cases where it has been badly shocked before death. In all cases, however, it finally reforms and reunites. (354–5)

This narrative of reconstruction suggests an anticipation of Judgement Day, with spiritual resurrection taking place within a discussion of bodies being made whole again.

Spiritualist texts in these instances are populated by seemingly benign ghosts who, by virtue of their continuing spiritual life, have not really died at all. Such ghosts appear to offer a form of redemptive consolation to grieving readers. However, these figures of spectrality are not without a Gothic imprint. The specific elisions between bodies and spirits that we find in the war spectres are not obvious features of pre-war spiritualist ghosts. These later spirit bodies reflect the physical fallibility of the body that has been destroyed. The spirits are a new type of dead undead, but they are frequently freighted by models of fragmentation and reconstruction which require acts of reassembly that echo those of the creature's in *Frankenstein*. Also, these spirits, like Mary Shelley's creature, also ask questions about their plight and struggle to understand the new world in which they find themselves. They, too, are innocent victims, born out of a delirium and egotism associated with the war (and with the Kaiser), which echoes the amoral, selfish ambitions of the conflicted creator–scientist that is Victor Frankenstein. Also, as Riquelme notes, texts like *Frankenstein* and *Dracula* are revenge narratives, and as benign as these soldier-spirits might seem, they too are out for vengeance (Riquelme 2014: 21). The cultural context of the Gothic is thus unconsciously co-opted culturally to shape the plight of the spiritualist soldier-ghost.

There is a clear moral view taken of the war in these narratives, which emphasise that it is necessary to eradicate evil from the world. The dead soldier claims that the war 'was necessary. In the great cosmic scheme of things, one can see that it could not have been otherwise [...] it is the best thing that could possibly have happened!' (H. C. 1915: 355). The war is thus reconceived as a moral necessity, in which sacrifices are made in the name of a good cause. In addition, the dead are not in need of mourning or memorialisation since their deaths constitute a necessary sacrifice that in reality was no sacrifice at all, seeing as they have merely entered a form of higher life. These narratives constitute a form of propaganda which patriotically asserts the presence of the combative spirit of the dead soldier, and yet, despite this jaunty optimism, there is a concern that the divine plan is not a clear one. The reasons why that might be are not simply associated with the Germans; it is also the fault of the Victorians.

The anonymous editor of 'Notes of the Month' in the January 1916 edition accuses the nineteenth century of having boasted vaingloriously of its progress, and while acknowledging that scientific and commercial developments have taken place, the editorial voice queries whether there has been a corresponding progress in morality. Such a view unsettles the idea of an ongoing spiritual progress that *The Occult Review* had previously endorsed as heralding the positive overthrow of satanic forces. The line taken has much in common with H. G. Wells's scientific romances of the late nineteenth century in arguing for a lag between scientific advancement and moral progress. The editor claims that 'material and intellectual progress have been out of all proportion to any corresponding moral development' (Anon. 1916: 2), so that there has been no hesitation in harnessing the destructive capacities of technology to help prosecute the war. The material world of the Victorians thus produces a material, technological solution to problems (about 'good' and 'evil') which are spiritual in nature. The editor concludes that the culture has been shaped by a model of social and economic power which has overshadowed the importance of morality and spiritual awareness:

> The strong have proved themselves to be not on the side of the angels, but on the side of the powers of hell, and each step upward that the race has made in its path of so-called progress has made the danger of a fall more imminent and more fraught with fatal consequences. (Anon. 1916: 2)

British culture of a specifically non-spiritual kind is now implicated in the war, and not just the demonised Kaiser. The above claim can also be read as a gloss on theories of degeneration which, at the *fin de siècle*, had argued that apparent economic progress, and a confidence in civilisation, had actually generated the possibility of a degenerate decline. The desire to apportion blame is clearly meant to be read against the backdrop of some reversals of fortune in the war, which had continued for much longer than commentators had anticipated and which, from the vantage point of 1916, seemed troublingly to suggest that any recent moral and spiritual gains have not been sufficient to fight off the malevolence of a longstanding pan-European technocratic mentality. There is near deadlock on the Western front, in which the forces of good and evil are 'evenly matched' (Anon. 1916: 4). This means that the Allies cannot be confident of success, and the editorial even goes so far as to entertain the possibility that the Allies could be defeated by the forces of evil:

> There are those who will tell us [...] that such an eventuality is not within the bounds of the possible. It would [...] be in effect, a defeat of God, and God is all-powerful in spite of the temporary triumphs of evil. The obvious reply is that we cannot know this. We know that in many ages evil has, for the time being at least, secured a triumph. (4)

However, having established this threat, the editorial argues that the current mood of pessimism about the war should be seen as the result of some 'temporary set-backs' within a wider 'desperate struggle of those predestined to failure against their inevitable doom', a very Gothic description (5). That the strategic advantages achieved by the Germans *are* Gothic, in fact, appears in the claim that their successes have been due to their employment of black magic. The struggle against Germany thus becomes all the more important because, if they were to win, 'This triumph would mean the triumph of the material over the spiritual, the victory of matter over light and the higher wisdom, throughout the earth' (3). Germany's defeat, however, is assured precisely because it has convinced itself of its invincibility, even when faced with the reality that this is not true: 'The belief on the part of any one nation in their universal superiority is [...] only another form of lunacy', so much so that the Kaiser will ultimately end up in 'a strait-waistcoat' (6). National claims to 'universal superiority', at least on the part of Germany, are debunked as delusional. The Germans represent an immediate foreign problem but the legacies of the Victorians create an additional complexity, which is reflected in how a Victorian Gothic world of divided amoral subjects, as in *Jekyll and Hyde*, or potentially corruptible versions of middle-class values, as in *Dracula*, becomes obliquely restaged within these wartime fears. The Victorians are there to cast off, even while the conflicts and divisions associated with the Victorian Gothic continue to influence the way in which the war was interpreted.

The January 1916 issue had been clear that Germany had created a false view of the world based upon its own egotism and that, in pursuing this reality, it had embarked on a literally lunatic path. The Germans' Gothic world, estranged from reality, is rooted in the occult (black magic) and doomed to failure. British losses should be seen as only temporary setbacks in a conflict in which the Kaiser's defeat is assured because of his association with the Antichrist and a lunatic egotism. The antidote to this corrupted world of malevolent Gothic threats is to be found within the possibility of spiritual renewal, in which the Allies need to cast off a Victorian material ethos in order to reconnect with their true spiritual selves. A direct and collaborative solution to this problem of spiritual connection is articulated through the transformative energies marshalled within the collective will.

In the December 1914 *Occult Review*, A. P. Sinnett had argued that the collective mental support of non-combatants could be sent to those on the frontline. It was an idea that J. W. Brodie-Innes returned to in 'Psychic Help for Soldiers and Sailors' in the April 1918 issue. Brodie-Innes was the author of popular Gothic romances with a Scottish setting, such as *Morag the Seal* (1908), *Old as the World* (1910), *For the Soul of a Witch* (1910) and *The Devil's Mistress* (1915). *The Devil's Mistress* centres on a battle between the forces of good and evil, which echoes *The Occult Review*'s evaluation of the war. Brodie-Innes was also a prominent member of the Hermetic Order of the Golden Dawn and a believer in occult realities. He was also keen to establish that the articulation of our inner spiritual world was analogously reflected in the modern communication systems of the day, which, in the case of radio, focused on the telepathic transmission of disembodied voices. Brodie-Innes approvingly supports the claim of Oliver Lodge, the leading physicist, spiritualist and pioneer of radio transmitters, that 'in every brain is the analogue of a wireless receiver and transmitter in embryo', and, 'if these be only developed and tuned to one another, messages may flash from brain to brain across any distance', a theory of spirit transmission 'that accounts for a vast number of recorded facts', with even periodic setbacks reflecting the 'failures [which] frequently occurred in the first experiments of wireless' (Brodie-Innes 1918: 212–13).[6] While Jay Winter argues that spiritualism seemed to reach out for an 'unmodern' impulse during a very 'modern' war (Winter 1995: 54), these references to technology endorse Jenny Hazelgrove's claim that 'Spiritualism's power of persuasion was rooted in its ability to elicit and co-ordinate a variety of fugitive and fragmented supernaturalisms buried in modernity' (Hazelgrove 2000: 23). The 'fugitive [...] supernaturalism' manifested by these modern ghosts opposes the conventional idea of the Gothic ghost as a tragic figure tied to the past. The advancements in the technology of communications which involved projected voices (as in the telephone and the radio) supported a penchant for scientifically scrutinising a spirit world which was trying to communicate with us.[7] Thoughts can be sent to us via dreams, it was assumed (in contrast to Freud), much as messages are transmitted via the radio. Brodie-Innes gives an example of this type of thought transference through a dream he had in 1916 about being on board a ship, where the crew had been guided by a guardian spirit through a sea of mines before a chance explosion led to Brodie-Innes being killed. A week later, he relates this vision to the Battle of Jutland and the death of a friend who was killed in the same way that Brodie-Innes had experienced in the dream. The channel of communication goes both ways, according to Brodie-Innes, meaning that it is possible to send messages of support psychically to those who are serving so that 'we *can* give psychic help to our soldiers and sailors' (Brodie-Innes 1918: 221, italics in original), even if the reasons for 'the laws governing these phenomena are still unknown' (221). Channels of communication to the spirits are thus open to us as our inner spirit communes with the 'dead' and with the living soldier. In effect, those at home are now psychically able to support those on the battlefield, turning the non-combatant into a type of armchair soldier in this spiritual conflict.

These ideas, in their reaching out for a positive, seemingly non-Gothic image of the spirit, are nevertheless dogged by Gothic contexts. This desire to communicate with the dead is foreshadowed in *Dracula*, for example, where the infected Mina Harker is placed in a mesmeric trance by Van Helsing in order to try to locate the infected Count. When, in the trance, Mina is asked where the Count is and what he is doing she replies '"I am still – oh, so still. It is like Death!"' (Stoker 1996: 313). There are echoes here of Poe's 'The Facts in the Case of M. Valdemar' (1845), when the dying Valdemar, placed in a mesmeric trance, asserts '"*I am dead!*"' (Poe 1982: 103, italics in original), shortly before his bodily dissolution. Mina is able to inhabit the 'dead undead' world of the vampire through this form of mesmerically induced astral travelling and so provide important clues concerning the Count's whereabouts. How to speak to the dead (or the undead) is thus a feature of the Gothic as well as the spiritualist text, with both indebted to ideas about telepathic communication with the living and the dead which gained cultural popularity through the work of individuals such as F. W. H. Myers, amongst others researching alleged psychic activity.

How to send and receive messages requires an account of influence and agency, and the issue of psychic influence was addressed further in the October issue of *The Occult Review* in an article on 'Mystical Substitution' by Montague Summers, who would later gain a considerable reputation as a scholar of the occult with his books on witchcraft and vampires, and an early history of Gothic literature, *The Gothic Quest* (1938). Summers defines mystical substitution as 'stretching forth a helping hand' (Summers 1918: 215), typically associated with prayer and forms of religious oblation. Such acts are usually carried out by religious mystics, but Summers emphasises that religion does not have a monopoly on these forms of service because there are 'many mystics of to-day' who are 'men and women outwardly leading just ordinary commonplace lives' (215) but can nevertheless send feelings of love and support to those in need. For Summers, 'If love be deep enough, if sympathy be true, it is often possible for those at home mystically to alleviate in some measure the pain and sorrows of those loved, and even to ward off evil from them' (217). According to Summers, there is an emotional drain generated by this type of commitment, one worth enduring to alleviate the suffering of others. The championing of the amateur mystic was central to the spiritualist credo in which lay spirits constituted a means of ghostly support for, and radio-like transmission to, those at risk during the war.

The December 1918 *Occult Review* issue reflects back on the war, regarding it as representing the triumph of spiritual values over 'man's lower nature, his passions, ambitions and animal desires' (Anon. 1918: 307). Finally, the animal instincts evoked by the war, discussed in Chapter 2, are laid to rest. The triumph of the real self over the artificial self demonstrates that, 'Like all evil, selfishness is based on an illusion' (307). If the Allies represent the triumph of a latent spiritual purity that was brought out during the war, so the enemies become associated with a Gothic malevolence that led to their defeat. As part of this post-war reflection, the Austrians become construed as haunted by specific Gothic narratives which heralded the war. The editorial claims that the Black Dwarf of Vienna, 'a strange emissary from the Unseen World' (311), would appear to the ruling Hapsburg family at times of crisis. It is asserted that this strange ghost may have been that of a court jester who was killed on the orders of one of the Emperors and was first seen prior to the Turkish siege of Vienna in 1683. The appearance of the ghost heralded various military and personal disasters that befell the Hapsburgs. This ghostly black dwarf had not been seen for a while until 'A few months [...] before the outbreak of the Great War, he appeared once more in the halls of the Hofburg, showing this time an angry and threatening mien' (312). According to an eye-witness, Princess Catherine Radziwill, author of *The Black Dwarf of Vienna, and Other Weird Stories* (1916):

> 'As soon as the war broke out [...] the dwarf has once more become a daily visitor at the Hofburg. He seems to have aged and he walks about as if carrying a burden too heavy for his shoulders to bear. No one molests him, but everyone tries to avoid him because it is known that his presence means death and sorrow.' (Anon. 1918: 312)

The black dwarf is not the only ghostly herald that haunts the Austrian ruling family; there is also the tradition of the Turnfälken, purported to be gigantic white birds which, if seen during the day, 'forebode misfortune to the reigning house' (313). The *Occult Review* editorial notes that only a few days before the assassination of Archduke Franz Ferdinand, his wife Countess Sophie Hohenburg saw above the cathedral 'a flock of enormous white birds such as she had never seen before, wheeling round and round in the sky and uttering weird and sinister cries' (313). These family-specific spectres demonstrate, at least for *The Occult Review*, that the world consists of signs and portents that require acts of interpretation. Given how consolidated these narratives are within family folklore, their presence is seemingly taken for granted, but they function more broadly to make sense of danger. There is a purpose to these visitations that suggests how powerless the individual subject is. The subject cannot mitigate the disaster that these visitations herald nor be confident about what the nature of the tragedy will be. Precautionary warnings can be truly rationalised only after the event.

During the war, *The Occult Review* repeatedly asserted that a benign spirit world was on the side of the Allies and that this world gained strength as it became added to by the ghosts of the fallen. In *The Occult Review*, the battle that is won in the spirit world over satanic forces ensures victory on the battlefield. Ghosts thus have meaning, and this is the fundamental message emphasised by spiritualists which is reflected in how signs, symbols and portents draw attention to the places where meaning is to be found and suggest ways in which seemingly cryptic symbols could be decoded. Making sense of ghostly messages becomes crucial in this emerging hermeneutics of spectrality. These issues about interpreting the ghost often require complex acts of analysis that also unconsciously suggest the literary nature of spirit communication; Oliver Lodge's *Raymond* makes these issues clear.

Reading *Raymond*, Decoding the Ghost

Lodge's book begins with an account of a cryptic precautionary warning concerning an impending tragedy.[8] A spirit message was allegedly sent by F. W. H. Myers (who had died in 1901) via another spirit and related to a medium, Mrs Robbins, at a séance at the New Hampshire home of Leonora Piper, a well-known medium. The message was that 'Myers says you take the part of the poet, and he will act as Faunus. FAUNUS'; this message is intended for 'Lodge' and concludes with the seemingly cryptic comment 'Ask Verrall, she will also understand. Arthur says so' (Lodge 1917b: 90). The reference to Verrall is to Margaret Verrall, a well-known medium and classics scholar whose husband, Arthur Verrall (who died in 1912), had been a Cambridge Classics scholar and Professor of English. Piper and Margaret Verrall correspond on this communication, which implies that some type of protection is present within what otherwise appears to be a warning. Lodge asks Verrall for clarification of what the line means, and she informs him that it is a reference to one of Horace's *Odes*, II. xvi, in which Horace describes having been saved by Faunus when a tree was about to fall on him. Lodge interprets the message as 'meaning that some blow was going to fall, though I didn't know of what kind, and that Myers would intervene, apparently to protect me from it' (92). Shortly after this interchange, his son Raymond was killed on the Western front.

Given Raymond's death, the message might seem misleading, but Lodge asks for another interpretation of it and its specific relationship to that particular Horatian Ode. He consults the Reverend M. A. Bayfield, a Classical scholar and former headmaster, who writes to Lodge that Horace

> says Faunus lightened the blow [...] As bearing on your terrible loss, the meaning seems to be that the blow would fall but not crush; it would be 'lightened' by the assurance, conveyed afresh to you by a special message from the still living Myers, that your boy still lives. (93)

Thus a reading of the text confirms that the dead are not dead precisely because the spirit of Myers could not have got this wrong. True spirit communications were often highly cryptic and their meaning consequently unclear until they were made sense of by subsequent events. There are repeated references made to the need to read analytically in order to decode spirit messages, which emphasises the difficulty in interpreting such communication. In the instance of cross-correspondences (when a message is sent in fragments to a range of mediums and then reassembled into a coherent text), for example, there was a laborious process of interpretation at work because, for Lodge, 'the puzzles and hidden allusions contained in these messages are not more difficult than literary scholars are accustomed to; that, indeed, they are precisely of similar order' (173). Still, the pursuit of coherence is guided by the conviction that meaning can be found. We have seen in the previous chapter how the wandering ghost seems meaningless, lost within his own traumatic experience precisely because he is unable to find a narrative structure which can, after the event, make sense of that trauma. This type of textual belatedness is echoed in these spirit narratives, which also only surrender their true meaning based on an interpretive act which reveals the hidden truth within a cryptic message. Ghosts, in a spiritualist context, thus give voice to meaning, even if an implied reader (or listener) struggles to make sense of their message – that is, until a subsequent action – or a death in the case of *Raymond* – resolves it.

The pursuit of coherence is the main theme which comes through *Raymond*. Messages appear to be fragmentary or incomplete, and the desire to make sense of them is in part linked to a desire to make sense of World War One as a whole. Acts of textual reconstruction also have links to the fragmented bodies of the war dead. We saw in 'What Happens in the Spirit-World over a Battlefield' by 'H. C.' the claim that the dismembered body is reformed as whole in a new spirit body which takes time to recompose itself. Lodge, via a medium, asks a question about how the fragmented bodies of the war dead are reassembled, and the response is relayed back to Lodge:

> I am told [...] that when anybody's blown to pieces, it takes some time for the spirit-body to complete itself, to gather itself all in, and to be complete [...] The *spirit* isn't blown apart of course [...] but it has an effect upon it. (Lodge 1917b: 195, italics in original)

As textual bodies are reconstructed to generate meaning so the fragmented corporeal bodies of the war dead are reformed into what overcomes the Gothic, new spirit bodies which start their life anew. Like the creature in Shelley's novel, these recomposed bodies are made out of dead bodies. They constitute a version of the dead undead that, like Victor's creature, need to be communicated with in order to make sense of the messages that they convey. The transmission of messages is influenced by the language of the séance, but the act of interpretation requires analytical skills in assembling these messages which we also find in the Gothic. Dr Seward, for example, notes in *Dracula* that the key to interpreting the vampire is to be found by placing the protagonists' individual accounts into a chronological order which generates 'a whole connected narrative' (Stoker 1996: 225), thus revealing what the Count is and how to defeat him. The Gothic monster, like the spiritualist ghost, needs decoding.

Narrative coherence and metaphysical coherence are elided as the trauma of war is effectively set aside in order to emphasise the continuing contribution that the dead make to the war effort. As we have seen, the plotless ghost has no narrative by which it can express and so contain its trauma, whereas an act of textual reconstruction generates the narrative coherence that, in this instance, denies that lasting trauma has occurred. Even those wounded before death are completed within the spirit world; the medium tells Lodge that Raymond knows a man that had lost his arm, but he has got another one now [...] He seemed as if without a limb when first he entered the astral, seemed incomplete, but after a while it got more and more complete, until he got a new one. (195)

These newly abled spirits are busily at work now that the spirit world resembles a university where new discoveries are made and are passed on to those working in the physical realm, so that they can increase the stock of earthly human knowledge. These underlying principles of evolutionary advancement emphasise the possibility of human perfectibility, in which the war dead are made physically whole again and acquire an intellectual mastery over those toiling on the physical plane. A type of platonic influence is established, in which books become imprinted on the minds of authors who support the spirit cause. Via a medium, Raymond informs his brother, Alec, that in the spirit world

> There are books there not yet published on the earth plane. He is told [...] that these books will be produced, books like these that are there now; that the matter in them will be impressed on the brain of some man, he supposes an author. (209)

This leads Raymond to conclude that 'Father is going to write one' (209).

Raymond was a bestseller during the war years and provided consolation to many. However, it was not beyond mockery from sceptics, largely due to the class-based parallels which could be discerned between Raymond's spirit world and the world he had left behind. In *Raymond* spirits can wear tweeds, smoke cigars and 'call for whisky sodas' (Lodge 1917b: 198), which made it sound like a gentleman's club to many. One notable critic of spiritualism was Charles Mercier, a leading psychiatrist, who, in *Spiritualism and Sir Oliver Lodge* (1917), sidesteps specific criticism of *Raymond* by attributing the book to misguided, but understandable, feelings of grief. At the same time, Mercier more broadly attacks the spiritualist enterprise as a dangerous folly which 'leads to a morbid frame of mind, and tends to render those who are at all predisposed to insanity an easy prey to the disease' (Mercier n.d.: vi). For Mercier, the spiritualist mentality is irrational and associated with a 'morbid', potentially diseased, Gothic gloom. He finds the claims for spiritualism especially surprising in a man of science such as Lodge. Spiritualism has no scientific validity for Mercier and simply speaks to the converted without being able to convert sceptics to the cause; Mercier even notes that 'I have not discovered any record of an occasion when a sceptic was present at one of his [Lodge's] own experiments' (7). In Mercier's view, what is at stake in the clash between science and spiritualism is what constitutes reality because, for him, what Lodge 'calls facts are not established as facts. They are for the most part hearsay, or they are interpretations of fact' (131) – a position which replicates the problem confronted by spirit messages which come through mediums in fragmented and cryptically symbolic forms. Nonetheless, Lodge defended his spiritualist beliefs in a number of articles intended for a popular readership, including 'How I Became Convinced of the Survival of the Dead: An Autobiographical Sketch', published in *The Strand* in 1917, in which he asserts that he believes in the spirit world 'on a basis of fact' (Lodge 1917a: 563).

Raymond is a text in which the medium of the message places it within a familiar Gothic terrain associated with how the ghost should be read. In the traditional ghost story the ghost is required to explain itself to clarify its mission – rather like Jacob Marley's ghost in *A Christmas Carol* (1843), to give just one example. Ghosts in spiritualist and Gothic contexts have a purpose and frequently that is an ethical one. *The Occult Review* focused on the privileged, moral and spiritual authority of the dead, which ensures their continuing commitment to the ethical purpose of the war. The examination of the moral character of the deceased occurs repeatedly in accounts of the war dead and becomes an issue when the soldier has led an unethical life and struggles to adapt to the ethical demands of the spirit world. Wellesley Tudor Pole's *Private Dowding* (1917) addresses this topic and also foregrounds the problem of communication between the spirit world and those on the physical plane. His is a self-contained spirit world, which draws upon many of the contexts and influences that we have observed in the work of Lodge and contributors to *The Occult Review*. However, it is a multi-layered world, which is also patrolled by forces which are explicitly indebted to an earlier Gothic tradition.

Private Dowding's Purgatory

Private Dowding purports to be a spirit memoir channelled through the spiritualist Wellesley Tudor Pole. The text is presented as a diary of communications from Dowding to Tudor Pole which charts Dowding's post-mortem journey on the spiritual plane and the various encounters and explorations that take place with spirit guides. This narrative is intended to demonstrate what is encountered in the spirit world and outlines how to prepare for those encounters. This non-officer memoir is clearly intended to be a counterpoint to the number of spirit narratives by officers, such as *Raymond*, which were published at the time.

Dowding, although a schoolteacher in life and so ostensibly middle-class, is, for Tudor Pole, initially defined by his demotic use of English, which links him to working-class culture. Tudor Pole finds Dowding's speech difficult to record because 'the thoughts were not my own, the language was a little unusual. Ideas were mainly conveyed in short simple phrases' (Tudor Pole 1966: 7). Dowding also highlights the challenge inherent in all spirit communication:

> It is not easy to get messages through with certainty. They are so often lost in transit or misinterpreted. Sometimes the imagination of the receiver weaves a curious fabric round the thoughts we try to pass down, then the ideas we want to communicate are either lost or disfigured. (13)

The problem of communication is therefore never far from the surface in *Private Dowding*. Dowding relays messages from the Messenger and an angel, who are his chief spirit guides, and he channels their views, tempered with his own reflections, via Tudor Pole, who in turn channels them to the reader. The structural similarities with *Frankenstein* are striking. In Mary Shelley's novel, the creature's story is told to Victor, who tells it to Robert Walton, who passes it all on to his sister, Margaret Saville. The creature, who is made out of death and who articulates a language of loss and emotional estrangement, repeatedly tries to tell his story. His is a voice which speaks about the experience of a death-like existence because the world cannot accommodate him, or understand him – which is reflected by Dowding's position, and *Private Dowding* structurally echoes Shelley's narrative because evidence is consistently mediated and remediated, so much so that this type of impacted communication throws doubt on many of the messages. How to read messages is a recurring issue in spirit texts which construe the ideal reader as a type of literary detective, a type of descendant of Mina Harker, who searches for narrative order in *Dracula*, who can restore an otherwise missing narrative coherence. Tudor Pole's caveat about Dowding's indirect communication aside, however, Dowding's text is remarkably clear in its communication of his death in demonstrably non-traumatic terms: for example, 'I had been struck by a shell splinter. There was no pain. The whole life was knocked out of my body', after which 'I found the whole of myself – all, that is, that thinks and sees and feels and knows – was still alive and conscious! I had begun a new chapter of life' (16). If Dowding expresses any regrets, it is that he had not prepared fully enough for this new life, and consequently it takes him some time to adjust to the spirit world. In civilian life, Dowding had been a bored schoolteacher with solitary pursuits that had estranged him from others. He provides a precautionary warning: 'Live widely.

Don't get isolated. Exchange thoughts and services. Don't read too much. That was my mistake. Books appealed to me more than life or people. I am now suffering for my mistakes' (21–2). Such a warning is in keeping with spiritualist narratives which emphasised that the subject must be appropriately prepared to enter the spirit realm by having led a spiritually meaningful life prior to physical death. Tudor Pole's later commentary references Dowding's apparent reliance on Alice Mortley's *Christ in You* (1910) (one book that Dowding clearly approved of) as providing the type of spiritual training necessary to enter the spirit world in a prepared way. In a manner typical of spiritualist tracts, the war is regarded as the consequence of the material ambitions of the pre-war period (a claim that we also saw in *The Occult Review*); Dowding reports that his dealings with the Messenger (his spirit guide) lead him to the view 'that lust for wealth (of one material kind or another) was the real cause of the war' (11). However, the road to hell is a more personal matter, and Dowding embarks on a journey there to see whether the soul of a soldier who, in life, was 'a degenerate, a murderer, a sensualist' might be saved (32). The encounters on the journey prompt a debate about the nature of reality. In hell, 'Those who enter it are led to believe that the only realities are the sense passions and the beliefs of the human "I". This hell consists in believing the unreal to be real' (34). As with other spirit narratives discussed here, this unreal world is a Gothic world, characterised by socially transgressive desires and populated by demonic forms, which reflects a war that is 'all based on illusion' due to its material nature and financial origins (29). Hell represents a degenerate sensual self-indulgence where 'All the thoughts of lust and passion, greed, hatred, envy, and, above all, selfishness, passing through the minds of men and women, generate the "condition" called hell' (34). Hell is thus a very human affair, as it is rooted within negative emotions rather than in a world presided over by Satan. The idea of an inner monster is suggested here and the type of doubling that characterises *Jekyll and Hyde* underpins the forms of conflict that we find in *Private Dowding*, which argues that war is the inevitable consequence of the conflict between material, financial ambitions, which has created this world of Gothic illusions, in contrast to the reality of a spiritual world, which engages with a higher morality. Degenerate Gothic bodies and corruptible inner worlds shape the conflict between the coarse material realm and the transcendent spirit world.

Private Dowding differs from other spiritualist tracts, which were often actively hostile to orthodox religion because the claims for the scientific standing of spiritualist beliefs did not require an act of faith. Dowding's cosmology, however, is a recognisably Christian one, in which, if we accept entry into the omnipresent 'Christ Sphere' (Tudor Pole 1966: 28), we will achieve salvation. The key message of Dowding's chief spirit guide, the Messenger, is that 'a spiritual revival was destined to take place within all the great world-faiths' (36) once the seemingly necessary purge occasioned by the war is complete. However, the principle of evolutionary progress, which runs through so many of the spiritualist narratives discussed here, is also developed in Dowding's reflection on the stagnation of his life when he argues for the need to 'Keep moving in some direction all the time. How was it that I lived so stagnantly whilst on earth? – Let my life be an example' (38). However, despite this insistent spiritual message from the spectre of a dead soldier, *Dowding* also becomes an exercise in doubt and hence is more Gothic than it ostensibly appears.

Dowding's concluding remarks include the comment 'Do not think that all I say must be true. It may be. I cannot tell myself' (37). Tudor Pole himself says of Dowding's narrative that

> I must treat the whole experience as real. Otherwise it would not have been worth while setting down. To me my communications with Thomas Dowding were so real that he seemed to be in the room sitting at my elbow, prompting my pen. (39–40)

However, he then paradoxically claims that although one 'cannot doubt the possibility of "spirit communication," as it is often called, it seems to me that there can be no final proof concerning these matters' (40). Tudor Pole does not doubt his own experience but finds 'I cannot prove the genuineness of the experience to anyone else. I cannot even prove it finally to myself' (40). The claim is evocative of Jonathan Harker's concluding Note in *Dracula* where he states:

> We were struck with the fact that, in all the mass of material of which the record is composed, there is hardly one authentic document! nothing but a mass of type-writing [...] We could hardly ask anyone [...] to accept these proofs of so wild a story. (Stoker 1996: 378)

The reality of experience in the end escapes the attempt to audit that experience bureaucratically. The problem is one of recoding testimony in a convincing way, an issue which also lies at the heart of *Frankenstein*. For Tudor Pole, there is an additional problem because 'Dowding, or whoever is speaking, has no clear idea of what truth is. He emphasises the fact that he knows nothing' (40) because he is simply a conduit for the spirit messages of others, and although 'He passes on the information he receives from the "Messenger" and the "angel", [...] he cannot very often endorse the truth of such information in the light of his own experience' (40–1). Tudor Pole's solution to this problem is to evaluate the messages 'in light of their own internal worth' (40), to celebrate their spiritual, rather than literal, truth. The problem with Dowding was 'His was not an enlightened soul' (43), so that 'He passes on fragments of a teaching which he only dimly understands' (43). Nevertheless, their worth resides within their reflection on the spiritual experience of the reader, so that 'the value of these fragments to us must lie in our reading their deeper meaning in relation to our own lives' (43). As in *Raymond*, these fragments, as in many Gothic texts, need to be reassembled to reveal their hidden truth; hence it is clear that Dowding, while the conduit for such messages, is also an obstacle, in that the spirit communications become warped by his limited spiritual understanding. In order to resolve this conundrum, Tudor Pole contacts the Messenger directly, who prophesies the emergence of a new post-war, and resolutely non-Gothic, world which will be disease-free and egalitarian, including equal rights for women. Tudor Pole is thus prompted to observe 'Your utterances are so utopian that I fear it impossible to secure a fair hearing for them' (53) because he senses that the world is more Gothically dystopian than this conclusion suggests.

Private Dowding reappears in a section added to the original 1917 text, with Dowding now speaking from the vantage point of 1919. Dowding's 1919 return is intended in part to scotch criticism of the earlier edition of the volume, which claimed that he did not exist, prompting him to assert 'Never mind if people tell you that "Private Dowding" has no existence outside your own imagination. It does not matter. The message matters, fragmentary though it is' (Tudor Pole 1966: 58). The 'message' is one of spiritual rebirth: Dowding's relatively unevolved spirit has placed him in purgatory, which makes him a type of potential everyman but with the capacity to evolve. In Dowding's configuration, purgatory 'is a condition to be welcomed, to be bravely faced and lived through. I am beginning to rise above my own purgatory; otherwise I could be of no real service to others' (28). The purgatorial space was, as we shall see, central to how ghosts of the war dead were represented in modernist texts, although in quite a different way.

Private Dowding in its own right, though, is an important spiritualist memoir, which does not, like *Raymond*, attempt to convince on the basis of concrete evidence; rather, it is the reality of spirit messages which is ultimately important, despite these epistemological uncertainties. At heart, such memoirs share a fundamentally Gothic view about the existence of a hidden reality which can be made visible only in symbolic forms. *Private Dowding*, with its angel, is closer to Christian symbolism than many spiritualist writings of the time. The tensions, however, between spiritual certainty and epistemological uncertainty position the ghosts of the war dead within a new liminality. These are ghosts which nuance those found in conventional ghost stories. Like them, they have a story to tell and a cause to promote. However, they are not malevolent or backward-looking, but rather demonstrate that the principles of a benign modernity, associated with spiritual and intellectual progress, are championed in the spirit world. The spirits might represent a note of optimism but the narrative structures in which their message appears are subject to ambivalence. The belief in Dowding's message requires an article of faith, given the absence of evidence. The question of knowing, as a matter of scientific principle, and of understanding, as a condition of spirituality, is the new gulf that is traversed by the ghosts of the war in these spirit narratives. Many of these issues were given treatment in J. S. M. Ward's *Gone West: Three Narratives of After-Death Experiences* (1917). However, *Gone West* engages with the war dead in an oblique way, as many of the spirits have passed over before the war. Ward, a spiritualist who would develop his own religious sect, followed this volume with *A Subaltern in Spirit Land: A Sequel to 'Gone West'* (1919), which reflects on his brother, who was killed during the war, and the later book provides a counterpoint to some of the issues raised in *Private Dowding*.

Ward's Subaltern Spirits

A Subaltern in Spirit Land consists of two parts. The first part centres on Ward's travel to the astral plane, where he meets his brother, Alex, who was killed in April 1916. Ward has numerous discussions with him and others about their war experiences and there is, in the second part, a lengthy account of the nature of the astral plane, which functions as a kind of purgatory. The representations of forms of purgatory have a rich cultural history. Notable within that history is Hamlet's father's ghost, who tells Hamlet that he is:

> confined to fast in fires,
> Till the foul crimes done in my days of nature
> Are burnt and purged away (I, v, 11–13)

As discussed in the Introduction, this is the type of purgatorial ghost which haunts Manfred in *The Castle of Otranto*, a novel which, like *Hamlet*, is about how to protect an aristocratic lineage when it is under threat. Manfred, haunted by his grandfather's ghost, is forced to atone for the past sins of his family, who have usurped the legitimate rulers of the principality of Otranto. Purgatory, 'my prison-house'

(*Hamlet*, I, v, 14), can be left behind only if sins are atoned for and it plays an important role in structuring Manfred's escalating feelings of desperation. Purgatory thus plays an important role in the foundational text of the British Gothic tradition and formulates a version of ghosts and purgatory that is inherited by spiritualist texts supposedly channelled by the ghosts of dead soldiers. Dale Townshend notes in his discussion of *Hamlet*'s influence on *Otranto* that, historically, 'To dismantle purgatory was [...] to impose an abrupt ending upon frequently drawn-out grieving practices' (Townshend 2008: 76). Purgatory is both a terrifying liminal state *and* the space which identifies the presence of a cultural need to mourn.

The astral plane functions as a purgatorial realm which can be visited by those who are earthbound and can find soldier spirits waiting on the astral plane to depart either for heaven or for hell. Alex, lonely after his battlefield death, is comforted by the presence of some of the spirit guides which had appeared in the earlier *Gone West*. The spirit world contains everything that has ever lived, set out in discrete zones, so that journeying through it takes Ward and his brother through areas populated by dinosaurs all the way to modern times. Alex's account of his death (he is blown up while bravely defending Allied territory) includes a description of how the dead carry on fighting in the immediate aftermath of a battle. They fail to realise that they are dead, so that, for Alex:

> 'I heard a savage shout [...] Then a whirling mass of struggling men, dark and shadowy, swept past me [...]. Next moment the tide of battle rolled up and engulfed me. I fired my revolver full into the face of a German, but it seemed to make not the slightest difference.' (Ward 1919: 16)

This is a Gothic world of shadows, in which the subject becomes subsumed by malevolent forces which they are powerless either to comprehend or to resist. Reality is in abeyance as even bullets have no material effect in this spirit world, which is clearly rooted within a Gothic sensibility. The astral plane is thus generated out of a Gothic vision which reworks the Gothic purgatory of Walpole's ghosts, who are also aware that there is unfinished business that will play itself out. In Ward's text, the initial chief difficulty for the guiding spirits is to convince those who have just been killed that they are really dead. Spirits, such as Alex's, need to spend time on this purgatorial astral plane helping those who are newly arrived to it. By helping the newly deceased adjust to their post-mortem selves, spirits, like Alex, acquire the necessary moral credit to overwrite past sins and so are enabled to depart the astral plane permanently for heaven. They may also meet spirits who attempt to persuade them to pursue sensual pleasures; these are mainly focused on alcohol, but sex is also referred to, which would ensure that they go to hell. These two spiritual forces constitute, in the second part of the book, clearly defined opposing factions. Fighting takes place, in which spirits are organised into regiments and prisoners are taken in a clear echo of the ongoing battle between the armies on the Western front. The conflict between good and evil is fought by '"ghostly armies"' (46) and is potentially ceaseless, as the book makes the biblical point (the presence of dinosaurs notwithstanding) that, although evil can be defeated, it cannot be destroyed. Lines allegedly dictated on 15 November that reflect upon the armistice also echo that view: '"Today the organised force of Germany has perished; tomorrow we shall have to deal with the evil wrought by anarchy. Our work is not done, but it will be different"' (157). Moral issues are thus elided with political imperatives.

The book reworks the model of spiritual progress that characterised *Private Dowding* and argues for a similar progressive evolutionary state in which '"there is no stagnation or decay, but out of corruption arises incorruption, and out of death, life"' (158). This ethical position is combined with the home comforts of *Raymond*, including whisky sodas, universities and theatrical productions. Yet beyond these familiar features, the book imagines a multi-faceted and non-mimetic afterlife. This is not a Gothic life, despite its unreality, but a world which is beyond the structures of conventional models of reality. The astral plane is a type of waiting room in which the spirit makes final decisions, which ensure either ascension to heaven or descent into a Gothically rendered version of hell. The war dead may be playing their customary role, settling the cosmic battle between good and evil which is physically played out on the Western front, but beyond them, this book embraces figures and formulations not seen in any of the texts previously discussed. Surprisingly, for example, the spirits of recently deceased Germans are present. These men are still fighting on the astral plane and their ultimate destination is unclear, while many of the British spirits of the war dead present themselves as red, which indicates that their too passionate nature would lead them to hell unless they acquire the necessary self-restraint. The spirit world is populated by monstrous animal-like forms called elementals, who are soulless and need to be fought. Such Gothic entities are augmented by the presence of 'very dangerous vampires' (53), who are imaged as female prostitutes who 'will pay for their fleshly joys with much suffering' (53). Set against this *demi-monde* is the celebration of a set of conventional class-bound British values which centre on art, culture and stately homes. Such houses are precisely rendered in illustrations of their layout, including their elaborate gardens which come complete with sets of specialist gardeners. There is a clear vision of Britain under attack here, wherein its history and culture are threatened by malign forces, echoing the war-induced anxieties of the time. To a degree, Dante's *Purgatorio* (the second part of his Divine Comedy [1320]) is, alongside *Hamlet* and *Otranto*, also a precursor narrative which structures the upward journey through a version of purgatory. Ward's purgatory is also a hybrid world of recognisable places and Gothic monsters, of gardeners and vampires. The spirit needs to decide to which world it belongs.

In *A Subaltern in Spirit Land*, consequently, ghosts are highly conflicted entities who are subject to physical desires unless they embrace the self-sacrifice that leads them to a higher plane of existence. The astral plane is effectively a war zone, where competing claims on the subject are developed as moral conflicts in which the dead must take sides and battle as soldiers against dark forces (in which they can still use their rifles). War is represented as a state of continuing human conflict beyond death because the presence of evil is necessary in order for the ghosts to show their moral worth. Any ultimate triumph is a largely personal rather than collective one, in which individuals embark on their moral journeys within a world dominated by regiments and battalions. As one spirit puts it, '"there is no armistice in the fight between good and evil. Neither in the fight which goes on within ourselves, nor in the greater struggle which is always raging. It shifts its ground, but does not disappear"' (157). This post-war sentiment is intended to keep alive the fundamental principles of the spiritualist agenda concerning the necessity of ongoing spiritual conflict, in which virtue wins by perpetually battling against vice. The principled nature of this conflict is also supported by the deaths generated by the post-war 'Spanish flu' pandemic. The end of the war is thus not the end of the matter, as one spirit puts it: '"The armistice has brought a big drop in the number of newcomers, though this spell of influenza has kept up the flow fairly well"' (157). Hence, morally improving the dead to defeat the elementals remains an ongoing affair.

The ghosts of the war dead in these spiritualist narratives provide reassurance about the continuation of life and confirm that the struggle for moral ascendance is ongoing. Many of these narratives focus on the evidence of a spiritual reality and the tensions between spiritual truth and epistemological uncertainty. They also represent an inward turn, in which the values of the inner life are closely scrutinised. The subject is sanitised when it casts off its worldly and bodily desires, so much so that this new puritanism may seem to be at odds with a modernist aesthetic which evolved before and during the war. However, the issue of epistemological uncertainty and a concern with the emotional turmoil of the subject suggests links between spiritualism and Freud which underpin the fractured world of the modernist text and its constructions of subjectivity. Ghosts wander through modernist texts to the point of widening this debate about the war dead and their ontological function. Their presence generates a newly formed, war-nuanced, Gothic.

Modernist Ghosts: A Resurgence of the Gothic

The links between modernism and the Gothic have been subject to some sustained critical scrutiny.[9] For John Paul Riquelme, the 'intersection' between the Gothic and modernism 'is memorable and revealing' (Riquelme 2014: 20), as the modernist text inherits a principle of exploring oppositional states which is rooted within the Victorian Gothic. The doubled and divided, conflicted, Gothic subjects which we find in the Victorian Gothic reappear in the emotionally lost and psychologically confused subjects which populate modernist texts. Riquelme also notes how an earlier Gothic tradition left its imprint on combatant texts such as Wilfred Owen's 'Strange Meeting', in which two opposing soldiers become united in death (Riquelme 2014: 26–7). Riquelme also argues that the war represented 'a Gothic narrative' (Riquelme 2014: 26) because it constituted a dystopian disruption of notions of social progress. The war, however, is not the principal critical focus of Riquelme's analysis and this chapter aims to make the war more central to any consideration of the modernist Gothic. The modernist self is lost, as Foley notes, due to its associations with a persistent state of mourning caused by the war, which clearly contrasts with the spiritualist view that death is not the end. Nevertheless, there are links between spiritualism and modernism and an earlier Gothic tradition.

The specific links between spiritualism and modernism are largely aesthetic and epistemological. Aesthetically, the fragmentary nature of spirit messages meets its corollary in the complex structure of the modernist text. Both also suggest that authentic experience is found in what lies beneath the seemingly superficial appearance of the everyday material world, and ask questions about how we might gain access to this spectral presence. Charles Ko, for example, has argued that F. W. H. Myers's spiritualist view – that complex multi-authored messages can be sent telepathically via subliminal interventions – is analogous to the type of multi-textuality found in the writings of James Joyce. For Ko, the 'unconscious' in Myers 'is unsealed, operating not only intrapersonally but also *interpersonally* as a kind of vast, decentralised, open-ended, palimpsestic writing machine linking one porous mind to another, continually rereading and rewriting itself as multiple messages intersect and overlap, circulate and recirculate' (Ko 2007: 747, italics in original). Roger Luckhurst has also argued that many modernists were indebted to the type of psychic investigations articulated within various occult theologies, such as Theosophy.[10] These occult religious beliefs were shaped by the type of psychology developed by Myers, which, as Luckhurst notes, prompted André Breton in 1933 to acknowledge that Surrealism 'owe[d] more than is generally conceded to what William James justly called the *gothic psychology* of F. W. H. Myers' (Breton 1978: 100, italics in original).

Spiritualism was hostile towards modernism because the modernist text's foregrounding of a fragmentary aesthetic did not reflect the profound experience of spiritual transcendence. Ultimately, the fragmented modernist subject retains its fragmentation rather than regaining the bodily and emotional unity that tends to triumph in spiritualism. The implicit presence of *Frankenstein* is, for example, key to shaping representations of the fragmented subject in *The Waste Land* (1922). The modernist subject thus becomes a Gothic subject, as Breton suggests, who is psychologically fragmented and emotionally frozen in a state of persistent grief.

There is a moment in Ward's *A Subaltern in Spirit Land* where he finds himself 'seized with a desire to do cubist drawings' (Ward 1919: 77). He seeks an explanation from a spirit guide, who tells him '"some cubist artist who has been killed lately is trying to continue to work through you"' (77). The spirit guide deprecates the ambitions of a ghost trying to produce cubist art because there is no money in it, noting that '"Personally I can't imagine anyone buying a cubist drawing, but there's no accounting for taste"' (77). A note at the end of the chapter records that 'This cubist phase soon passed' (77). The overall tone of this passage is one of comic denigration, since it is clear that cubist art has no spiritual, or financial, worth, and the scene is merely introduced in order to move beyond it. The refutation of a modernist aesthetic, albeit brief, is revealing. Modernism, seen from a spiritualist perspective, is characterised by shallow aesthetic interests, whereas spiritualism explores experience founded in metaphysical depths that aims for a reunified psyche at metaphysical heights.

For spiritualists, there is no need for mourning because the dead have not really died, merely moving to another realm where they begin a higher spiritual life than any found on the physical plane. The reality of mourning is denied in this embracing of an eternal life, and this belief is augmented by a patriotic narrative in which the dead continue either to fight on the battlefield or to help resolve the wider spiritual conflicts taking place on the astral plane. Conflict is necessary and constitutes a moral good, seeing as it provides an opportunity for spiritual growth.

The modernist impulse is different in kind because the modernist text's foregrounding of fragmentation emphasises that unity or resolution is not possible. This disjunction explains why psychologically complex texts such as West's *The Return of the Soldier* focus on loss and the attendant feelings of mourning, which spiritualism denies. Nevertheless, the modernist ghost should be seen within the context of a culture of mourning the war dead at the time. The modernist ghost, as we shall see, represents a failure of mourning practices that are associated with a model of purgatory from which the ghost cannot escape. This version of the purgatorial is different in kind from how the astral plane is represented as a transitional state in spiritualist texts. These conflicting views of the war dead are thus fought over, with Gothic affect, the semantic terrain of purgatory.

Liminal Modernism: Purgatorial States

We have seen how spirit narratives such as *Private Dowding* and *A Subaltern in Spirit Land* refer to the astral plane as a state of purgatory from which the soul can ascend if the spirit carries out good works such as helping those who have newly arrived to settle in. Such a position acknowledges that those who have just been killed in the war might not have led as moral a life as they should have, but with a commitment to ethical behaviour they are able to achieve redemption; death is thus not the end, but a waypoint on a spiritual journey. This purgatorial state also appears in modernist writing about ghosts. Matt Foley's *Haunting Modernisms* has addressed the modernist representation of purgatory in depth. He argues that, in writings by Richard Aldington, Ford Madox Ford, T. S. Eliot, Wyndham Lewis and Virginia Woolf, 'such haunting modernisms are indeterminably bound by purgatorial models of selfhood so that ghostly modernism becomes virtually defined by its resistance to recuperation and transcendence' (Foley 2017: 4). The modernist ghost evidences the presence of an unhealthy melancholia rather than a healthy, because temporary, form of mourning. In modernism there appear 'anti-consolatory and purgatorial modes of subjectivity' (Foley 2017: 5), which suggest a version of World War One 'in which paradigms of normative, life-affirming mourning are eschewed' (9). These modernist ghosts are not simply conventional Gothic figures, however; they are entities that represent certain liminal ontological states in figurative form. The Gothic is subtly recalled in the representation of lost and persistently traumatised selves that we find in such modernist texts; as Townshend notes in his discussion of

Otranto, 'In Gothic that which has not been adequately mourned is likely to return as a ghost' (Townshend 2008: 77) and this is reworked within a modernist context in order to generate a new type of Gothic in which the self becomes spectrally haunted by traumatic feelings that it cannot resolve. The new type of Gothic that emerges is centred on how to cope in a world which is ontologically disorientating. More specifically, modernism becomes defined by a persistent from of mourning that Freud associated with melancholia in 'Mourning and Melancholia' (1917), an essay shaped especially by the mass deaths occasioned by World War One. For Freud:

> The distinguishing mental features of melancholia are a profoundly painful dejection, cessation of interest in the outside world, loss of the capacity to love, inhibition of all activity, and a lowering of the self-regarding feelings to a degree that finds utterance in self-reproaches and self-revilings, and culminates in a delusional expectation of punishment. (Freud 1991b: 252)

Freud notes that all of these attributes also characterise mourning, although, crucially, in mourning there is no 'disturbance of self-regard' (252). Foley uses this sense of melancholia to argue that modernist ghosts do not conform to Freud's 'The Uncanny' (and, to a degree, evade the conventions of the literary Gothic) because, for Foley,

> conflating the ghostly with the uncanny does not capture the persistent nature of the haunting experienced by the purgatorial subject in modernism. The uncanny, by definition, is a transitory experiential moment; whereas purgatorial subjectivity [...] is an on-going mode of (non-)being, during which neither lasting transcendence nor extended consolation is possible. (2017: 27–8)

The argument is that modernism tacitly inherits this model of an unresolved, and so purgatorial, mourning. Freud's account of mourning and the modernist text are thus both shaped by wartime grief. In modernism, as in melancholia, the dead are thus not quite dead but permanently trapped in limbo as grief makes the dead emotionally present. This state can be consciously read against the spiritualist position on the war dead, which argues that they are not really dead: hence the largely negative way in which spiritualism is represented in modernism.

Foley notes that, in Woolf's *Mrs Dalloway* (1925), the shell-shocked Septimus Smith seemingly hears the voice of Evans, a dead soldier that he had fought with. Septimus's wife, Rezia, records what Septimus tells her Evans is saying:

> That man, his friend who was killed, Evans, had come, he said. He was singing behind the screen. She wrote it down just as he spoke it. Some things

were very beautiful; others sheer nonsense. And he was always stopping in the middle, changing his mind; wanting to add something; hearing something new; listening with his hand up. But she heard nothing. (Woolf 2019: 154)

This spirit message does not quite bring the consolation that Septimus is searching for and, when he is unable to reach Evans again, he commits suicide 'in order to avoid the very painful work of mourning' (Foley 2017: 118). Septimus displays many of the features of Freud's definition of melancholia, including the loss of positive emotional affect reflected in his incapacity to feel. Rezia takes him to a tea-shop, 'But he could not taste, he could not feel. In the tea-shop among the tables and the chattering waiters the appalling fear came over him – he could not feel' (Woolf 2019: 96). He is also unable to reconnect with his love of literature. His experiences of the war explain why he reads literature for cryptic messages which confirm his pessimistic view of the world. Septimus, a once avid reader of Shakespeare, reflects that the beauty of Shakespeare conceals a darker message 'now revealed to Septimus; the message hidden in the beauty of words. The secret signal which one generation passes, under disguise, to the next is loathing, hatred, despair. Dante the same. Aeschylus (translated) the same' (97). Earlier, it was noted that there exists a Gothic genealogy around purgatory, which can be seen in *Hamlet*'s influence on Walpole's *The Castle of Otranto*. Septimus's sense of a hidden message which works through Shakespeare and Dante into the modern world also traverses that history. We also saw in *Private Dowding* that the spirit of the dead soldier urges 'Live widely. Don't get isolated. Exchange thoughts and services. Don't read too much. That was my mistake. Books appealed to me more than life or people. I am now suffering for my mistakes' (Tudor Pole 1966: 21–2). Septimus's pre-war fascination with books, by these lights, distances him from the world and from Rezia, but they are also perceived by Septimus as the conveyors of hidden signs of despair which mirror his jaded view of the world, to such an extent that Septimus's melancholia is reflected back by everything that he has read and sees.

The principal cause of his unhappiness is his inability to feel anything about the death of Evans: 'He had not cared when Evans was killed; that was worst' (Woolf 2019: 99), worse even than loss of his love for Rezia. Septimus's apparent inability to feel is paradoxical because it is feeling itself that has worn him out. He has reached this point not because he feels too little, but because he has felt too much – but in highly abstract terms which are generated by his briefly and obliquely expressed experience of the war. In Freudian terms, his absent/present feeling of loss 'is the expression of an exclusive devotion to mourning which leaves nothing over for other purposes or other interests' (Freud 1991b: 252). Septimus notes at one point that 'he could add up his bill; his brain was prefect; it must be the fault of the world then – that he could not feel' (Woolf 2019: 96), which corresponds to Freud's idea that 'In mourning it is the world which has become poor and empty', whereas 'in melancholia it is the ego itself' (Freud 1991b: 254). However, the novel is clear that, while Septimus might see the world as being the problem, this is not how others sees Septimus: most notably, Rezia who refers to a 'Septimus, who wasn't Septimus any longer' (Woolf 2019: 71). His response to Rezia's despair becomes the measure by which we witness his descent from mourning into melancholia: 'His wife was crying, and he felt nothing; only each time she sobbed in this profound, this silent, this hopeless way, he descended another step into the pit' (Woolf 2019: 99). It is not clear if he registers this descent or not. His medical treatment focuses on his shattered nerves, but ultimately Septimus is unable to cast off the ghosts of the dead, illustrated by his periodic haunting by Evans and by Septimus's writings. He destroys his journals, which centre on 'how the dead sing behind rhododendron bushes; odes to Time; conversations with Shakespeare; Evans, Evans, Evans – his messages from the dead' (Woolf 2019: 162). Gabrielle Myers has noted that 'the manic fragmentation' (Myers 2011: 217) of Septimus's spirit messages are evocative of post-traumatic shock and so represent a symptom of shell-shock rather than its possible cure. Septimus's suicide is also a moment ghosted by the war when he jumps from the window to escape the medical intervention of Dr Holmes, whom he does not trust and whom he regards with hostility. The language used in the scene implicates the war. When he jumps, Septimus cries out as if he were attacking an enemy position '"I'll give it you!"' and Dr Holmes, forcing open the room's locked door, shouts out '"The coward!"' (Woolf 2019: 164) as he enters the room. Elaine Showalter has noted that military attitudes, which often regarded shell-shock 'as a form of cowardice or malingering', inform the representation of Septimus (Showalter 2019: xxxvii). Holmes's intervention can therefore be read as both a diagnosis and an unsympathetic judgement. The manner of Septimus's suicide is also notably Gothic. Judith Wilt states that 'when we who regularly read the Gothic later learn that those railings were piercing spikes, and reconsider the invasion of the doctor and the staking of the madman, we find in fact the classic vampire death scene', albeit one that is 'meaningfully inverted' (Wilt 2001: 68), as Dr Holmes is the destructive agent. In Wilt's reading, Septimus is a representative figure of the dead undead who escapes this limbo world and his suicide is thus a way out of the purgatorial realm identified by Foley.

Ultimately, his death functions as a critique of a post-war world which was quick to judge rather than to cure. Foley's main focus is on Septimus; however, he is not the only haunted character in the novel because Clarissa Dalloway's intimation of a world of apparitions is also used to implicate a generation of non-combatants who also, like Septimus, feel lost.

Clarissa, while walking up Shaftesbury Avenue, in a scene immediately following Septimus's suicide, contemplates the people whom she encounters on a regular if impersonal basis (such as shopkeepers or other habitués of urban locations), which

> ended in a transcendental theory which, with her horror of death, allowed her to believe, or say that she believed (for all her scepticism), that since our apparitions, the part of us which appears, are so momentary compared with the other, the unseen part of us, which spreads wide, the unseen might survive, be recovered somehow attached to this person or that, or even haunting certain places, after death. Perhaps – perhaps. (Woolf 2019: 164)

This passage is constructed from a short series of hesitant expressions, which culminate in the final double use of 'perhaps'. The hesitations can be related to the sense of purgatory as Foley defines it. Clarissa is metaphysically uncertain about which world she belongs to. Her 'apparitions' are not ghosts, but 'the part of us which appears', whereas 'the unseen part', while properly ghostly, suggests the prospect of immortality. At the same time, this is an immortality which is subjected to a principle of redistribution, which implies that it is manifested through the lives that we touch. The issue of fragmentation which informs representations of the war dead is potentially replaced by a possible positive redistribution of continuing influence. The ghost is dispersed and able to haunt multiple sites. This both evokes and challenges the conventional aspects of the literary ghost – it haunts places and people, but it does so not out of a principle of revenge, but through a desire to inhabit the diverse contexts of a life that has touched many. There is a desperation to this newly formed Gothic ghost as it desires to hang on to the people and places that were important to it in life. In short, it represents a desire to be remembered, which is a common aspect of the traditional Gothic ghost which, like Walpole's ghosts, indicates that the past wants to touch the present. Wilt has also noted Woolf's indebtedness to Henry James, arguing that, like him:

> Woolf went to the Gothic pantheon for 'agents' of the marvellous because these agents traditionally enforce in characters and readers that sudden opening, widening, shattering of consciousness, that dissolving of boundaries, which was one of the goals of her fiction. (Wilt 2001: 62)

The fragmented modernist subject that we witness in Clarissa's own 'shattering' and 'dissolving of boundaries' breaks down the barriers between the material world and one founded in feeling by employing the ghost to bridge these worlds projectively. The question posed is whether this shattered self can, at some point, be 'recovered [...] after death'. Clarissa's confusion is reflected in how the living become apparitional and the spectral imbued with life ('the unseen might survive'). This liminal limbo echoes Septimus's purgatorial melancholia.

That Septimus and Clarissa function as doubles has been noted by Gabrielle Myers (Myers 2011: 215) and Elaine Showalter, who argues that Septimus 'is linked to Clarissa through his anxieties about sexuality and marriage; his anguish about mortality and immortality; and his acute sensitivities to his surroundings, which have gone over the line into madness' (Showalter 2019: xxxvii). Septimus's suicide becomes a topic for discussion in the final scenes of the novel, which occur at Clarissa's party. At the party, there is some general debate about the plight of shell-shocked soldiers, but Clarissa is struck by two seemingly conflicting impulses. One is a feeling of discomfort that death has been introduced into the life of her party: 'Oh! thought Clarissa, in the middle of my party, here's death, she thought' (Woolf 2019: 201); the other is that Septimus, who is unknown to her, has, in committing suicide, rebelled against the type of emotional deadness which characterises her post-war social milieu. She is led to conclude that his suicide demonstrated that 'Death was defiance. Death was an attempt to communicate, people feeling the impossibility of reaching the centre which, mystically, evaded them; closeness drew apart; rapture faded; one was alone. There was an embrace in death' (Woolf 2019: 202). Her conclusion complicates the view that she saw the discussion of death as an unpalatable topic at her party, since death now looms as already 'in the middle of my party' because the moribund social relations and faded emotional connections between its attendees indicate that this is a dead world. As Showalter notes of the party, 'People arrive to be announced by the hired butler like ghosts of the past' and 'As Woolf takes us into the minds of the various guests, we see that their facades of festivity and good breading conceal a terror of ageing and death' (Showalter 2019: xliv). Read in this light, Septimus's '"I'll give it you!"' can be read as a gesture of defiance which symbolically asserts agency against deadening conformity and false companionship, explaining Clarissa's view of her relationships in which 'closeness drew apart; rapture faded; one was alone. There was an embrace in death', so that 'She felt somehow very like him – the young man who had killed himself. She felt glad that he had done it; thrown it away while they went on living' (Woolf

2019: 202). Septimus's journey and Clarissa's are thus related and Wilt notes that 'Clarissa's ghost story plot has always encircled Septimus's' (Wilt 2001: 69). However, while Septimus's death is transformed into a life-affirming radical gesture, Clarissa returns to the inescapable purgatorial realm of her party because, ultimately, she is not a convert to the spiritualist cause.

Mrs Dalloway, then, provides evidence that modernism represents spiritualism in a predominantly negative way. Septimus dabbles in spiritualist practice when he repeats what the dead Evans says to him so that Rezia can write it down, although she hears nothing. Before they destroy his spiritualist papers, Rezia recalls that they had discovered their cleaner 'reading one of these papers in fits of laughter' (Woolf 2019: 154). The type of spiritualism that indicates that transcendence is possible and that one may ascend from purgatory is denied in a modernism which culturally represents, as in the case of Septimus, an ongoing mourning that slips into melancholia. The spiritualist spectre is thus an ambivalently disruptive presence because, although spiritualism is represented negatively, it nevertheless articulates a possible post-mortem life which Clarissa both yearns for and cannot quite believe in. The spirits raised through versions of spiritualist practice are thus negative figures in modernism, and these ideas can be related to that most ghost-laden of modernist narratives, T. S. Eliot's *The Waste Land*.

The Waste Land

Allyson Booth has noted that, while a number of modernists such as T. S. Eliot were non-combatants, they nevertheless incorporated the experience of war into their texts, in the main from their reading of war poetry. She asserts that 'No doubt soldiers taught post war poets lessons [...] well: T.S. Eliot's *The Waste Land* is commonly understood to incorporate the sounds and images of trench warfare and its aftermath' (Booth 1996: 6). Eliot's poem is also, as many of the texts in this chapter are, ghosted by the Gothic presence of both *Frankenstein* and *Dracula*. In part five it is noted:

> A woman drew her long black hair out tight
> And fiddled whisper music on those strings
> And bats with baby faces in the violet light
> Whistled, and beat their wings
> And crawled head downward down a blackened wall
> And upside down in air were towers

> Tolling reminiscent bells, that kept the hours
> And voices singing out of empty cisterns and exhausted wells. (v. 1.377–85)

The lines are based on the scene in *Dracula* when Harker sees the Count descend from his tower in pursuit of a baby, which he will deliver to the three female vampires. The high modernist text thus, again, acknowledges an engagement with the popular Victorian Gothic text. Eliot's poem also refers to a world of carnage populated by rats, the bones of the dead, and feelings of emotional and physical despair, all of which evoke the trenches and *Frankenstein*. Tellingly, the poem begins with a discussion of what to do with the dead and how to remember them. The landscape is, paradoxically, about death *and* renewal, reflected in a view of whether memory keeps alive the past or simply entombs it:

> April is the cruellest month, breeding
> Lilacs out of the dead land, mixing
> Memory and desire, stirring
> Dull roots with spring rain. (ll. 1–4)

The landscape is a composted composite of life, death, memory and desire, which are principal themes of the poem. Eliot is confronted by the problem of the persistence of memory, which maintains a hold on those who have survived the war. The narrator asks:

> What are the roots that clutch, what branches grow
> Out of this stony rubbish? (ll. 19–20)

The sense that the past has the subject in its clutches indicates the extent to which modernist subjects are restrained by the type of unresolved mourning identified by Foley. There is, however, another issue here relating to trauma and the impossibility of articulating an experience that those who had not fought in the war could understand.[11] In *Mrs Dalloway*, Rezia does not hear the voice of Evans and records Septimus's account as 'nonsense'. The war veteran cannot articulate his experience of the war via the medium of a dead soldier, whereas in spiritualist narratives this very transmission is turned into something positive. *The Waste Land* is about what is held back, not what can be loquaciously channelled via a medium. Indeed, this poem is about a traumatised silence which gains a stylised eloquence through its refusal to speak of, or visually conjure, the experience of memory. In the section entitled 'The Burial of the Dead', this is expressed in the encounter with '"the hyacinth girl"' (l. 36), who functions as the type of lover that a veteran returns to, only to find:

> ... when we came back, late, from the Hyacinth garden,
> Your arms full, and your hair wet, I could not
> Speak, and my eyes failed, I was neither
> Living nor dead, and I knew nothing,
> Looking into the heart of light, the silence. (ll. 37–41)

The speaker is a ghost-like figure whose spectrality contrasts with the physicality of the girl with her 'arms full' and her 'hair wet'. He is both there and not there, and this liminality is repeatedly associated in the poem with an enforced silence. Later, in 'A Game of Chess', a similar scenario is evoked in which the woman asks:

> '"Speak to me. Why do you never speak? Speak.
> What are you thinking of? What thinking? What?
> I never know what you are thinking. Think."' (ll. 111–14)

The subject of her interrogation mentally evokes an image from the trenches:

> I think we are in rats' alley
> Where the dead men lost their bones. (ll. 115–16)

For Randy Malamud, these lines (and others in the poem) evoke Victor Frankenstein's work in the charnel house, where he assembles the creature out of the dead (Malamud 1988: 42). Riquelme also notes that Eliot's poem 'can be compared to Frankenstein's monster as a creation made from damaged parts, a "heap of broken images (l. 22) and "withered stumps of time" (l. 104)' (Riquelme 2014: 25). For Malamud, the poem engages with the abyss associated with the veteran but also with the type of emotional abyss confronted by Victor's creature (Malamud 1988: 42). The creature, like Eliot's narrator, struggles to find the words which can convince their interlocutors about their experience. Eliot's narrator is trapped in a memory of war which cannot be articulated and which leaves the baffled woman exasperated by the silence: '"Are you alive, or not? Is there nothing in your head?"' (l. 126). The answer is that the subject is not sure, in part because reality itself now seems to have shifted from life-after-death to death-in-life, as in the references to what goes on within the 'Unreal City' (l. 60) of London, where the ghosts 'flowed over London Bridge, so many,/I had not thought death had undone so many' (ll. 62–3). The poem inherits a problem with communication from *Frankenstein*, in which voices, such as the creature's, are lost within the narrative mediations of others. The issue was discussed in relation to Tudor Pole's *Private Dowding*, where Dowding's voice is in danger of being lost because of this mediation. There, the spirit message was in danger of becoming obscured and in *The Waste*

Land this shift is also, significantly, articulated through the figure of the clairvoyant Madame Sosostris, whose Tarot cards suggest that nothing is progressing: 'I see crowds of people, walking round in a ring' (l. 56). She senses that she is surrounded by a figurative range of possible realities, which suggests the erosion of a stable world that may, or may not, be restored, even though 'One must be so careful these days' (l. 59). Her particular set of possible futures echoes a problem with reality, rather than any restoration of it, and indicates that Eliot is sceptical about spiritualist models of reality.

The problem of communication is that it is private and isolating, and this view contrasts with spiritualist writings which dwell on how messages from the spirit world can, as in *Raymond* and the spirit texts discussed earlier, be widely shared. In the modernist text, the focus is not communal; Septimus Smith, in the main, suffers alone and the war-worn figures in *The Waste Land* are isolated by their silence. Eliot supports this position by citing, in his notes to the poem, from F. H. Bradley's *Appearance and Reality* (1893): 'In brief, regarded as an existence which appears in the soul, the whole world for each is peculiar and private to that soul' (Eliot 2001: 56). This is a type of purgatory, but one which reflects on the nature of what it means to be either dead or alive, or in the world, or of it. In the spiritualist texts discussed here, it is clear that the living can commune with the dead on the purgatorial astral plane. While this reassurance is supposed to emphasise the possibility of communicating with the spirit world, it also suggests that the living can also be seen as in purgatory. To the families of the missing, this suggestion must have captured the emotional reality for those waiting for news that would confirm either a death or a life. Eliot moves beyond the spiritualist position as he sees the trauma of the war dead as incommunicable, so that metaphors of death proliferate because the dead cannot be granted the type of closure that conventional mourning bestows. This is why *Frankenstein* is a key Gothic precursor to *The Waste Land*. The figure of the fragmented dead, who cannot tell their story directly, is inherited by Eliot as way of thinking about the traumatised soldier who, like Mary Shelley's creature, is unable to escape images of death and cannot be accommodated within conventional romantic or family structures. The poem's explicit evocation of *Dracula* also indicates associations with the dead undead figure that the veteran has become.

The dead persist for Eliot, but not as they do in spiritualism. The dead have a veneer of life that generates an unresolved grief. Figuratively speaking, death is granted a life of its own, an issue raised in the poem as 'That corpse you planted last year in your garden,/Has it begun to sprout?' (ll. 71–2). Booth argues that, in the poem, 'death seeps out of its container, disrupting verb tenses, the connection between the conscious self and the body it inhabits – even a speaker's ability to tell whether he or she is living or dead' (Booth 1996: 60). Booth asserts that in modernism the corpse maintains a hold over the living so that the 'past [...] remains stubbornly present [and] flummoxes the ability of characters to create new selves' (63). This very liminality populates *The Waste Land*, as Michael Levenson has noted, with its ghosts, making the poem 'a kind of ghost story with protagonists both haunted and haunting' (Levenson 1984:174). These are not empty ghosts (or hollow men, as Eliot might also have it); rather, they should be seen as on the cusp of generating meaning, and their failure to do so reflects the wider inability to engage with a necessary mourning that is required before the world can move beyond the war. This problem of death, as a problem of continual grieving, generates new forms of narration which resist the aesthetic unity of a post-mourning world. Such disunity can be seen in modernist poetry which reflects rather more directly on the war than *The Waste Land*, and David Jones's epic poem *In Parenthesis* (1937) provides an illuminating example of that.

In Parenthesis

It is difficult to define *In Parenthesis* generically, since it consists of a variety of narrative forms: poetry, prose and, above all, memoir. It is both a highly impressionistic, modernist view of war and an account of day-to-day activities. It is arguably unfinished, seeing as it ends in July 1916 (Jones was at the front until 1918), and this abrupt conclusion may have been occasioned by the mental breakdown Jones suffered when writing his hybrid text. The poem weaves together different narratives, including references to Shakespeare, Coleridge, Celtic myths and, above all, Malory's *Morte d'Arthur* (1485). To that degree, it echoes the textual complexity of *The Waste Land*, including thirty-five pages of notes to explain the various references and to clarify certain phrases and contexts. *In Parenthesis* centres on Jones's experiences as a private soldier, and the heroic and quasi-heroic literary contexts that he evokes grant the private soldier a form of cultural dignity which is blended with their demotic speech patterns and quotidian frustrations.

The publication of Jones's text was, in fact, overseen by T. S. Eliot, whose 1961 Introduction acknowledges Jones's place within the modernist canon in part because of the poem's range of literary allusions. Eliot asserts that 'When *In Parenthesis* is widely enough known – as it will be in time – it will no doubt undergo the same sort of detective analysis and exegesis as the later work of James Joyce and the Cantos of Ezra Pound' (Eliot 2014: vii). Eliot was keen to claim that Jones's work was comparable not only to that of Joyce and Pound but also to his own work, while acknowledging a key difference – Jones had been a combatant. Jones's Preface makes it clear that his poem attempts a textual resurrection of those whom he had fought alongside in the 'war landscape' that he refers to as 'the Waste Land' (the reference to Eliot seems deliberate), in which 'the sudden violences and the long stillnesses, the sharp contours and the unformed voids of that mysterious existence, profoundly affected the imaginations of those who suffered it. It was a place of enchantment' (Jones 2014: x). His text, moreover, illustrates that it was a notably Gothic form of enchantment, in which the dead appeared to have a form of life, although one repeatedly expressed through their physical remains rather than by a continuing spirit. His focus is on the presence of the bodies of soldiers and how they are freighted by images of death as they frequently appear as corpses in waiting. As in the previous texts discussed here, the emphasis is on the soldier as a type of dead undead, in which they die but are subject to possible forms of resurrection. *Frankenstein* again appears as an unspoken influence, but there is also an interest in ghosts as Walpolean harbingers from the past who have unfinished business. The liminality of the ghost in Jones's poem is closely associated with the composite liminality of his text. His Preface explains some of the linguistic influences which shaped his narrative and explains why the title flags liminality as an essential experience of the war, although in typically provisional terms. He notes:

> The writing is called 'In Parenthesis' because I have written it in a kind of space between – I don't know quite what – but as you turn aside to do something; and because for us amateur soldiers (and especially for the writer, who was not only amateur, but grotesquely incompetent, a knock-er-over of piles, a parade's despair) the war itself was a parenthesis – how glad we thought we were to step outside its brackets at the end of '18 – and also because our curious type of existence here is altogether in parenthesis. (xv)

The bracketed-off experience represents both a hiatus from life and an attempt to contain the trauma of the war, a task which Jones ultimately felt to be impossible. The inter-textuality of *In Parenthesis* also reflects the difficulty of writing trauma, discussed in the previous chapter. How to find the right idiom involves reaching out for an inter-textual synthesis which cannot quite overcome a sense of fragmentation, which means that Jones's text should be seen as a bridge between those fragmented war memoirs and the experimental ambitions of the modernist text which struggle to grasp the current nature of reality epistemologically. The idea of writing as a form of in parenthesis also has a clear Gothic provenance. Walpole's *The Castle of Otranto* was, as Walpole's second edition preface testifies, written between waning and rising forms of writing. He acknowledges the ambition 'to blend two types of romance, the ancient and the modern' (Walpole 1998: 9), and so bridging an older fantastical romance which traded in unreality and an emerging new form of Gothic romance in which reality can be discerned within symbolic forms. In Walpole's novel, the dead are manifested in fragments and in images of the dead arising out of enclosures and walls. The dead, the waning narrative forms, intrude into the new but in such a way that invites a reading of their symbolic significance. *In Parenthesis* is indebted to the Walpolean Gothic tradition as it too wrestles with making symbolic sense of what the dead represent.

Jones's view that 'the Waste Land' of the battlefield was also an 'enchanted' place, after all, means that it, like the Gothic, produced a sense of unreality. He notes of his experience of moving on to the frontline that 'It had all the unknownness of something of immense realness, but of which you lack all true perceptual knowledge' (15–16). As we have seen before, in Blunden and Sassoon, no-man's-land becomes a spectral place in which the landscape, destroyed by shelling, nevertheless retains an overwhelming vitality. Damaged buildings also evoke spectres, with Jones noting of a house which had been partially destroyed by shelling that, from it, 'Three men, sack-buskined to the hips, rose like wraiths out of the ground' (41). These ghosts are associated with place and, like them, these apparitions are intended to startle and make us stop and think. These figures are seemingly harbingers of death (wraiths) but have also survived death, manifested, quite Gothically, out of 'the mason work' of the building. These figures are solid but also apparitional, alive and yet heralding death. Jones is using the idea of 'in parenthesis' to map the spectral liminality of life on the real, but unknown, battlefield. Soldiers survive death but become symbolic of a death that is yet to come – a horrifying inheritance of and prelude to what might happen next to any soldier. Jones also recalls the sight of dead soldiers seemingly being brought back to life as a fog settles on them, which confuses the viewer's perception of whether they are alive or not, an ambiguity reflected in the images and the language used to describe the moment:

> Fog refracted, losing articulation in the cloying damp, the word of command unmade in its passage, mischiefed of the opaque air, mutated, bereaved of content, become an incoherent uttering, a curious bent cry out of the smarting drift, lost altogether – yet making rise again the grey bundles where they lie.
> Sodden night-bones vivify, wet bones live. (60)

The vivification of 'wet bones' evokes *Frankenstein*, as does the 'incoherent uttering' which struggles to relay the import of the moment. This is a complex scene in which the dead reach out to the living in ways which are familiar from Walpole's ghosts. The issue of war and legitimacy is raised here, which also glosses Walpole's focus on legitimate and illegitimate forms of inheritance. Jones's ghosts are thus inhabited by earlier Gothic ghosts but they are also subtly nuanced. Walpole's ghosts are symbolic bearers of messages from the past, whereas here, formal language becomes emptied of coherent meaning, with commands being 'unmade' by another type of reality reflected in the 'wet bones' which have evaded language. There is bereavement here, both for the dead and for the broader failure of a poetic language which attempts to resurrect the dead. These are bodies without spirit, automatons whose resurrection confronts the subject with the horror of war. These are not the reunited, reformed war dead of the spirit world but 'grey bundles' and bones brought back to horrifying life. Ghosts in Jones are palpable forms, not invocated spirits, and as such they are figures without transcendence who invite mourning because they are also soulless or 'bereaved of content'. As the dead become perceptually alive, so the living become representationally dead. Jones notes of a group of mud-spattered soldiers:

> They stretched encumbered limbs to take their rifles, listless, bemused, to slowly scrape away the thicker mire caked, with deadness in their eyes and hands as each to each they spoke – like damned-corpse-gossiping, of hopeless bleedin' dawns – then laught to see themselves so straitened, tricked out in mudded stiffening. (63)

The soldiers are figured as talking corpses because the mud that they are covered in suggests their burial. Like the mud, they too will become stiff. Their already dead eyes conjure the earlier figure of the 'wraiths' as portents of death. For Jones, death is something that you terrifyingly head towards and horrifyingly overcome by turning into resurrected bones, rather like Frederic's encounter in *Otranto* with the ghostly but skeletal remains of the hermit of Joppa, with his 'fleshless jaws and empty eye sockets' (Walpole 1998: 106), who warns Frederic that he needs to follow a moral path rather than carnal pursuits. In Jones's poem, it is the war which constitutes a type of carnal pursuit in which, however, death has no obvious moral function but is simply inevitable. The combatants in *In Parenthesis* are thus spectral figures who are awaiting death and an imaginative resurrection of their body. Life itself is just a prelude to physical dissolution, but there is no sense of a soul here, merely the feeling of waiting for the inevitable transformation in which the living are already to be mourned, but in which – typical of modernist texts – mourning is perpetually deferred.

Jones produces a notably nuanced version of the spectral in *In Parenthesis*. The alive are waiting to die, and the resurrection of the dead is subject to a purely physical – indeed, mechanical – process which he outlines in 'The Preface', when he recounts that, after their basic training, 'From then onward things hardened into a more relentless, mechanical affair, took on a more sinister aspect' (ix), when the mechanised nature of the war and frontline routines effectively depersonalise the soldiers, rendering them both bodies *and* spectres. Very much in this vein, too, the poems of Richard Aldington provide another way of thinking about death and mourning during the period with ghosts which also reveal a Gothic imprint.

Aldington's Corpses[12]

Matt Foley has argued that Aldington's *Images of War* (1919) reaches beyond a modernist Imagist aesthetic which failed to reflect the emotional experience of fighting in the war (Foley 2017: 62–9). Aldington has clear modernist credentials: he was married to H. D., knew Ezra Pound and published in modernist journals, but he was not a slavish adherent to modernist principles. Aldington's aesthetics are, as Foley notes, important to consider as part of a wider trend of writing which struggles with the representation of trauma. It is, however, also important to address Aldington's representations of death and mourning, which, like Jones's *In Parenthesis*, require an engagement with the mood and spirit of the Western front. In his 1948 Introduction to *The Complete Poems* Aldington states that his intention was to engage with a spectre-like presence 'which is outside of me' and which 'is far greater and more interesting than I am' (Aldington 1948a: 16). For Aldington, this mysterious presence is, as in Jones, related to a sense of time and place. Aldington asserts that 'By the sense of mystery I understand the experience of certain places and times when one's whole nature seems to be in touch with a presence, a *genius loci*, a potency' (16, italics in original). This is a figure that we explored in depth in the previous chapter. It is a ghost which captures a sense of place, but also one which articulates feelings of loss and ongoing melancholia which we have witnessed in Woolf, Eliot and Jones.

Aldington's sense of being haunted by the past is represented by the horror of memories rather than by clear configurations of spectrality. While, in Jones, the bones of the dead seem to spring to puppet-like life, in Aldington any sense of even an imaginative post-mortem existence is flatly denied. In the 'Epilogue' to *Images of Desire*, Aldington states:

> [...] we who do not drug ourselves with lies
> Know, with how deep a pathos, that we have
> Only the warmth and beauty of this life
> Before the blankness of the unending gloom. (ll. 3–6)

The absence of spirit here turns mourning into a grievance for the brevity of life. For Aldington, desire appears as the counterpoint to the war because it is the only emotion which makes the subject truly alive and self-present. In *Images of War*, this failure of desire leads the poet to question whether he is alive, especially when a vision of the dead intrudes on what is intended to be a voyeuristic erotic spectacle. In 'Concert', the poet looks at women:

> Seeing them naked on that paltry stage
> Stared at by half a thousand lustful eyes. (ll. 4–5)

However, this is not a shared spectacle. Rather, the poet confronts a series of questions:

> Am I dead? Withered? Grown old?
> That not the least flush of desire
> Tinges my unmoved flesh,
> And that instead of women's living bodies
> I see dead men – you understand? – dead men
> With sullen, dark red gashes
> Luminous in a foul trench? (ll. 7–13)

Lust is replaced with a vision of the fragility of life. However, this should also be read as another version of the type of Gothic melancholia which characterises the modernist texts discussed earlier. As in Jones, images of life (here lust) evoke the bodies of the dead. These are images which incorporate one sense of the Walpolean ghost who persists and argues for their presence within moments of seeming, although amoral, celebration (such as the anticipated wedding ceremony with which the novel begins), but they also diverge from this figure because the dead function as memories which obscure and so make life impossible, rather than heralding a need for revenge.

The war dead repeatedly haunt Aldington in *Images of War* and *Images of Desire* and taunt his inability to engage with life. Mourning cannot take place because of this haunting presence which compromises the attempt to form a positive post-war life because all that he is left with, as he notes in 'The Blood of the Young Men', is a state in which he and fellow survivors are 'Crying for our brothers, the men we fought with,/Crying out, mourning them, alone with our dead/ones;' (Stanza 8, ll. 7–9). The dead are inescapable, as in the description of the moon in 'Meditation' from *Images of Desire*, which appears like 'the face of a six days' corpse' (l. 5), itself an echo of the persecutory haunting that we witnessed in Aldington's short story 'The Case of Lieutenant Hall', discussed in Chapter 2. These are ghosts who are beyond the appeasement of the ghost from the Walpolean tradition; here the ghost functions to ensure that the living feel dead because they cannot embrace life.

Aldington's poems are thus haunted by traumatic memories, and this problem of memory will be explored in greater depth in the following chapter in an account of how a post-war culture attempted to move beyond the traumatic memories of the war. This cultural impulse can also be witnessed across Aldington's poetry, which often honours the dead, including two poems to fallen soldiers, 'Epitaph 1' and 'Epitaph 2' in *Images of War*. His later poem, 'In Memory of Wilfred Owen' (1931), includes the lines 'But I have never quite forgotten, never forgotten/All you who lie there so lonely, and never stir' (ll. 10–11), a view which contrasts with those who are dead: 'Do you remember … but why should you remember?/Have you not given all you had, to forget?' (ll. 13–14). There is a growing ambivalence here, especially in the suggestion that it is the living who have become victims of the war due to their inability to forget. The war lives on in the memories of the participants. In these circumstances, to try to forget becomes a pre-condition for finding a meaningful, trauma-free, post-war life. If there is grief here, it is for the living who are dogged by these memories of death. In his long poem *The Eaten Heart*, published in 1929, the same year as *Death of a Hero*, Aldington records a visit to a grave, which provokes the admonishment 'Hush, you dead man. Act a dead man's part/And leave to the living the life you lost' (Verse 8, ll. 37–8). The final lines of '1933' (1935) state 'I mourn, I mourn alone for a world dying;/In vain I yearn for a world to be born' (ll. 13–14). Such a view, that one can, perhaps from the vantage point of the 1930s, renounce one's mourning for the dead because their ghosts simply hold you back, is reflected in the opening stanza of 'To One Dead' (1934):

> It is pleasant to me to know that I have done with you.
> If I owed you a debt. I have paid it;
> If I mistook you, I have set it right;
> If you wronged me, I have obliterated the wrong.
> And so we are quits and at peace. (ll. 1–5)

Finally, a form of the Walpolean spectre appears to have been appeased, but this is only apparent because the poet still speaks to the dead as if they were still alive. All of this is expressed as a would-be final farewell to the ghosts of the war dead. The last three lines record a gracious act of separation in which 'Nevertheless I am glad to be done with you,/To say: "It is all finished",/And to wave a last, but never indifferent farewell' (ll. 12–14). The ghosts of war are seemingly laid to rest as a form of mourning is completed, if only in this particular poem.[13]

Ghosts of the war dead in Aldington are passive and memories of corpses and battlefield sites haunt the poet. These ghosts lack agency and do not speak back to the living but rather exist as a series of memories which constitute a robustly secular model of death. Aldington invokes Gothic figurations which are familiar from the Walpolean ghost story, in order to lay them to rest so that the poet is beyond accusation and untouched by demands for revenge. He also tries to move beyond the type of persistent melancholia that we have witnessed modernist writers contend with. However, the physically dead might be formally laid to rest, but how to represent and banish traumatic memories is more problematic.

This chapter has explored how the purgatorial realm in spiritualism, the astral plane, provides the possibility of redemption, whereas the modernist wartime ghost finds itself lost in this purgatorial world. A new type of Gothic, indebted to older forms, is manifested by modernist ghosts who find themselves configuring a persistent state of mourning that is denied in spiritualism. The spiritualist version of purgatory is not without its Gothic influences, but these are manifested through a patriotic metaphysical battle between forces of good and evil, with only one optimistic outcome possible. We have seen how ghosts from a Walpolean tradition and the presence of *Frankenstein* and *Dracula* have all, in various ways and at different levels of explicitness, shaped the figurations of these wartime spectres. The spiritualist ghost and the modernist ghost meet in purgatory but they have little in common, other than that they incorporate and attempt to move beyond pre-existing Gothic tropes. Memories of the war are impossible to cast off in modernism, even while figures such as Aldington try to reach out for a post-war world that requires a necessary forgetting of the war dead. How to envision a future free from the ghosts of the war requires a different cultural strategy from that found in either spiritualism or modernism. It means, paradoxically, demonising the war dead in order to move beyond them. The ghost stories of M. R. James and E. F. Benson, discussed in the following chapter, demonstrate how such a reversal might be achieved.

Notes

1. Matt Foley sees in the haunted modernist text new, and non-Gothic, formations of the spectre. I have some sympathy with this reading (as not all ghosts are Gothic) but in this chapter I wish to examine how a new form of the Gothic might be discerned within these models of persistent grief, as well as considering the cultural significance of evoking and then moving beyond older Gothic tropes.
2. For an account of spiritualist debates about the war which appeared in *The Light* see Leo Ruickbie's *Angels in the Trenches: Spiritualism, Superstition and the Supernatural During the First World War* (London: Robinson, 2018).
3. For an overview of spiritualist links between the Kaiser and the Antichrist, see Owen Davies, *A Supernatural War: Magic, Divination, and Faith During the First World War* (Oxford: Oxford University Press, 2018), pp. 48–52.
4. See also Owen Davies's discussion of Sinnett in *A Supernatural War: Magic, Divination, and Faith During the First World War* (Oxford: Oxford University Press, 2018), pp. 89–90.
5. Max Nordau's *Degeneration* (1892) is one of the most important examples.
6. See also Owen Davies's discussion of Brodie-Innes in *A Supernatural War: Magic, Divination, and Faith During the First World War* (Oxford: Oxford University Press, 2018), p. 92.
7. For an early story which addresses these points see Rudyard Kipling's 'Wireless' (1902).
8. My account of *Raymond* further develops my reading of it in *The Ghost Story 1840–1920: A Cultural History* (Manchester: Manchester University Press, 2010), pp. 110–14. For an account of other memoirs produced by spirit guidance see Owen Davies, *A Supernatural War: Magic, Divination, and Faith During the First World War* (Oxford: Oxford University Press, 2018), p. 86.
9. See Andrew Smith and Jeff Wallace, eds, *Gothic Modernisms* (Basingstoke: Macmillan, 2002) and John Paul Riquelme, ed., *Gothic and Modernism* (Baltimore: Johns Hopkins University Press, 2008).
10. Roger Luckhurst, 'Religion, Psychical Research, Spiritualism and the Occult', *The Oxford Handbook of Modernisms*, ed. Peter Brooker, Andrzej Gąsiorek, Deborah Longworth and Andrew Thacker (Oxford: Oxford University Press, 2010), pp. 429–44.
11. See Kate McLoughlin's *Veteran Poetics: British Literature in the Age of Mass Warfare, 1790–2015* (Oxford: Oxford University Press, 2018), pp. 226–35, where she summarises the problem of veteran testimony.
12. This chapter focuses on Aldington rather than Siegfried Sassoon, given the extent of critical coverage on Sassoon, although the latter's poems deal with similar themes. See especially Sassoon's 'Banishment' (1917), 'Sick Leave' (1917), 'To Any Dead Officer' (1917), 'Memorial Tablet' (1918) and 'On Passing the New Menin Gate' (1928).

13. Aldington also explored how the memory of the dead persists (despite the tale's title) in 'Farewell to Memories', in *Roads to Glory*, when the narrator imagines seeing '*the dead youth of Europe march down the Road past the silent sentry, past the ruined house, march back, march home*' (1930b: 270, italics in original). What type of welcome they might receive is unclear.

Chapter 4

Aftershock: Malevolent Ghosts and the Problem of Memory

In previous chapters we have witnessed how the Gothic shaped the types of ghosts which are associated with the uncanny, trauma and mourning. These ghosts have different characteristics and either incorporate, or head towards and then reject, elements from an earlier Gothic tradition. We have seen how ghosts might come alive again in the home, are forced to roam restlessly, seemingly beyond hope, or articulate versions of purgatorial mourning. These ghosts are frequently objects of sympathy but this chapter focuses on the presence of the malevolent ghost, who is clearly part of a recognisable Gothic tradition of vengeful ghosts: the sort we see in the work of Algernon Blackwood and Vernon Lee, to give just two examples. These malevolent ghosts represent in projected form the aspiration of a post-war culture which casts soldier-ghosts, or those closely associated with them, as evil entities because they inhibit the emergence of the post-war world. Clearly, this kind of ghost construction is not without ambivalence. These are ghosts who are familiar from the Walpolean tradition, who are seemingly trapped between the pull of the past and the desire to reach out for the new. This is a tension which characterises the *fin-de-siècle* Gothic world of *Dracula*, in which vampire hunters confront the feudal remnant that is Count Dracula – and yet they are beguiled by the vampire's erotic freedoms, so that they too find it difficult to cast off the past. This established a notably Freudian framework for a Gothic subject who, in forms of war-induced melancholia, also cannot leave the past behind. These frameworks underpin many of the narratives discussed in this book and the presence of the malevolent ghost emphasises the ambivalence with which the war dead are regarded – as Gothic villains *and* as victims. In M. R. James, for example, there is a desire to memorialise the dead, but also the need to other them and so cast them off. Ultimately, to lay these Gothic ghosts to rest requires a demonisation of the war and those who perpetuated it, but it is difficult for the culture to forget the nature of their sacrifice, which explains the persistent ambivalence. As throughout this book, we need to understand the key role that the Gothic plays in shaping these forms of cultural representation and grasp where, and how, the Gothic becomes embraced as a way of capturing the horror that is associated with the continuing legacies of war. After discussing the representations of malevolent ghosts, the chapter concludes with readings of Dorothy L. Sayers's *The Nine Tailors* (1934) and Dennis Wheatley's *The Devil Rides Out* (1934), both of which demonstrate how the symbolic representation of the bodies of dead soldiers is informed by figurations of malevolent spectrality that illustrate how important it became both to remember, and to forget, in the post-war period. Before looking at the ghost stories of M. R. James and E. F. Benson, however, we first need to establish the wider parameters of remembrance and forgetting during the period of World War One, an issue which reappears in the Walpolean ghosts which haunt the poetry of Robert Graves.

Memorialising the Dead

The previous chapter explored melancholia as a limbo state of perpetual mourning. The war dead cannot be left behind by the modernist, although, as we saw, Richard Aldington's poetry registered an optimism about this possibility. How to leave the dead behind was not without ambivalence, however, and the cultural response to war memorials helps to illustrate that. David Cannadine has explored how, in the immediate post-war period, the establishment of war memorials provided a focus for national and community grieving, which became progressively erased after the Second World War when the two-minute silence on 11 November was moved to the preceding Sunday.[1] Cannadine is right to point to the period immediately after World War One as one in which memorials emphasised that the contributions of the war dead should not be forgotten, yet even here conflicting feelings emerged. Cannadine notes of the war: 'Shock, guilt, anguish, grief, remorse: these were only some of the emotions which such an experience left behind: above all, a desire to forget, and yet also a recognition that such experience should not be, must not be, forgotten' (Cannadine 1981: 217). This paradoxical impulse, to forget and to remember, has been charted by Paul Fussell, who notes Britain's long cultural tradition of associating the poppy with forgetting. Fussell argues that, although the poppy, as a symbol of battlefield remembrance, was in part established by John McCrae's poem 'In Flanders Field' (1915), it was a flower that was also symbolically freighted with ideas of forgetting, which was why the British Legion chose it as an icon of remembrance in 1921 (Fussell 2009: 314). We need to flesh out the reason for this paradox.

McCrae's 'In Flanders Field' is narrated by a ghost, who asks the reader to contemplate the mass grave in which it and the other spectres find themselves, one in which 'the poppies blow/Between the crosses, row on row' (ll. 1–2). The narrator emphasises that:

> We are the dead. Short days ago
> We lived, felt dawn, saw sunset glow,
> Loved and were loved, and now we lie
> In Flanders Field. (ll. 6–9)

The poem is a cry not to be forgotten, so that the next generation will 'take up our quarrel with the foe' (l. 10), with the warning that 'If ye break faith with us who die/We shall not sleep' (ll. 13–14). The implication is that they will haunt those who fail to take up the fight. These are ghosts who are potentially out for revenge, not so much against the Germans as against those who have broken faith with their loss.[2]

McCrae's ghost is the product of 1915, so the spectral narrator's emphasis on continuing the fight implicates a different form of memorialisation from that found in post-war spectres. Nevertheless, the anxiety that the dead must be remembered or they will seek retribution also taints the post-war spectre. The war may be over for those ghosts (unlike McCrae's), but only in a temporal sense, since they too seek to impress the nature of their sacrifice on the living. In order to begin again, however, this post-war world needs to resist this pressure to remember, and the resulting inconsistency of demands shapes this new, often conflicted, model of the ghost. These are ghosts with agency because they are motivated to haunt the living with their loss. Such a final Gothic turn, in which these ghosts are manifested as malevolent entities, does not fully take place until the post-war era. Hence these ghosts exist alongside the spectres which we have explored so far, in a cultural mesh of highly diverse, and frequently incompatible, views about the war.

McCrae's ghost is of a recently fallen soldier, whereas Robert Graves's post-war poems are haunted by a different order of spectrality, which indicates a desire to cast off the ghosts of the war to establish an age of peace. 'From Our Ghostly Enemy', a poem in *Welchman's Hose* (1925), centres on a man holding a prayer book consisting of 'Spelt prayers for the sick and needy' (l. 18). His reading is interrupted by a malevolent ghost, who recomposes some of the lines so that the narrator reads 'When you have endured your fill,/Kill!' (ll. 9–10), rather than a message of spiritual support. The ghost causes considerable metaphysical disturbance because it 'Twists the ill to holy, holy to ill' (l. 28), which

'Confuses me' (l. 29). Those who suggested a religious basis for the war are clearly a target here. The ghost also stalks the speaker with threats of mortality, so that, when walking near some flower beds, he sees '"Death within twelve hours"/Written in flowers' heads' (ll. 44–5). His wife, however, knows what to do and tells him '"That whom you fear the most/This ghost, fears you"' (ll. 49–50). She advises him on what to say:

> 'Ghost, my anguish equals yours,
> Let our cruelties therefore end.
>   Your friend let me be.' (ll. 53–5)

The final stanza runs:

> He spoke, and the ghost, who knew not
>   How he plagued that man,
> Ceased, and the lamp was lit again,
> And the dumb clock ticked again,
>   And the reign of peace began. (ll. 56–60)

There is manifestly a malevolent Gothic ghost which is cast out at this point. It is not clear who this ghost is but, because it causes metaphysical and temporal disturbance, it needs to be laid to rest for the haunted man to move on – a shift that occurs when he is reinserted back into time ('And the dumb clock ticked again'). The reaching out to the ghost is staged in an ambivalent language of friendship suggested in the use of 'Your friend let me be,' which acknowledges both friendship and a desire to be free of the ghost. Ultimately, friendship is not possible and the ghost disappears, but the telling last line, which refers to a 'reign of peace', implies the end of war. In Graves's poem, the ghosts are no more, and time can restart for those who have been left behind by the dead. However, this seems like a provisional position. The ghost is exorcised but it is not thereby clear that they are lost to memory.

Graves returns to the topic in 'No More Ghosts', included in *Collected Poems* (1938), with a title that anticipates his 1940 collection, *No More Ghosts*. This poem begins with the destruction of ancestral ghosts, symbolically present within a soon-to-be-dismembered four-poster bed, who are thereby located within a space conventionally associated with the haunted house:

> The patriarchal bed with four posts
> Which was a harbourage of ghosts
> Is hauled out from attic glooms
> And cut to wholesome furniture for wholesome rooms ... (ll. 1–4)

The past becomes utilised to help the present, which now effectively erases the past and lays the ancestral ghost to rest. Older forms of authority (that 'patriarchal bed') are destroyed because they are now powerless to resist the demands of the present and yet the present is thereby built out of the remnants of the past, which indicates ambivalence. These are not war ghosts *per se*, and in the poem the weight of history is superficially little more than a manageable object rather than a horrifying intangible presence. Ghosts are, however, trapped within an object associated with ancestral inheritance. They appear as the product of a literary ghost tradition, which is both evoked and seemingly exorcised:

> Where they (the ghosts) confused, abused, thinned,
> Forgetful how they sighed and sinned,
> Cannot disturb our ordered ease
> Except as summer dust tickles the nose to sneeze. (ll. 6–9)

This sighing ghost evokes Manfred's grandfather's ghost in *The Castle of Otranto*, who 'uttered a deep sigh and heaved its breast' (Walpole 1998: 26), as it acknowledges its sins and what it is that Manfred has illegitimately inherited. In Graves, the traumatic presence of the ghost is here rendered as little more than a minor irritant in a moment of comic deflation that undoes any latent Gothic energy that the ghost – here 'forgetful' of all that – may once have possessed. Yet, for all this forgetfulness, they are vivid forms in the poem and are not so easy to forget. They are 'confused, abused, thinned', as if they are already abandoned, but their very presence cannot be denied, even if the scale of their impact is seemingly diminished. There is the claim that these ghosts' projected 'confused' state stands in contrast to 'our ordered ease', an image of calm which, ultimately, the ghost cannot disrupt. There is, however, ambivalence here, which is also registered in the tone of the poem, in which comedy and the figure of the abandoned ghost are at odds. Walpole's ghosts continue to sigh at the nature of their treatment, which indicates that their past has not quite been left behind, despite the attempt to overlay the Gothic ghost with a comic inflection.

So far, the Gothic ghost (as a figure of the past) is evoked in order to try to lay them to rest. This is the ostensible narrative traversed by these poems. However, these ghosts are not so easy to eradicate. They are haunting presences, figures of an ancestral Gothic past who cannot quite be seen off by a comic tone. These are ghosts who seem to keep coming back. The past, as we have seen repeatedly in Gothic texts, is not quite so easy to leave behind, although the adoption of a non-Gothic register, such as comedy, represents an apparent genre shift designed to move beyond the Gothic world of the sighing ghost.

The wrestle with the ghost is a battle with the past and this becomes particularly acute when issues of grief (as a form of memory) intrude. Ghosts provide an outlet for grief, although not for the type of melancholia that was explored in the previous chapters. Here, grief is temporary and associated with a healthy mourning, which anticipates a point at which the ghost might finally be laid to rest. Yet there are gender implications too, as noted in Graves's 'patriarchal bed', which also touch upon this issue of grief and the type of ghost with which it is associated. Grief, like the Gothic ghost, is not so easy to leave behind.

The poetry of May Wedderburn Cannan provides an important counterpoint to the masculine voices found in Sassoon, Blunden, Aldington and Graves. Cannan, like Vera Brittain, served in the war and lost a fiancé on active service (Bevil Quiller-Couch, who died of pneumonia in February 1919 when he was part of the British Army of occupation in Germany). Her poetry collections, *In War Time* (1917), *The Splendid Days* (1919) and *The House of Hope* (1923), include many poems which reflect on wartime loss, an issue also addressed in her novel *The Lonely Generation* (1934). In 'Women Demobilised' (1919), she explores feelings of grief on Armistice Day in 1919. The opening stanza notes:

> Now we must go back again to the world
> Full of grey ghosts and voices of men dying,
> And in the rain the sounding of Last Posts,
> And Lovers' crying –
> Back to the old, back to the empty world. (ll. 1–5)

Women like her have been 'demobilised' by their loss, left bereft and unable to move on. These 'grey ghosts and voices' are difficult to forget, and this line anticipates her posthumously published memoir, *Grey Ghosts and Voices* (1976), in which she explores her profound feelings of post-war grief. However, the memoir also suggests ways to move on from these ghosts. She notes of her loss that 'Losing one's world one still wanders in it, a ghost. It is for long, more real than the new world into which one knows (but does not want to know) one must presently move and live' (Cannan 1976: 150). These ghosts are not of the men who have been killed but are of the women who have been left behind and for whom the death of a loved one 'was the end of the world' (144). She recounts a pivotal encounter with Stephan, a Serbian journalist, while on holiday in Rome in the early 1920s. She insists on showing him various ancient monuments to the dead and he asks '"Why [...] do you spend your mind, and yes, mademoiselle, your heart on the dead? [...] It is to the living that you should give your mind and heart"' (168). When she returns to London, she realises that the time has come to move on, 'But though I had lost the zest and the gaiety and the hopefulness of first youth, I was still young and there were still things to be done' (187), so she finally finds a way of casting off the 'grey ghost' that she had become. Despite Cannan employing the ghost to figure her grief, Graves and Cannan have much in common. They both attempt to leave their ghosts in the past, although in a way which does no violence to the memory of the dead. Cannan's grief makes her into a ghost, as the world becomes empty and ghost-like for her. While she acknowledges the ambition to find 'things to be done', it is clear that grief retains a continuing presence in her life (as the recollection, the memory, of her earlier poem in the title of her memoir suggests).

In Graves and Cannan we witness the presence of an ambivalent view of the war dead. Their ghosts are like those of Walpole, in that they cannot be cast off, but rather retain a place within memory. Like Walpole's non-ghostly characters, they wish to reach out for the future but are aware of the pull of the past and the responsibilities which it imposes. These figures from the past are not always horrifying ghosts but they share something in common with the Gothic ghost because they cannot be evaded, are not capable of being appeased, and keep the subject trapped in the type of limbo which was literalised in the spirit narratives we explored in the previous chapter. There is a mood of pathos which touches the ambivalence that we find in Graves and Cannan and shapes their memories and ambitions to forget.

The focus here is on how a Gothic discourse of subjectivity, in which subjects are held back by the needs of ghosts, produces the emotional framework in which the war dead are ambivalently remembered. The cultural reach of the complex tension between remembering and forgetting can also be discerned in scenes of emotional disturbance, which owe a debt to the Gothic, within texts that are conventionally thought of as classic realism.

The anxiety that the war disturbingly – and thus Gothically – persists can be discerned not only in accounts of ghosts but also in realist fiction such as Winifred Holtby's *South Riding* (1936). Holtby was a close friend of Vera Brittain (whose *Testament of Friendship* [1940] recounts their relationship), and had served in the war as part of the Women's Army Auxiliary Corps in France in 1918.[3] *South Riding*'s opening chapter centres on the fourteen-year-old Midge Carne, the daughter of the emotionally disturbed war veteran Robert Carne (whose mentally unstable wife is in an asylum). It thus addresses several typical Gothic themes concerning emotional instability, madness and incarceration. The novel is set in the aftermath of the war and focuses on a community readjusting to the post-war world. Midge is described as emotionally unsteady during the opening of the book, where she symbolically represents the continuing turmoil of the war. She is possessed by the spirit of the war and it is noted that

> she flew into horrible passions that made her lie on the floor and kick and scream. A fiend entered into her [...]. One moment she would feel nothing but good and gentle and polite and then these storms would seize her for no purpose, lashing her into fury [...]. It was no fun having an evil spirit. (Holtby 2010: 14)

Midge is possessed by an evil spirit, apparently the Gothic inheritance of her mother's congenital instability. It becomes clear, however, that she is equally a product of her father's war traumas. One form of emotional instability is inherited and the other acquired, but Midge's emotional state is generated from within this tense family drama, which makes her life a haunted one. This disturbing Gothic drama becomes reflected in Midge's capricious moods, which in turn represent the difficulty of adapting to the peacetime world, the very problem confronted by her father. Midge is thus haunted by traumas which properly belong to others. This, in other words, is a form of Walpolean inheritance, whereby the sins of the father fall on their progeny. Midge is in need of a cultural exorcism to make her fit to enter the domestic world because she representationally inhabits the world confronted by the returning soldier (there is much emphasis given to how she acts in the home), here displaced from her father to her. It is noted that 'Her terrors, like her tempers, descended without warning out of calm and safety, sending her screaming, frenzied, towards the kitchen, the dining-room, wherever were lights and fires and grown-up people' (Holtby 2010: 19). The implication is that the horrors of war might be Gothically inherited by the next generation unless, like Midge, it can find a way of laying the war to rest. Society, it is suggested, cannot move on unless it can forget, and formally memorialising the war dead provides a highly ambivalent opportunity for that. More widely, the district of South Riding also needs to move beyond the war so that it can politically build a version of the future untainted by the traumas of the past (as Midge needs to get better, so the novel argues, by going to school). Exorcising the past of this 'fiend', or 'evil spirit', becomes one way in which to move beyond the 'terrors' of the war. The presence of war-induced trauma in Midge suggests that the war cannot be quite so easily left behind. The trauma of war becomes inherited by the next generation, who, like Midge, challenge those who have bequeathed a seemingly insane world to them.

The ghosts and images of emotional turmoil discussed so far have been shaped by the shared ambition to move beyond the grief, and the horror, of war. The Gothic reappears in these forms of representation, influencing how images of loss, horror and madness are harboured within the post-war world. These ghosts are dealt with in diverse ways but all suggest that the war cannot quite be left behind. The horror of what might persist from the war is given full treatment in the ghost stories of M. R. James, whose ghosts will not go without a fight.

Gothic Ghosts: M. R. James

Patrick J. Murphy and Fred Porcheddu have explored how James's 'A Warning to the Curious' (1925) obliquely references the trauma of the First World War.[4] They note that the discovery of an Anglo-Saxon crown, which needs to be returned to its barrow to maintain its legendary function of protecting the Norfolk coast from German invasion, has dire consequences for Paxton, who has removed it. The narrator records that although Paxton has returned the crown, he discovers Paxton's body and that Paxton's 'mouth was full of sand and stones, and his teeth and jaws were broken to bits' (James 1970d: 585). Murphy and Porcheddu read this Gothic horror as representing the plight of the mangled dead of World War One. How much James had this link in mind is indicated by the fact that the real world journey taken by the principal protagonists as they walk from their hotel to the barrow would have taken them close to a war memorial. The tale's images of close, high hedges, through which the characters nervously move, is symbolically read by Murphy and Porcheddu as an evocation of trench warfare. The tale thus functions as a memorial for the dead of the First World War and provides a precautionary warning to those who might be tempted, if somewhat inadvertently in Paxton's case, to jeopardise the country's defences.

'A Warning to the Curious' was published in the 1925 collection of the same name, and there are a number of other tales from the collection which can also be read as addressing these concerns about the war. Murphy and Porcheddu note that M. R. James's seemingly serene academic world was considerably disrupted by World War One. James was Provost of King's College Cambridge at the start of the war and in his memoir, *Eton and King's* (1926), refers to his involvement in negotiations over emergency legislation that would place the university at the government's disposal in the event of a hostile invasion.[5] Various parts of the university were turned into temporary hospitals to treat the wounded and quite quickly the university shrank to less than a third of its normal numbers, with King's left with only forty undergraduates. In his Vice-Chancellor's oration in October 1914, James emphasised the importance of a business as usual approach: 'Let our advanced work – however irrelevant it may seem to the needs of the moment – be unremittingly and faithfully pursued' (cited in Pfaff 1980: 242). However, the consequences of the war could not be overlooked, with the lack of undergraduates placing a considerable financial strain on the college. Also, as biographers have noted, James kept up a correspondence with a number of his students who were serving abroad and was aware of the dangers and privations they faced. Murphy and Porcheddu refer to an important memorial address given by James in 1916, when he unveiled a roll of honour at the Cambridge Tipperary Club. In his speech, he dwelt on the ghosts of the war dead and how they continue to provide meaningful service, even in death:

> It is, then, somewhat thus that I think of our dead. They are God's soldiers, as they were the King's. They are training for the front. The things for which we held them dear, their kindness, truthfulness, courage, unselfishness, cheerfulness, these are being brought out: that which was faulty in them is being done away. The time will come when they will be able to help other souls – it may be, the souls of the very men whom but now they fought and slew – to better knowledge and clearer sight. (Cited in Pfaff 1980: 245)

These spirits of the war dead have a new life and sense of purpose, in which they 'go to school once more in a new life' (cited in Pfaff 1980: 245). James's claims about these spectres have much in common with the spiritualist view of the dead soldier discussed in the previous chapter. These are ghosts which have become purified and peaceable but they also need to be memorialised, and James's contribution to remembering the dead was reflected in his role on the committee appointed to create the inscription for the memorial scroll that would be sent to the war dead's next of kin. Richard Pfaff's biography of James includes the text of the original scroll written by James, with changes made by other members of the Commission:

> He whom this scroll commemorates was numbered among the sons of the British Empire [sons of the British Empire changed to those] who at the bidding of their country [changed to call of King and country] left all that was dear to them, endured hardships, faced danger, and finally passed out of sight of men by the path of duty and self-sacrifice, giving up their own lives that others might live in freedom.
> The remembrance of them shall be honoured in the land which they loved and died to save [this sentence changed to Let those who come after see to it that his name be not forgotten]. (Cited in Pfaff 1980: 247)

Murphy and Porcheddu note that this inscription was often reproduced in slightly amended form on other war memorials and that it graces the real-world war memorial at Aldeburgh that Paxton's walk to the burial mound in 'A Warning to the Curious' would have taken him past. There are thus two versions of James that parallel one another. One is the man of public office who wants the war dead to be remembered with affection, while the other is the writer of ghost stories in which images of the soldier-dead are not recalled in such a benign, or sanitised, way. Paxton's body is violently damaged by a malevolent force, associated with the war, which represents the type of aggression associated with British nationalism and its view of the Germans. The disparity between these two versions of James represents a pull between the need to remember and the desire to forget, and they illustrate, in a highly polarised way, the cultural tension between these worlds that we have seen in a more muted way in Graves and Cannan. The legacy of war also colours other tales in James's 1925 collection, most notably 'The Uncommon Prayer-Book', 'A Neighbour's Landmark' and 'A View from a Hill'. The issue of memorialisation is a highly ambiguous and conflicted matter in James, caught as he was between the man of public office *and* the Gothic author. In his tales, the dead come back for restitution and revenge and are not appeased by public memorials, their presence repeatedly questioning whether the culture can ever move beyond the shadow cast by the war.

'The Uncommon Prayer-Book' centres on the attempt to retrieve some rare prayer books stolen from the chapel of Brockstone Court, an imposing country house. Before their theft, a holidaying antiquarian called Davidson, who narrates the tale, visits the chapel, which is of some historical interest. The chapel holds eight prayer books, which were published during the period of Cromwell's Protectorate and so represent a bold assertion of faith from a time when prayer, and the printing of prayer books, would have constituted a penal offence. Davidson is intrigued to hear that the housekeeper's wife, Mrs Porter, always finds the eight prayer books open, despite the fact that she always closes them, covers them with a protective cloth and then locks the chapel when she leaves. She is the custodian of the sole key to the chapel, so it is a mystery how the opening of the books can occur. Brockstone Court, which is attached to the chapel, meanwhile, is closely associated with the ancestral figure of Lady Sadlier. Shown round the Court, Davidson is struck by the painted ceiling representing 'the Triumph of Loyalty and Defeat of Sedition', in which he notes 'The portraits of Cromwell, Ireton, Bradshaw, Peters and the rest, writhing in carefully devised torments' (James 1970b: 495). This assertion of faith was central to James's 1916 speech concerning how the war dead were now part of God's army.

Those dead have moved from being loyal to the King to serving God, and this idea of the triumph of loyalty becomes central to James's tale. Every morning, the payer books are all found open at Psalm CIX, which centres on lies and deceit, and how they spread an evil which is opposed to the loving kindness of God. The idea of deceit is further manifested in the tale when the prayer books are stolen by an unscrupulous conman and replaced with less valuable editions.

Davidson first encounters the eventual thief whilst enquiring about train times at a local pub. A small car pulls up outside, 'and out of it came a small man in a fur coat, who stood on the steps and gave directions in a rather yapping foreign accent to his chauffeur' (501). Davidson strikes up a conversation with the man, an antiques dealer named Homberger, who is seeking directions to the house and chapel that Davidson has just visited. Homberger seemingly adjusts his accent for Davidson's benefit when claiming that '"we English have always this marvellous talent for accumulating rarities in the most unexpected places, ain't it?"' (502). The suspicious Davidson decides 'He did not really like Mr. Homberger' (503). One of the mysteries of the prayer books is that they all indicate that Psalm CIX should be read on 25 April, or St Mark's day. This reference initially makes sense because it also invokes Oliver Cromwell's birthday and since the Psalm is popularly known as the 'cursing psalm', its royalist rejection of Cromwell is clear. Davidson notes that the real-life 'figure of old Lady Sadlier became more substantial to his imagination, as of one whom love of Church and King had gradually given place to intense hate of the power that had silenced one and slaughtered the other' (503). Davidson sees in Lady Sadlier a model of what of it truly means to be English. The support for King and Church is clearly also a support for an idea of England that James had extolled in his 1916 Tipperary Club speech. As in 'A Warning to the Curious', theft poses a national danger. Paxton might put the Anglo-Saxon crown back but he needs to be punished for his, albeit temporary, compromising of England's boundaries, which would have left England vulnerable to a specifically German invasion. Consequently, Homberger, who purloins the prayer books, needs to be subject to punishment and, as in 'A Warning to the Curious', it is one which involves a war memorial. Homberger, posing as a Mr Henderson, has taken the prayer books, with his departure witnessed by Mr Avery, Mrs Porter's father. Avery tells Davidson that Henderson:

> 'was working his own motoring car himself [...] And as he drove away under the big yew tree by the monument, I see the long white bundle laying on the top of the coach, what I didn't notice when he drove up.' (507)

This 'long white bundle' and its proximity to the war memorial suggests that the spirits of the war dead are indeed capable of the kind of restitution that James had suggested in his 1916 address, although here that 'return' is played out as a vengeful intervention into the physical world.

At the centre of the tale is the ludicrous way in which Homberger tries to pass as English, almost as if he were an obvious spy bent on stealing documents (here prayer books) of national importance. Towards the end, the tale shifts to a police investigation in London, which reveals that Homberger had been working under the equally foreign name of Poschwitz. The commissionaire, one Mr Watkins, tells the police about Poschwitz's death, which he witnesses through a glass door kept locked by Poschwitz to exclude any unwelcome visitors with designs on retrieving the stolen prayer books. The 'long white bundle' seen earlier now comes to life. Watson recalls that Poschwitz was taking out a package from the safe (which contained the books), when:

> 'I see what looked to be like a great roll of old shabby white flannel, about four to five feet high, fall for'ards out of the inside of the safe right against Mr. Potwitch's shoulder as he was stooping over [...] this roll had a kind of a face in the upper end of it [...] And the eyes, well they was dry-like, and much as if there was two big spiders' bodies in the holes [...] it fell right over on to Mr. Potwitch's shoulder, and this face hid in his neck [...] about where the injury was.' (511)

Poschwitz dies of blood poisoning as a result of this vampiric assault, and the strange figure which had inflicted the bite turns into a dust that covers the floor. Read in this way, the war dead assert some form of revenge against those who have sought to appropriate a version of British values, and the Germanic Homberger/Poschwitz is clearly an enemy in that regard. However, there is ambivalence here. Murphy and Porcheddu note that, at the end of 'A Warning to the Curious',

> Paxton's death by the battery wall is by no means glorious, and the tale's final sequence is focused intensely on the agonizing inability of the well-intentioned mentors to alert the curious youth to the danger he faces: in other words, to deliver a desperate 'warning to the curious'. (Murphy and Porcheddu 2014: 222)

The tale does not quite cohere, and Murphy and Porcheddu note that this discordance is reflected in how the tale fails to complete the mystery properly. However, they also note that 'James's own reticent intentions are often difficult to pin down, but we should not under-estimate his dedication both to artful misdirection and scholarly precision' (Murphy and Porcheddu 2014: 222). This contradictory dedication suggests both a general ambivalence about the war dead and a specifically alternative way of thinking about the importance of reading Psalm CIX on 25 April, or on St Mark's day.

The psalm represents King David's idea of suffering and whether he holds God responsible for it. Stephen Ahearne-Kroll has argued that St Mark's discussion of Christ in Mark's gospel passion-narrative alludes to David's psalms and effectively queries whether Jesus needed to be sacrificed, given that David's suffering would have sufficed as an example of God's authority.[6] In other words, has the sacrifice been a necessary or proportionate one? And, if so, who should be held responsible for it? The war memorial captures that sense of sacrifice, and the Germanic Homberger/Poschwitz is implicated in it. The wider question is whether there is a need for a continuing retribution amongst James's ghosts. 'The Uncommon Prayer-Book' is an obvious revenge narrative which uses the ghost, and a vampiric one at that, in a way quite different from what we find in Blunden, Graves and Brittain, where it is often used as a device to emphasise the new, fantastical, realities generated by the metaphysical turmoil of the war. James's tales also differs from the ghost stories in *The Strand*, discussed in Chapter 1, which evoked and then moved beyond the conventions of the form effectively to contain, and so neutralise, trauma. James's ghosts are out for revenge, not sympathy. The sense that James may also have had revenge on his mind is indicated in a letter he wrote three days after the armistice to his friend Clive Carey, in which James states that 'I want to go on saying to a German till he is sick in my presence [that] We who have not been out to fight or do anything have no right to be noble and forgiving' (cited in Pfaff 1980: 335).[7] Pfaff has also noted that in the conclusion to James's pamphlet *The Wanderings and Homes of Manuscripts*, which was probably written in the Spring of 1918, James wrote about the Germans as unforgivably destructive:

> They are, undoing their own work now: they have robbed the world of beauties and delights that can never be given back. It will be long before any of the nations can forgive Germany: longer still, I earnestly hope, before she can forgive herself. (Cited in Pfaff 1980: 336)

This hostility explains the violence meted out to Poschwitz because the 'The Uncommon Prayer Book' appears to hold Germans responsible for the sacrificial deaths of the British war dead. Revenge is therefore unfinished business for James, which is reflected in how his restless spirits enforce the boundaries between the legitimate and the illegitimate at a moral, legal and territorial level. These are ghosts which are not memories in the way that ghosts are presented in Graves and Cannan, for example, but they do represent the collective memory of the nation. Here, the soldier-ghost-vampire defends British history (of a specifically royalist kind) against a foreign invader and arguably fulfils a political purpose. However, there is ambivalence here; this ghost is an overdetermined Gothic entity whose very presence indicates that the war dead have not been laid to rest. They are conjured out of a war memorial, with its affectionate and benign public recollection of the dead, and become transformed into a Gothic monster. This shift indicates that the ghosts of the war dead are associated with violence and death, rather than with compassionate loss – even though Poschwitz needs to be stopped. This is not a ghost that one would want to grieve for in the way that Cannan does. James sought to resolve this paradox of the revengeful ghost by exploring how these spirits become clearly troubling when they demand a restitution which is closer to home, an issue that is addressed in James's 'A Neighbour's Landmark'.

The tale begins with an account by an anonymous book collector about their initial appraisal of some books held at a house, Betton Court, in an unnamed English county. The house name is evocative of Bettencourt, the small French village in the Somme region caught up in the fighting during the war. The book collection includes a number of items which, although published during the reign of Queen Anne, have titles pertinent to the First World War, including *The Late Peace*, *The Late War* and *The Conduct of the Allies*. That the tale wishes to emphasise this as a context is indicated by the narrator stating that it was this material, rather than some sermons, which constituted his initial reading matter. Later, he reads some religious pamphlets which address a concern about territorial location that also appears in the war publications. These texts all refer to the area around Betton Court and other places where forms of military activity had taken place. A letter referring to an act of territorial 'Abuse' cites an apparent riddle which reflects on the ownership of woodland close to Betton Court:

'That which walks in Betton Wood
   Knows why it walks or why it cries.' (James 1970a: 517)

The riddle refers to an alleged spirit which ghosts the area of a wood that was cut down because of its associations with death and is now inhabited by an apparently restless spirit. It is a ruin of a wood and its linguistic link to the Somme, combined with the reading of war pamphlets, suggests a symbolic battlefield that is reflected in the tale's emphasis on the plot of territorial ownership, one which explains the presence of the restless spirit which still inhabits this ghost of a wood whose ownership had been fought over.

The tale emphasises the 'cry' of the ghost, which in reality is more of a scream. The unwitting narrator had visited this landscape and, while contemplating a view of the village from it,

> All at once I turned as if I had been stung. There thrilled into my right ear and pierced my head a note of incredible sharpness, like the shriek of a bat, only ten times more intensified – the kind of thing that makes you wonder if something has not given way in one's brain. I held my breath, and covered my ear, and shivered. (521)

The subhuman scream means that he cannot appreciate the bucolic pleasures of the village, and specifically its church, in the same way as they become replaced by 'images [...] of dusty beams and creeping spiders and savage owls up in the tower, and forgotten graves and their ugly contents below' (521). Instead of enjoying an old-world charm, a different type of history, associated with death and decay and symbolically the war, is evoked. The function of the scream is important to note as it is a recurring motif in post-war representations of the war, present in *South Riding* in Midge's 'Terrors', which send 'her screaming', and, as we shall see, in the auditory responses to an intolerable recollection of battlefield noises in Dorothy L. Sayers's *The Nine Tailors*. The problem confronted by James's narrator is that the ontological status of the scream is unclear; as he notes, 'Hideous it was beyond anything I had heard or have heard since, but I could read no emotion in it, and doubted if I could read any intelligence' (522). This link between screaming and the wood echoes a moment in Robert Graves's tale 'The Shout' (1924), which has implicit links to James's story that are worth developing before returning to James's tale.

'The Shout' centres on a narrator who is helping to keep score in a cricket match against an asylum team, whose scorer, Crossley, is a murderer subject to various delusions. Crossley embarks on a rambling story in which a character named Richard meets a figure called Charles, who claims that he has a shout that is so terrifying that it can kill people, which he argues is a known natural force referred to as the 'terror shout' (Graves 1984: 17). Richard outlines a cultural history of the shout, which suggests an oblique link to James's tale:

> I have read of the hero shout which the ancient Irish warriors used, that would drive armies backwards; and did not Hector, the Trojan, have a terrible shout? And there were sudden shouts in the woods of Greece. They were ascribed to the god Pan and would infect men with a madness of fear [...] and the animals and trees, the earth and the waters were left barren. (17)

The shout is related to war and destruction, as it is in 'A Neighbour's Landmark', but in James the shout, or scream, has no obvious purpose.

It transpires that the shout in James's tale is a legacy matter, relating to a historic territorial dispute over ownership of the wood, and it is a trace of an old battle cry, a ghost of it, but one now devoid of any significance for the present day. Yet that seems to be the point of James's tale: it becomes impossible to cast off the traumas of the past as they linger as old ghosts around dead places. Graves's tale of the destructive shout is, at one level, the ramblings of an apparent lunatic, but that the universe may contain a continuing destructive force is apparent at the end when the narrator flees from the scoring box as Crossley appears to launch his own killer shout. The narrator covers his ears and runs, the scoring box is struck by lightning, and Crossley and his doctor are killed. The lightning, like the scream in James, is a seemingly amoral force rather than an act of God which determines who lives and dies and is reminiscent of an artillery barrage, with the narrator recalling, 'I had run perhaps twenty yards, when an indescribable pang of fire spun me about and left me dazed and numbed. I escaped death somehow' (Graves 1984: 30). This moment would be echoed in Graves's account in *Goodbye to All That* of being wounded in July 1916:

> [I] felt as though I had been punched rather hard between the shoulder-blades, but without any pain. I took the punch merely for the shock of the explosion; but blood trickled into my eye and turning faint, I called [...] 'I've been hit.' (Graves 1967: 181)

In James's tale, the scream captures a feeling of horror about the war; it is a trace of a previous conflict that cannot quite be shaken off. The horror of a past event is made present through the shout so that the past speaks to the present in a deranged way. The horror of war is unspeakable and is figured within the rage of the inarticulate shout which noises pain, but also clearly hate. Here is another example of how the memories of war become difficult to cast off and the nature of those memories becomes associated with an unappeasable feeling of grievance, which, in the end, is amoral and illegitimate; that is why it is so horrific.

The shout in 'A Neighbour's Landmark' is used to emphasise an issue about territorial legitimacy. It is revealed that, in the 1680s, one Lady Ivy had attempted to claim the wood as belonging to her, having successfully appropriated land in this way in the past. Her fraudulent claim is easily exposed, but the scream in the now non-wood registers her continuing disappointment and drives others away, so that in spirit she has taken possession of this now dead place. Again, there is ambivalence here because Lady Ivy has somehow managed to be acquitted of forgery and lived to an old age. The idea of legitimate and illegitimate ownership of territory is an issue that Walpole addresses in *The Castle of Otranto*, but in James ghosts appear as demented Gothic entities who have no rational claims on the present. This echoes the anti-Enlightenment impulse of Walpole's novel even while the Walpolean spectre's association with a possibly appeaseable (if violent) past is denied. The implication is that, instead of providence, there is an amoral force at work in the world and this is what is shared with Graves's tale, a sense that the usual forms of justice are in abeyance and, in James, this in turn is linked to a post-war view of the war dead as having an amoral and illegitimate claim on the present.

James's spectral presences are clearly working beyond representations of the spiritualist spectre or modernist melancholia. In 'A Neighbour's Landmark', the dead *do* come back, but as Gothic figures who have been deranged by their experience of war and for whom there can be no place in the post-war world. Revenge may, at one level, seem to be justified in some of these tales, as we saw with 'The Uncommon Prayer-Book', but it is also aligned with something demonic and supernatural, as if revenge comes out of a demented sense of rectitude in which the dead demand to be honoured, so that the horror of the war cannot quite be left behind. Lady Ivy's scream may be illegitimate from a certain perspective, but it articulates a sense of fear and pain in a symbolically dead battlefield that transcends the ostensible plot about territorial rights and expresses an ongoing horror about the war and its dead, which are issues addressed further in James's 'A View from a Hill'.

This tale is set in an unnamed south-western English county, in which a holidaying academic named Fanshawe, staying with his friend, Squire Richards, explores the area's countryside. Fanshawe finds himself caught up in a series of ghostly encounters, which culminate in an explanation of why these vengeful ghosts have been conjured. As in 'A Neighbour's Landmark', there is a fascination with terrain which, in this instance, is expressed through a military-like reconnaissance of it. Richards tells Fanshawe, '"We'll have a map, and I'll show you where things are; and you can go off on your machine"' (James 1970c: 535). To give him help with this reconnaissance, Fanshawe requests a pair of binoculars and is provided with a heavy, old-fashioned pair that Richards inherited when he bought the house, a typically Jamesian small stately home. That there is something sinister about these binoculars is indicated when Fanshawe is cut prising open the box they are stored in. Although he says, '"I don't begrudge a drop of blood in a good cause"' (536), it is indeed the idea of shedding blood for a good cause that the tale takes issue with. The terrain they explore is not so much the country as an implied battlefield: 'the Squire, who was great on earthworks, pointed out the various spots where he detected or imagined traces of war-ditches and the like' (537). Whilst this terrain is meant to be linked to sites of Roman occupation, these too suggest the presence of a now lost model of civilisation and echo ideas of invasion which were suggested in 'A Warning to the Curious', 'The Uncommon Prayer-Book' and 'A Neighbour's Landmark'.

The key figure in this tale, moreover, is one Baxter, from whom Richards bought the house, who had mapped the terrain on an Ordnance Survey map and there noted places where he found indications of Roman settlements. The landscape is a peculiar mixture of partially concealed battlefield and bucolic England, in which

> the eye picked out red farms and grey houses, and nearer home scattered cottages, and then the Hall, nestled under the hill. The smoke of chimneys was very blue and straight. There was a smell of hay in the air: there were wild roses on bushes hard by. It was the acme of summer. (539)

This emphasis on what the eye picks out is developed further through what Fanshawe sees through the binoculars, which is a vision of justice and judgement from long ago. He sees what he takes to be a dummy gibbet with '"a man hanging on it"' (541): Richards sees nothing, and Fanshawe indicates that '"The gibbet is perfectly plain, and the grass field, and there even seem to be people on it, and carts, or *a* cart, with men in it. And yet when I take the glass away, there's nothing"' (541). The binoculars are a Gothic device which enables you to see into the past and invites you to consider how it impacts on the present. Beneath the bucolic vision there is a history associated with death and punishment. James's tales are indebted to this longstanding Gothic impulse in which subjects find themselves caught between the pull of an unappeasable past and the superficial, and fragile, versions of the past which appear to linger idealistically in the present – here represented by the pictorial charm of village life. The type of pastoralism which forms a version of a cultural home, discussed at the end of Chapter 2, is denied by the presence of these malevolent spectres. The modern envisioning of the past attempts to sanitise a more sinister version of the past associated with violence. Bucolic views of the village therefore function in much the same way as war memorials, which also produce sanitised recollections of those that died. These visions of the past suggest a continuing menace in which the gibbet appears to play a central role. Later, Fanshawe has a dream in which he removes a stone in a garden, only to find a note that reads '"On no account remove this stone".' The stone has disappeared and Fanshawe looks down into the hole that it occupied:

> Something stirred in the blackness, and then, to his intense horror, a hand emerged – a clean right hand in a neat cuff and coat-sleeve, just in the attitude of a hand that means to shake yours. He wondered whether it would not be rude to let it alone. (544)

This welcoming hand is culturally familiar to Fanshawe, who clearly contemplates shaking it, only for the hand to be replaced by something more sinister:

> as he looked at it, it began to grow hairy and dirty and thin, and also to change its pose and stretch out as if to take hold of his leg. At that he dropped all thought of politeness, decided to run, screamed and woke himself up. (544)

So the scene progresses from the civil to the barbaric, from friendship to aggression, and from peace to war. What is noteworthy is the insistent presence of this dangerous hand, which civilisation has not supplanted. It is like the view of bucolic England becoming obscured by the gibbet. There is, so the tale suggests, other histories at work beneath the level of appearance, and those histories need to be discovered (indeed, formally explored in Baxter's excavations) – which also evokes the anti-Enlightenment impulse which we have witnessed in *Otranto*. At the same time, doing so is not without considerable danger. These dead but somehow alive hands reaching out of the earth indicate that the dead wish to claim us, as if they are owed some form of restitution by not allowing them to rest in peace (as in Fanshawe's moving of the stone). James might want to honour the war dead – one reason why he helped construct memorials at both Cambridge and Eton – but there is the persistent suggestion that, horrifyingly, the dead might not leave us alone in the cultural aftershock following the war. In this tale, ghosts are unappeasable spirits who insist on being remembered in a certain way. The polite hands symbolically represent the way in which the culture would like to remember the loss of benign and civilised subjects, but the other hands are feral, muddy and thin, and are symbolically associated with the battlefield. These two recollections of the dead are incompatible: the first vision represents a forgetting of the second which implicates the way that the soldier has died and the state to which war had reduced them. Behind one memory lurks another, as in the war memorial in 'The Uncommon Prayer-Book'. The dead do not leave us alone because we cannot quite forget the manner of their horrific passing and so, James suggests, we are also responsible for not being able to forget the war, or those hands that reach out of the mud, first in friendship and then in enmity.

Fanshawe realises that the binoculars give him complete visions of now destroyed buildings. Like the wood in 'A Neighbour's Landmark', they are places which have been levelled to the ground, and he notes of one building that 'There's absolutely nothing left [...] but the bases of the piers which supported it' (James 1970c: 548). Beneath the superficial charm of the English landscape lies a desolate one associated with war, war going back to the Roman occupation but also recalling World War One. Fanshawe senses that trying to find the place where the gibbet stood might provide the key to understanding these visions, only to discover that the terrain is hostile to his investigation, puncturing his bicycle tyres to impede his progress and leaving him with a feeling of being watched. At one point he hears 'steps crackling over twigs behind me, indistinct people stepping behind trees in front of me, yes, and even a hand laid on my shoulder' (550). These ghosts are multiple, semi-tangible, just about felt and seen, but also blurred and indistinct. Like the past, they are both there and not there, like a negative version of James's conceptualisation of the spirits of the war dead in his 1916 Tipperary Club speech. It is therefore appropriate that Fanshawe finds himself in 'an unholy evil sort of graveyard' (550), from which, just barely, he manages to escape. James's message is clear: it is because we cannot leave the dead alone that they come to claim us, and this is spelled out in the plight of Baxter, which explains why the binoculars enable the viewer to see back into the past.

Baxter's decline has been initiated by his unearthing of the bones of the dead who had been buried near the gibbet. He, in fact, boiled up their bones and put the fluid into the binoculars, which enabled him to see the village through their eyes and so identify the places once occupied by now ruined buildings that Baxter could locate and excavate for their rare and valuable artefacts. The dead spirits drag Baxter up Gallows Hill, where he is subsequently found with his neck broken. Squire Richards decides that the only thing to be done is to give the binoculars a decent burial.

The tale is a morally ambiguous one, in which, at the start, the binoculars do not seem to work in church, with an implication that the dead were godless, but at the end they seemingly do function in the church. These prevarications reflect the central concern about gauging the moral status of the dead, who might be the ghosts of the executed but are also justified in their revenge. They are partially visible, can at one point speak, and yet they are also dead and gone.

The moral standing of the war dead is an ambivalent one in James. Their ghosts have a claim on the present, from which they demand justice. These ghosts are also monstrous and touch not just the lives of those who have deliberately done them harm, such as Baxter, but also the life of those who appear to be more innocently caught up in their drama, such as Fanshawe. The amorality of the ghosts, in this instance, makes them horrifying and Gothic, which is why James, despite his work on commemorating the war dead, suggests that they would be better left undisturbed. At heart, James's war memorials should also be seen as a way of forgetting the violent reality of the war. Murphy and Porcheddu note that, in 'A Warning to the Curious', the disfigured face of the dead Paxton evokes images of facial mutilation that are rooted within the experience of war, and that this suggestion constitutes 'an image of violence memorials strive to forget' (Murphy and Porcheddu 2014: 220). The principal protagonists' walk past such a memorial questions whether these acts of forgetting (an act which is omitted, or 'forgotten' in the tale) are not quite enough to cast off the horror of war because forgetting requires an amoral distance from the war which is, so James implies, both socially necessary and totally abhorrent. This strand of amorality in James's ghost stories about the war becomes developed even further in E. F. Benson's ghost stories.

E. F. Benson: The Amoral Ghosts of War

E. F. Benson was, like his brother, the ghost-story writer A. C. Benson, one of the auditors of M. R. James's Christmas ghost stories at Cambridge. E. F. Benson had a keen interest in the war and was the author of *The Outbreak of War, 1914* (1933) and *The Kaiser and English Relations* (1936), as well as the popular Mapp and Lucia series of novels published between 1920 and 1939.

Many of Benson's ghost stories explore mediumship and séances, including 'Outside the Door' (1912), 'The Thing in the Hall' (1912) and 'Mr Tilly's Séance' (1922). Most of the pre-war stories have a jocular tone to them, quite different from the tenor of the post-war ghost stories which are populated by either malign or amoral spectres. A pre-war ghost story such as 'How Fear Departed from the Long-Gallery' (1911) conjures a version of British pragmatism which accepts the presence of ghosts as a matter of course, so that, for the Peveril family who occupy the haunted house of Church-Peveril, 'the appearance of a ghost is a matter of hardly greater significance than is the appearance of the post to those who live in more ordinary houses' (Benson 2012e: 77). The house is populated by many harmless and eccentric ancestral ghosts. However, among the spectres there emerges a more sinister story centred on the murder of twin babies in 1601. Their ghosts appear only occasionally and then only in the Long Gallery, but if they inspire negative emotions in those who encounter them (such as fear or even derision), then those people will die. This narrative is brought to an end when the ghosts are encountered by a house guest, Madge Dalrymple, who reaches out to them with feelings of empathetic compassion so that 'her pity, her sympathy, touched and dissolved and annihilated the curse' (Benson 2012e: 89). Positive emotions lead to redemption, so in Benson's pre-war tales ghosts are not noticeably malign. They are ghosts which inspire positive emotions as they reach out for help from the living. In 'Caterpillars' (1912), for example, 'Most ghosts, when all is said and done, do not much harm; they may perhaps terrify, but the person whom they visit usually gets over their visitation' (Benson 2012b: 91). But a post-war tale such as 'The Face' (1924) indicates that Benson's post-war ghosts are not so harmless.

'The Face' centres on a recurring dream of Hester Ward, who, from an early age, has been plagued by a nightmare in which she is pursued by a man with a war-damaged face: 'One side of it, soft-curved and beautiful, trembled into a smile, the other side, thick and gathered together as by some physical deformity, sneered and lusted' (Benson 2012d: 383). The adult Hester is terrified by these nightmares, in which this ghostly figure indicates that he will soon be with her. These dreams are set in a churchyard that has been subject to significant coastal erosion, meaning that much of the graveyard has toppled into the sea. Hester, on visiting a private gallery to look at some van Dycks, discovers among them a portrait of one Sir Roger Wyburn, whom she recognises as the person who haunts her dreams. Dr Baring, who treats Hester for her nightmares, recommends sending her to the country for rest, and so she and her husband, Dick, take a holiday in a hotel in an east coast seaside town. Dick has to return to London for work, and Hester visits a dilapidated churchyard that she quickly realises is the one in her dreams. She discovers that a grave which is about to topple over the cliff is that of Sir Roger Wyburn. His ghost later abducts her from the hotel and Hester is never seen again. Sir Roger's body is later discovered on the beach, 'untouched by corruption and decay, though two hundred years had elapsed since it was interred there' (Benson 2012d: 395), so much so that he seems to have been restored by his dream-world encounters with Hester.

Such a ghost is clearly of a different order than those found in a pre-war story such as 'How Fear Departed from the Long-Gallery', where there is a purpose to the twins' ghosts, who are hungry for love. There is a point to their presence, which is to elicit empathy and concern; in 'The Face', however, it is not clear why Hester is pursued by the spirit of Sir Roger, and the end of the tale suggests that he has somehow triumphed. The most chilling aspect of the story is the very arbitrariness of Hester's selection by Sir Roger and the inexplicability of his motivation. Her disappearance seems pointless, and this shift in Benson from pre-war to post-war ghost can be read as reflecting a culture attempting to make sense of the seemingly inexplicable deaths occasioned by the war. Superficially, the tale possesses the classic structure of the Walpolean ghost story in which ancestral revenge is apparently the cause of the haunting. Here, however, that convention is challenged because Sir Roger has no associations with Hester, so that the tale evokes a classic ghost story formula in order to break its rules. The ghost is not an aristocratic purveyor of family secrets, but a randomly malevolent spirit. This now horrifying ghost resembles those found in M. R. James's tales, which also frequently evoke the Walpolean ghost in order to undermine its function as a purveyor of secrets even while they appear to endorse Walpole's view in the first Preface to his novel, that the seemingly dead presences of the past can still reach out to us. The arbitrary nature of the abduction and implied killing of Hester evoke an amorality which increasingly appears in both the tone and the content of Benson's post-war tales. It is, for example, noted of a ghost story told by a vicar in 'Expiation' (1923) that 'his communication was very impersonal. It was just a narrating voice, without identity, an anonymous chronicle' (Benson 2012c: 464), so that emotional affect has disappeared from the voice of an unempathetic vicar. This is a world without spiritual salvation, in which a waning of affect gives way to a stark materiality. Benson's 'And the Dead Spake –' (1922), in a similar vein, provides an alternative way of letting the war dead speak to that found in spiritualism, which Benson satirises in 'Mr Tilly's Séance', published in the same year.

'And the Dead Spake –' foregrounds a materialist brain-science which points to a cultural numbing about death and a horror about a newly affectless world. The narrator of 'And the Dead Spake –' recounts the activities of one of their London neighbours, a renowned physicist named Sir James Horton, who had been working on a machine that would enable the dead to speak. The British physicist Oliver Lodge would appear to have influenced this characterisation in a tale which addresses a physicist's pursuit of a scientifically proven method for helping the war dead to speak. At the beginning, the narrator notes a disjunction between the peace of the street and the possibly 'vast and terrible forces' which might be at work behind the houses' facades (Benson 2012a: 200). The tale indicts a world which cannot be taken at surface value, which indicates that other hidden worlds, such as those of the dead, might be almost immediately accessible. Horton is an amoral scientist who has no human interest in the subjects under his care, and, although he is referred to as a physicist, he is also a pioneering brain surgeon able to save the lives of the people about whom he cares so little. The narrator notes of Horton that 'Men and women were to him like fossils to the geologist, things to be tapped and hammered and dissected' (201). He is a scientist who had once 'made an artificial being formed of the tissue, still living, of animals lately killed, with the brain of an ape and the heart of a bullock, and a sheep's thyroid' (201), making him a literary descendant of Mary Shelley's Frankenstein and H. G. Wells's Dr Moreau. Horton, like Victor Frankenstein, appears to have been horrified by his creation and left an envelope referring to the experiment which was not to be opened until after his death. He is a leader in his scientific field but, like Victor Frankenstein, he has no ties with any of his peers, whom he leaves 'to grope along unaided' because he was 'utterly absorbed in his own investigations' (Benson 2012a: 201). The beginning of the war and the excitement that it generates does not encroach upon Horton's world. The narrator recalls of their street:

> The Terrace had been stirred into volcanic activity by the news of war: the vendor of some late edition had penetrated into its quietude, and there were half a dozen parlour-maids fluttering about like black and white moths. But once inside Horton's door isolation as of an Arctic night seemed to close round me. (202)

Horton's detachment from the world feels complete, recalling Victor Frankenstein's ultimate isolation in the icy Arctic, because his contemplation of other people is entirely conditioned by his interest in material science, which suggests that death is only a matter of degree because some bodily organs may die while others retain a bare semblance of life, at least for a time. Horton discusses his ideas with the narrator, but only because speaking out loud to a non-scientist enables him to reflect on the nature and scope of his scientific interests. When he is at his most excitable, these fundamentally Gothic impulses are symbolically suggested to the narrator, who recalls that, when animated, Horton resembled 'some magician or perhaps the afrit which a magician of black arts had caused to appear' (204). Horton, however, does not acknowledge this type of supernatural conjuring because he sees brain science as the key to tapping the memory in a purely material way.

In previous chapters we have witnessed how memory of trauma needs to be substituted by an earlier memory of the non-traumatised self. Spiritualism, for example, denies trauma because it erases the distinction between the living and the dead. Horton's science appears to offer a blend of material and spiritual impulses as he suggests an analogy between the brain and a recording device in which the brain, if tapped by an appropriate machine, can, like a record, repeat what is deeply ingrained within it. This view suggests that the technology of modernity is a haunted one and evokes Lodge's work on radio transmitters and its associations with the disembodied voices of spiritualism. Horton, however, despite this cultural context, is no spiritualist and is more interested in the relationship between technology and the sheer materiality of the dead. For his experiment to work, it must be conducted with the brain of the recently deceased, since a physically corrupted brain loses the structure that the machine needs to tap. Dying soldiers provide Horton with the opportunity to work on fresh brains, so that 'Despite his utter indifference to the issues of the war – for, in his regard, issues far more crucial demanded his energies – he offered himself as a surgeon to a London hospital for operations on the brain' (206–7). He is able to save many lives, although that is not his principal motivation. Conversely, for the narrator, the war is never very far away, as when he notes the warning whistles of an air raid on a night in which 'The moon was brilliantly bright, the square quite empty, and far away the coughings of very distant guns' (207). That night, Horton experiments on the speech centre of a brain that he had removed in trying to cut out a piece of shrapnel from a fatally wounded soldier. Horton sets up his machine, which, like a gramophone, has a listening trumpet attached to it. The narrator recounts, 'I heard something begin to sing. Though the words were still inaudible there was melody, and the tune was "Tipperary"' (209). The tale emphasises that it is only the speech part of the brain that can be accessed and that the more a thing has been said, the more audible the echo of it. The soldier's sublinguistic trauma is missing and there is no sense in which he is spiritually alive; representations of trauma and spiritualism are simply excluded. This subject can speak, in a way, but is not conscious. All that can be accessed are verbal tics, recorded as memories only, because of the frequency with which things have been said or, in this instance, sung. Yet again, *Frankenstein* appears as an influence here, not just in the model of a Gothic scientist, but also in how Shelley's novel records the voice of the creature's, which is memorialised through Victor's account and Walton's letters. The creature is generated out of a world of death brought back to life, and although he possesses agency, his voice is interred within the records of others – just as Walpole claims in the first Preface to *The Castle of Otranto* that the dead voices of a seemingly lost age can still speak to us.

Horton refines his apparatus, Benson's narrator tells us, so that 'many and many an evening during the next year did I listen to voices that were dumb in death' (210). The amorality of Horton is not shared by the narrator, who is initially horrified by these experimental results. But his use of 'dumb' in this instance is revealing. The dead voices of the soldiers are brought into the home while, at the same time, they are not fully reanimated. Their voices are captured through a mechanical process which reveals very little about them, other than their verbal habits. These are not the war dead that reach out to us, but voices that are empty, dead and ultimately (due to the process of physical decay) going to be lost unless their words are preserved through possible recordings on Horton's device, which evokes Dr Seward's phonograph in *Dracula*. Only in one instance do they become revelatory, but even that is not quite the shock that it promises to be.

Horton's housekeeper, Mrs Gabriel, has, some time before, been tried for the murder of her husband and acquitted. Horton knows that she is guilty but is confident that he is safe because another unexplained death would incriminate her. She is overheard muttering to herself on several occasions and then, due to a fall, bangs her head and dies. Horton takes the opportunity to employ his machine on her brain, and she can be clearly heard reliving the moment in which she slit the throat of her husband, after having endured repeated drunken physical abuse. The tale finishes on Horton's death as he slips and accidentally electrocutes himself with his machine.

'And the Dead Spake –', then, is populated by the dead, who die either in the war or by accident. There is no providence at work in these deaths, which are all, so the tale suggests, fundamentally meaningless. The war dead may speak again but only to utter popular phrases or snatches of song; they are not genuine resurrections. The circumstances of their deaths are traumatic but that trauma is not registered in their voices. The war dead speak but in a way which has effectively erased much of the war experience. The voices record what has already happened and what cannot be changed. These voices can be left in the past and constitute little more than an archive because, as Horton tells the narrator, '"There is stored within a man's head the complete record of all the memorable things he has done and said"' (205). All this may be of historic interest but is not, as accounts of real trauma are, an ongoing concern. As in M. R. James, the suggestion is that the war dead might be better left behind. Benson's ghosts have no agency; they are not vengeful and their voices will eventually fade, but their possible recordings keep some version of their plight alive. Benson's tale thus finds a way of evoking the war dead, letting them speak and letting them go as subjects but retaining their experience as dead history. The horror is not in the soldiers but in the amorality of those, such as Horton, who are implicated in their care. The war has an effect on those who are left behind, depending upon how they choose to remember (here, record) the dead combatant.

How to move beyond the war dead constitutes a strand emerging at the time, one which sits alongside the more empathetic engagements that we have seen in Cannan and, to a degree, in Graves. In M. R. James, the symbolic ghosts of the war dead are terrifying because of the claims that they make upon the living. In Benson, the tone is different; the dead voices are not horrifying (even Mrs Gabriel's post-mortem confession has been anticipated); they are simply the voices of the dead who can, at last, be left behind, even if a record of their familiar expressions can be made. The Gothic horror of the ghost is projected on to those who raise these ghostly voices, not in a spirit of empathy, but out of scientific curiosity. In the end, Horton is killed by his own machine, with the suggestion that his amorality is part of a problem associated with the war which also needs to be consigned to the past.

This impulse either to demonise the war dead or to render them neutral and beyond making claims upon us appears elsewhere in popular fiction at this time and Dorothy L. Sayers's *The Nine Tailors* and Dennis Wheatley's *The Devil Rides Out*, both published in 1934, provide other examples of that. These are not novels which include representations of the ghosts of the war dead, but they do represent, in more physical form, bodies which have been damaged by war. They provide a different way of culturally thinking about the war dead. Whereas the ghost represents a continuing presence which the culture tries to lay to rest, so these novels represent the dead bodies of the war as physical expressions of the problem of what do with the body of the dead soldier. Ghosts, as part of their cultural exorcism, can be aligned with an alternative representation of the dead which reflects on the need for symbolic burial, as in the case of Sayers, or emphasises the importance of a resurrected and restored masculinity, as in the instance of Wheatley. The trauma associated with the mobile and malevolent ghost is replaced by a concern about the static corpse, albeit one which, like the ghost, requires a narrative to make sense of its death. These embodied bodies of the dead should therefore be seen as an example of how forms of popular culture in the 1930s also attempted to move beyond the restless, malevolent spirit of dead soldiers. These dead still speak, but their tales need to be told by others and are different in degree rather than kind to the ghosts that we have explored here. These dead are made representationally, rather than spectrally, present, but they still pose the problem of how to bury the dead properly in order to leave them behind.

Gothic Detectives: *The Nine Tailors*

Sayers's *The Nine Tailors* was published in what is regarded as the Golden Age of detective fiction but it is a mode which owes some debt to the Gothic. Links between the Gothic and crime fiction have been noted by Catherine Spooner, who states 'the two forms […] share a similar structure in their preoccupation with the return of past upon present' (Spooner 2010: 248), as both are focused on exposing how the misdeeds of the past (ancestral secrets and crimes) haunt the present and invite acts of analysis and exposure to make sense of them. This view accords with the Walpolean Gothic, in which the past comes back as a return of the repressed. Michelle Miranda has also noted that figures such as the criminologist Cesare Lombroso influenced Gothic representations of degeneration by asserting the pathological tendencies of supposed criminal types – an issue addressed in texts such as *Jekyll and Hyde* and *Dracula*.[8] Shared cultural context means that the two forms blend at various points, most notably as they attempt to make sense of the legacies of social crises, such as those engendered by the legacies of war. Critics like Gill Plain and Alison Light have noted that, during this period, detective fiction reflected post-war attitudes to death which demand that death (a murder) is explained, even whilst a form of cultural numbness appears in how the dead are represented, as if their plight is of little concern to others and merely constitutes a device that enables detection to take place. For Alison Light, the novels of Agatha Christie function as a form of therapy, providing 'a sedative for nerves' and so constitute 'the literature of emotional invalids, shock-absorbing and rehabilitating' (Light 1991: 71). Taryn Norman identifies clear Gothic motifs, such as séances, in Christie's first Poirot novel, *The Mysterious Affair at Styles* (1920), arguing that the novel's mourning for 'the conditions of modernity […] fail(s) to expel the Gothic' (Norman 2016: 90), as the war intrudes despite Christie's ostensibly escapist agenda. For Plain, such narratives make death safe, even while they attempt to move beyond the wartime anxieties that they implicitly evoke: 'The dismembered bodies of the battlefield become the tidily reassembled corpses of Christie's fiction. There is a transition from fragmentation to wholeness that replicates a wider social need for the reinstatement of the rituals of death' (Plain 2001: 33). This overcoming of fragmentation in Christie (whose husband was a highly decorated Royal Flying Corps pilot) echoes what we found in spiritualist texts, discussed in the previous chapter, which emphasised that the dead were made whole again in the spirit world and so provided a form of consolation for the bereaved.

It also evokes *Frankenstein*, where the living become resurrected through the reassembly of dead parts.

Plain further argues that it was detective fiction which enabled a culture to grieve for its dead and so move on. The familiar generic patterns of the detective story enable the detective to triumph over death and so progress to the next case. The form is thus centred on an essential paradox which combines 'rituals of remembrance and the self-preserving necessity of forgetting' (Plain 2001: 41). This also explains why Sayers would represent Lord Peter Wimsey as a shell-shock victim who is often troubled by his wartime experiences, which are evoked most completely in *The Nine Tailors*.

While Sayers would make direct reference to the war in the fourth Peter Wimsey novel, *The Unpleasantness at the Bellona Club* (1928), in which the two-minute silence on Armistice Day provides an opportunity to conceal a body, there is little actual evocation of the traumas of war, which appears in the later *The Nine Tailors*. The later novel is not about malevolent ghosts, but it is about how the war continues to blight the lives of individuals and communities who cannot find a way of moving beyond it, which means that war continues to haunt the post-war world malevolently. It also demonstrates ways in which the war is remembered by those who have been traumatised by it. The novel is populated, too, by symbolic spectral forms which owe much to the Gothic.

Helen Conrad-O'Briain has identified clear Gothic influences in *The Nine Tailors*, with references made to Le Fanu's *Wylder's Hand* (1864) and to many of M. R. James's ecclesiastical stories, such as 'The Treasure of Abbot Thomas' (1904), 'The Stalls of Barchester Cathedral' (1910) and 'An Episode of Cathedral History' (1914). Conrad-O'Briain also notes, 'There has always been a connection between the detection of crime and supernatural powers' (Conrad-O'Briain 2011: 22), a link that Sayers also observed in her Introduction to *Great Short Stories, of Detection, Mystery and Horror* (1928), where she acknowledges the influence of the Newgate novel and the writings of Poe and Le Fanu on her work.[9]

In *The Nine Tailors*, Wimsey, after a car crash, finds himself spending New Year's Eve with his servant, Bunter (a former sergeant who had served with Wimsey during the war) in the Fenland village of Fenchurch. Wimsey and Bunter are put up for the night by the Rector and his wife, Mr and Mrs Venables. The Rector is planning an extended ringing of his church's steeple bells to see in the new year and Wimsey, who is an enthusiastic campanologist, joins the team when one of its members, William Thoady, falls ill. Some time after this event, Wimsey returns to the village and helps to investigate the mysterious presence of a disfigured corpse (the face has been smashed and the hands amputated), which has been interred in the grave of Lady Thorpe and discovered when the grave had been reopened to include the body of Lady Thorpe's husband. Some years before, the Thorpes had held a house party, at which a necklace had been stolen from a guest by Deacon, the Thorpes' butler, who, with his accomplice, Cranton, was sent to prison. Deacon had been married to a maid of the Thorpes, who remarried a local man, William Thoady, after Deacon was pronounced officially dead on the discovery of his decayed body, found two years after he had escaped from prison. It transpires, however, that Deacon is alive and that the dead man was a soldier named Cobbleigh, whom Deacon had murdered and whose identity Deacon had assumed. This was in 1918, and in order to maintain his disguise, Deacon found himself having to report to a regiment and proceed to the front, where he is caught up in heavy fighting; seemingly shell-shocked, he stumbles on a French family, who take him in. Some years later, he returns to Fenchurch after contacting Cranton, his old accomplice, to retrieve the stolen necklace from its hiding place in the church. He is discovered by Thoady, who agrees to pay Deacon £200 if he will leave Fenchurch; Thoady, who is worried that Deacon might be recognised and so expose his marriage as bigamous, locks Deacon up in the church belfry while he goes to the bank, but after withdrawing the money, falls ill with influenza. Thoady's brother, Jim, realises from William's fevered ramblings that he has left someone tied up in the belfry and finds the body of Deacon. Jim relates his encounter with the dead Deacon to Wimsey: "'his face! My God, sir, I've never seen anything like it. His eyes staring open and a look in them as if he'd looked down into hell. It fair shook me'" (Sayers 1984: 281). Jim, thinking that William has murdered the man, conceals the corpse's identity by disfiguring it and interring the body in Lady Thorpe's grave. The facially disfigured corpse echoes that of Paxton in 'A Warning to the Curious' and Sir Roger in Benson's 'The Face'. Dr Baines reports at the inquest that "'The face had apparently been violently battered in with some blunt instrument, which had practically reduced all the anterior – that is, the front – part of the skull to splinters'" (85). The missing hands anonymise the body and align it with the mutilated bodies of the war dead, but there remains the question about how exactly he has been killed.

The war repeatedly ghosts the plot of *The Nine Tailors*. Before his death, it is noted of Sir Henry Thorpe that he '"got badly wounded in the Salient and was invalided home, but he's never been the same man since, and they says he's in a pretty bad way now"' (43). Deacon becomes an accidental victim of the war when his disguise as a soldier puts him at the front without any experience or military training. Cranton takes up the tale of war in which Deacon:

> 'lost his party and something hit him on the head and laid him out. Next thing he knew he was lying in a shell-hole along with somebody who'd been dead some time [...] after a bit he crawled out [...] He wandered about, and fell in and out of mud and holes and wire, and in the end he stumbled into a shed where there was some hay and stuff. But he couldn't remember much about that either because he'd had a devil of a knock on the head and he was getting feverish.' (247)

Deacon is a victim of shell-shock, but uses this condition as a cover to conceal his true identity and pretends to have lost his memory permanently. He masquerades as a French soldier, but one with a mumbling stammer who cannot easily be interrogated. Deacon's somewhat partial shell-shock enables him to claim a total loss of memory and so he eludes the authorities and settles on the French farm, marrying into the family which had discovered him, until he sees an opportunity to return to Fenchurch and retrieve the necklace. Deacon's war experience is brief, but his understanding of the symptomology of shell-shock is advanced and underlines his role as part victim and part conman. The wider question concerns the manner of his death because it becomes clear that he has not been murdered and did not die of neglect, seeing as William Thoady had made sure that he had provisions during what was intended to be a brief incarceration in the belfry.

Wimsey returns to the belfry at a moment when the bells are rung and discovers that it was the noise of the bells that had killed Deacon. For Wimsey:

> All the blood of his body seemed to rush to his head, swelling it to bursting-point [...] It was not noise – it was brute pain, a grinding, bludgeoning, ran-dan, crazy, intolerable torment. He felt himself screaming, but could not hear his own cry. His ear drums were cracking; his senses swam away. (305)

What is striking about this moment is its emotionally overwhelming nature. Within the context of a detective novel, this is a Gothic escalation of feeling that cannot be made sense of by rational discourses of detection and analysis. Wimsey is left screaming and, as we have seen in James and Graves, screaming and shouting became two ways in which the horror of the war is registered. The following lines both evoke and deny the war when it is noted that the noise 'was infinitely worse than any roar of heavy artillery. That had beaten and deafened, but this unendurable shrill clangour was a raving madness, an assault of devils' (305). The noise of war is here placed in close proximity to a noise that could induce 'a raving madness'. The horrifying conjuring of both war and its persistence is registered in this instance. The 'shrill clangour' is that memory of the past which the clearly traumatised Wimsey is unable to cast off. War becomes a form of disorientating Gothic madness which threatens the subject with complete dissolution as Wimsey's 'senses swam away'. Deacon's war experiences are also evoked here. Bryonny Muir argues that this scene's linking of the bells to an artillery bombardment effectively repeats Deacon's experience of coming under fire and that Wimsey's recovery from the bells echoes Deacon's recovery from his brief, terrifying experience of the war, after which Deacon's French wife confirms that '"his nerves were shattered"' (Sayers 1984: 172).[10] Read in this way, the novel works through a series of displacements between characters and their war experiences but also doubles Wimsey with Deacon. What lurks beneath the detective story is thus another narrative about the horror of war and its cultural persistence, which culturally echoes how, in M. R. James, the war memorial becomes inhabited by the horror of war (associated with a vampire-ghost) that the memorial denies. Deacon is represented as a continuing victim of the war, but he is also a murderer who appears to have been providentially punished, not least by Wimsey, who had taken Thoady's place at the New Year's bell-ringing and had pulled on the ropes of the bells that had caused the hidden Deacon to die. Punishment suggests the presence of some form of justice and the idea of providence, a key feature of the Radcliffean Gothic, is developed but ultimately challenged in the novel because, as in Wimsey and Deacon's experience in the bell tower, this feels like an unjust world and so is more evocative of the violence which characterises the Walpolean Gothic. What is recalled here is the malevolence of the war itself, which renders problematic any attempt to see value within the prevailing models of justice.

The issue of punishment is therefore an ambivalent one in *The Nine Tailors*. The church's history, which is given in some detail, evokes an anti-republican British history that manifests as an anti-Cromwellianism, which accords the church bells religious and political agency. A bell, it turns out, fell and killed one of Cromwell's soldiers when they were breaking into the church, which reflects the type of anti-Cromwellian attitude struck in James's 'The Uncommon Prayer-Book', where a model of royalist British history is also asserted. The engagement with history evokes a discourse of national unity and identity which reflects a version of Britain reaching out for older values that can be re-established in the post-war era. However, this retrospection is not without some cultural ambivalence. The past is not quite dead, and one Fenchurch resident in *The Nine Tailors* notes of the bells, '"I never have liked the sound of bells. There's something – you'd think they were alive, sometimes, and could talk"' (Sayers 1984: 283). Another resident claims of the particular bell that had killed Cromwell's soldier, '"You'll think I'm loopy, but I tell you that bell was alive"' (253). A Gothic presence lurks within these bells, and it becomes difficult to know if they represent the violence of British history or if they are intended to be seen as defenders of the nationalist cause. There are points of contact with the type of ambivalence which we witnessed in 'The Uncommon Prayer-Book', where the defender of British history and its values is a vampire-ghost. The killing of Deacon by the bells superficially looks like a providential intervention in a novel that culminates with a flood of symbolically biblical proportions which, however, kills both the just and the unjust alike.

Deacon is a murderer who appears to have been punished for his crime, but this picture is more complicated than it seems. The police discover that the man Deacon murdered was called Arthur Cobbleigh, and the Superintendent notes that Cobbleigh has '"Not a good record. Labourer. Been in trouble once or twice with the police for petty thieving and assault. Joined up in the first year of the War and considered a good riddance"' (Sayers 1984: 227). Also, Wimsey's war experiences are echoed in Deacon's, which suggests a possible doubling between them that breaks down any notion of a coherent model of justice that can be applied. Spooner notes that 'The doubling of the detective with the criminal is another feature of crime fiction drawn from Gothic convention' and that, in such tales, 'exposing the crime does not provide resolution and the restoration of order, but seals the detective's own damnation' (Spooner 2010: 251). Wimsey is not notably damned by his discovery of the means of Deacon's death, but it is the war which continues to generate its own version of damnation. This is reflected in the random way that the flood at the end engulfs the area around Fenchurch, resulting in the death of William Thoady and another resident, both of whom were caught between a barge and the river bank and '"were smashed like egg-shells"' (Sayers 1984: 303), a physical destruction which again references the war dead. Thoady has tried to protect his wife against a possible accusation of bigamy and otherwise appears to be an honourable man. These deaths are therefore subject to a highly ambivalent form of providence – or, more radically, the novel as a whole questions the very providential frame that it ostensibly works within. The language of providence is really little more than a narrative device which structures how characters operate within the world because, in the end, these deaths feel more accidental than providential. Muir argues that this type of tension creates the aporia that Derrida saw as central to Western texts' inability to represent trauma, so that 'metaphysical thought does violence to the text, searching for certainty of meaning while refusing to confront the fact that such certainty is impossible' (Muir 2017: 308).[11] Muir proceeds to argue that, because detective fiction demands closure, Wimsey's discovery of the cause of death provides a solution to the mystery. In reality, however, Wimsey is tacitly doubled with Deacon and the text foregrounds how a series of chance encounters mean that the truth is stumbled upon, rather than exposed by a pre-existing divine plan. Wimsey can explain how a death has occurred but the process of deduction is not foregrounded; rather, it is the accidental, and so seemingly unattributable and apparently amoral, death of Deacon – and the near-death of Wimsey, both from bell-ringing and a symbolic bombardment – that is emphasised. The accidental nature of this suggests the continuing presence of an anti-Enlightenment influence that, in keeping with the Walpolean Gothic, indicates that reason does not provide all of the answers.

The key post-war message in *The Nine Tailors* is that the dead will not stay dead and will return from their graves. This is a Gothic world which references the dead becoming undead as revenants of memory that relate to the war. Prior to the flood, William Thoady, under police interrogation, admits that he regarded Deacon's return as a troubling resurrection: '"here's that devil come out of his grave to trouble us again"' (Sayers 1984: 261). Later, he tells Jim about how horrified he had been when Deacon's body '"come up out o' that grave, like Judgement Day"' (275). As we have noted, the novel has points of contact with an earlier Gothic tradition of M. R. James and his ghosts are often seen in this novel. Rosie, a child, tells her friend Polly that she has seen a ghost near the newly dug grave of Lady Thorpe, which Polly's father relates to Wimsey, claiming '"Rosie's seen what she took to be the spirit of Lady Thorpe a-flittin' about her grave"' (143), but appears to have been '"a light just a-rising out of where the grave would be"' (143). The light belongs to Jim Thoady, who is burying Deacon in the grave. Deacon thus becomes the true ghost of the war which haunts the community. When Deacon is reinterred, before his identity is revealed, it is noted of Wimsey that 'he went and stood in the churchyard. The grave of the unknown victim still stood raw and black amid the grass' (241), which, given the way that the war repeatedly intrudes into the text, aligns the unknown Deacon with the unknown warrior unveiled in Westminster Abbey on Armistice Day in 1921. Muir argues that Cobbleigh's body also corresponds to the war dead because it was 'found in the dene-hole where Deacon shoved it, misidentified as so many were on the battlefield, and re-buried as Deacon' (Muir 2017: 299), but this layered description also applies to the anonymous body of Deacon. To identify the body requires giving it a biography, which divests it of its mythic symbolic significance. The exposure of identity unfixes all myths and returns the body to real time, in a novel which resolves its mysteries in a chronological reconstruction so that the past can be moved beyond.[12] How to recollect World War One and attempt to leave it behind are thus central to the novel, as they have been to all the texts discussed in this chapter.

There are other timescales in the novel that also evoke a British history of village life and superficially suggest a continuity with the past that is referenced through the historical changes in the village of Fenchurch and in particular the parish church, St Paul's, which incorporates within it a layering of history from its early abbey foundations to its modern alterations. The bells ring out time and make aurally present the idea of continuity with the past. Muir sees this linkage as an idealised history in which there is a 'great escapism to be found in an imagined village still ordered by medieval habits, patterns, and time-reckoning' which 'separated it from the mechanized and precise modern time-stream, and therefore from the pace of modern life' (Muir 2017: 296). However, as in M. R. James's 'A View from a Hill', appearances are deceptive, since the village is also a crime scene, there is an initially unaccountable death, and amoral forms of retribution undermine the novel's putative providential structure. It is noted, for example, that, before death, 'Lord Henry haunted the Rectory like an unhappy ghost' (Sayers 1984: 240), seeing as he too functions as a restless presence who is subject to his own traumatic memories of the war and who therefore cannot easily be accommodated within the ecclesiastical sensibilities of Fenchurch.

The Nine Tailors can also be read as an exploration of recuperated forms of masculinity to the degree that it is about trying to make emotionally damaged men, like Wimsey, well again. Monica Lott argues that 'Through detection, Wimsey regains the masculinity that had been wounded by his experiences in the war' (Lott 2013: 104). Detection thus 'becomes Lord Peter's cure for his shell shock' (Lott 2013: 110). Lott's view is that detection provides a cure that enables Wimsey to marry, whereas Ariela Freedman argues that Wimsey's detection offers a partial cure which is only fully achieved *when* he marries (Freedman 2010: 381). However, what is clear is that Wimsey's 'cure' is both public (his role as a detective) and private (his eventual marriage), which repeats the narrative we have witnessed earlier, in Chapter 1, about the reaccommodation of the damaged soldier into the domestic space. As in so many of these texts, however, the war cannot quite be shaken off; like the Walpolean ghost, it retains an insistent presence which permeates the repeated images of ghosts that we find in the novel, even while it lampoons Radcliffe's notion of a providential design. Again, elements of the Gothic tradition are asserted, or worked beyond, for quite specific cultural reasons which, in the main, relate to the assertion of secular values that reflect the influence of a war which is beyond transcendence. Wimsey might seem to regain some version of a masculine role through marriage and it is the issue of masculinity, and how best to restore it, which are central to the final text discussed in this chapter, Dennis Wheatley's *The Devil Rides Out*.

So far we have seen how the war becomes manifested as a malevolent force which inhabits various forms of spectrality. These are forces, and often ghosts, which require cultural exorcism in order for the post-war world to move beyond the legacies of the war. The Gothic plays a special role in shaping these images of deranged malevolence. Satanism also becomes associated with the war but, in the instance of Wheatley, provides an opportunity for men to band together and see off these malevolent forces, in a way that echoes the type of teamwork which characterises the vampire hunters in Bram Stoker's *Dracula*.

Casting out the Devil: Dennis Wheatley

Gill Plain's view of Agatha Christie's detective fiction could actually stand as a synopsis of *The Devil Rides Out*. For Plain, as we have noted, 'The dismembered bodies of the battlefield become [...] tidily reassembled corpses' in Christie's fiction, and this reassembly constitutes 'a transition from fragmentation to wholeness that replicates a wider social need for the reinstatement of the rituals of death' (Plain 2001: 33). As we have seen in the previous chapter, the fragmented bodies of the war dead repeatedly appear in spirit narratives which reach out for a type of *Frankenstein*-like piecing of dead bodies together, also underpinning the fascination with narrative fragments in Eliot's *The Waste Land*. Such acts of recomposition (both textual and physical) represent ways of mourning a complete body in order to leave it behind to embark on a new, post-war, life. The mangled bodies of those seemingly senselessly killed in the war, however, traumatically continue to haunt the culture. How to recompose the dead out of these fragments lies at the heart of Wheatley's novel, which insistently recalls the myth of the dismembered body of Osiris, the Egyptian ruler of the underworld (the novel references Frazer's *The Golden Bough*), who was murdered by his brother, Set, who wanted his throne. The body is dismembered by Set, and Osiris's wife, Isis, seeks out the body parts to reassemble him and bring him back to life, albeit briefly; during this period, she conceives Horus, the god of the sun, and Osiris dies. This mythological narrative of death, fragmentation, resurrection and birth can be read as reflecting the type of post-war concerns that we have witnessed in this chapter. The dead of the war need to be left behind in order for the culture to move on, but those dead can be more easily left behind if they are made whole again. Such dead are a comfort and represent an alternative to the anxiety generated by the malevolent ghost. Ghosts need to be appeased and their demands can be tempered by replacing their presence with a version of the peaceful corpse. The making whole, in this instance, functions as a form of cultural restitution that also permits fond, rather than traumatised, memories of the dead.

The potential recomposition of Osiris's body is, in Wheatley's novel, about the restoration of masculinity, but it is also concerned with what type of body may be restored. It transpires that Osiris is not capable of completion because Set has kept back a memento (referred to as the Talisman of Set), which is Osiris's phallus. Whoever owns the talisman governs the world, and that is why a group of Satanists, headed by Mocata, are in pursuit of it. If they are successful, the wrong type of body could be symbolically resurrected, which would lead, so the novel argues, to another world war.

Wheatley, who was invalided out of the army in May 1918, reworks the Osiris myth in *The Devil Rides Out* by transfiguring it into the adventures of four principal figures, all of whom simultaneously echo characters in *Dracula*: the French Duke de Richleau (a type of Van Helsing figure), the American Rex Van Ryn (who is an echo of Quincey Morris) and the Englishmen Simon Aron and Roger Eaton (who both resemble Jonathan Harker). These figures combine as a version of the crew of light from *Dracula*, who this time battle against the sinister figure of Mocata, whose skills as a black magician mean that he bears some resemblance to Stoker's Count, whose family is described by Van Helsing as having '"had dealings with the Evil One"' (Stoker 1996: 241). The novel is the second in a series after *The Forbidden Territory*, published in 1933 (Wheatley's first novel), which centred on the quartet's adventures in 1930s Soviet Russia. The novel also reflects upon their experiences of fighting in earlier conflicts, de Richleau having fought on the side of the White Russians during the revolution. Whilst *The Forbidden Territory* sees communism as an illegitimate post-war settlement, *The Devil Rides Out* explores a broader sense of legitimate and illegitimate post-war European reconstruction linked to models of legitimate and illegitimate versions of masculinity. As post-war Europe is represented as fragmented, so the novel addresses this condition through the fragmented body of Osiris. De Richleau explains that Osiris was murdered by his brother, Set, and his body cut into fourteen pieces, with Osiris's phallus taking on talismanic properties so that the possessor of it could create a gateway granting earthly access to the Four Horsemen of the Apocalypse and push Europe into another world war. According to de Richleau, those four horsemen have more recently been unleashed by the arch-Satanist Rasputin in Russia, who is held responsible for starting World War One.

Osiris is described as a man of peace who was the victim of a power struggle, which is echoed in post-war European political tensions. Significantly, Osiris's fragmented body is not made whole again as the bodies in Christie are; rather, a series of memorials mark the places where the fourteen pieces are buried. In *The Devil Rides Out*, these symbolically evoke war memorials, which mourn for the dead rather than indicate that the body can be made whole. This means that those killed by violence retain a place within a culture through Freud's version of melancholia or, as de Richleau puts it, 'the blood that was shed still lives' (Wheatley 1965: 35). The point is that trying to reconstitute a version of Europe that pre-dated the war merely places you back into the circumstances that led to the war in the first place.

An illegitimate version of unification is represented at the start of the novel in the gathering of the Satanists who meet under Mocata's supervision. It is illegitimate because the Satanists' pursuit of the phallus is intended to create war, not peace. Also, for de Richleau (and, one suspects, for Wheatley), there are some troublingly mixed-race individuals present at this meeting, such as 'A native of Madagascar [...] half negro and half-Polynesian [...] He's a bad black if ever I saw one' (10). There is also another issue here relating to masculinity. As we saw in H. D. Everett's 'A Perplexing Case' (1920), discussed in Chapter 1, national masculinities need to be restored, since they are now, so she implies, required at home and not on the frontline. The Satanists are representative figures of a violent masculinity that leads to war, and the repeated aggression of the six-foot-eight Madagascan, plus their desire to possess a magical phallus, represents this excess. It is also captured in a demonic manifestation of a phallus which besieges the Satanist hunters when they sit within the confines of a protective magic circle. It is noted of this figure:

> The Thing had a whitish pimply skin, leprous and unclean, like some huge silver slug. Waves of satanic power rippled through its spineless body, causing it to throb and work continuously like a great mass of new-made dough. A horrible stench of decay and corruption filled the room; for as it writhed it exuded a slimy poisonous moisture which trickled in little rivulets across the polished floor. (Wheatley 1965: 183)

This monstrous form of masculinity is implicated in the war and is here turned into a Gothic image of subhuman agency. The manliness is associated with death and represents the type of masculinity that takes people into war. Tellingly, our Satanist hunters do not, in themselves, represent an ideal form of masculinity since their own talents for violence (all are described as having killed in various conflicts) disqualifies them from a post-war peace settlement that can bring unification, even as their respective national identities represent the allies who had won the war. It would be difficult to claim Wheatley as a liberal, given the racism and consistently anti-socialist principles of his work, but, in the final showdown with Mocata, Mary Lou, Eaton's wife, cites some lines from the Red Book of Appin (a probable reference to Ethan Allen Hitchcock's *The Story of the Red Book of Appin* [1863]), which invokes the Lord of Light, a figure who stands in clear counterpoint to Mocata's earlier invocation of the Angel of Death. It also represents a spiritually abstract form of masculinity that embodies a positive example of racial unification which was demonized in the earlier image of the Madagascan:

> a full-grown man stood before them. From his dress he had the appearance of a Thibetan Lama, but his aesthetic face was as much Aryan as Mongolian, blending the highest characteristics of the two; and just as it seemed that he had passed the barriers of race, so he also appeared to have cast off the shackles of worldly time. (241)

He is described as possessing an 'angelic compassion' and to be 'nearing perfection after many lives' (241). This angelic figure stands in clear counterpoint to the Gothic imagery that is associated with Mocata and his followers. He defeats Mocata and his satanic powers, and so it is that an abstracted, immortal and racially unified version of masculinity brings peace into a world which had been so troubled by images of masculine violence and the wars with which it was associated. In the final scenes of the novel, de Richleau throws Osiris's phallus into a furnace, remarking that '"it is a concrete symbol of all that we have fought"' (243). Peace at last can be achieved.

The Devil Rides Out does not include ghosts in any obvious form but it does repeatedly make Gothic reference to spirits, some of which are evil and some not. De Richleau explains to Rex, '"There is no such person as the Devil, but there are vast numbers of Earthbound spirits, Elementals, and Evil Intelligences of the Outer Circle floating in our midst"' (45). Elementals have already played a key role in J. S. M. Ward's account of the spirit world in *A Subaltern in Spirit Land* (1919), where they constitute a type of necessary enemy because, as discussed in Chapter 3, there is the view that '"there is no armistice in the fight between good and evil"' (Ward 1919: 157). In Wheatley, these evil elementals have infiltrated the physical plane and occupy the negatively drawn racial figures outlined above. For Wheatley, it is necessary to discern the true enemy that lurks within these apparently human forms because that makes the moral and political ambitions of these spirits clear. To do so requires a reconsideration of the forces which were responsible for the First World War.

Rex mentions the role of Germany in starting the war, a view that receives a hostile reaction from de Richleau:

> 'You fool! [...] Germany did not make the War. It came out of Russia [...]. The monk Rasputin was the Evil genius behind it all. He was the greatest Black Magician that the world has known for centuries. It was he who found one of the gateways through which to let forth the four horsemen that they might wallow in blood and destruction [...]. Europe is ripe now for any trouble and if they are loosed again, it will be final Armageddon.' (Wheatley 1965: 121)

Mocata has inherited Rasputin's mantle and therefore '"We've got to kill Mocata before he can secure the Talisman and prevent him plunging the world into another war"' (121). Wheatley's pointing of a finger towards Russia indicates that communism, notwithstanding Rasputin's associations with a pre-communist Russian court, is the real, and seemingly continuing, threat.

Phil Baker has referred to *The Devil Rides Out* as 'an Appeasement novel' (Baker 2011: 335) because it emphasises that the true danger confronted by Europe in the 1930s is not Nazi Germany but Russia. This link also explains why the novel was published in instalments in Lord Rothermere's appeasement newspaper *The Daily Mail* (Baker 2011: 326). Ultimately, the novel suggests that it is love that conquers evil, and Wheatley's politics are shaped by a view of occult practice which celebrates the nobility of spirit against a world of crude materialism and animality. It is noted of one black elemental that it is (with Wheatley borrowing a phrase from William Hope Hodgson) 'ab-human' and 'embodied evil' (Wheatley 1965: 38). This invocation of a newly constituted form of Gothic degeneracy depends upon a fear of physical and racial hybridity and attendant forms of miscegenation. Wheatley asserts the sanctity of physical, racial and moral purity against ab-human Gothic figures which threaten the world with a future war. At a satanic ritual it is noted that the attendees wear masks that align them with animals: 'One had a huge cat mask [...] another the headdress of a repellent toad [...] Mocata [...] had webbed wings sprouting from his shoulders which gave him the appearance of a giant bat' (89). De Richleau later explains that these are the types of animals over which Satanists have some control '"They can control all the meaner things – bats, snakes, rats, foxes, owls – as well as cats and certain breeds of dog"' (107). Again, Count Dracula is evoked here, but also the type of relationship between animality and the war which was explored in Chapter 2. The fellow travellers for Satanists are these 'meaner things', whereas those defying the Satanists have more spiritual virtues and a masculine honour code which asserts that only violence used in a good cause is a good thing.

Baker has noted that *The Devil Rides Out* accorded Wheatley considerable fame and that after its publication Wheatley became culturally regarded as 'Agatha Christie's demon brother' (Baker 2011: 336). While that suggestive link relates to his popularity, there are, as suggested earlier, some links in Wheatley's work to Christie in terms of the reassembling of the dead as a means of engaging with the present and challenging future difficulties. Wheatley's veterans have all fought in conflicts during the war and are not notably nervous or sensitive types. Theirs is a model of a restored masculinity that can be of use in the post-war era, as long as it ultimately sets violence aside. Wheatley's often Gothic view of the world is crude in its construction of good versus evil but reflects some of the impulses found in spirit narratives, explored in Chapter 3, which argued that a conflict between warring spiritual entities is inherent to the world and was exposed in its rawest form during the war. Wheatley also engages with that most Gothic of themes – the past and how to find ways in which it can be defeated, which implicates attitudes about the First World War even while it establishes that this is a battle won by a defiant collaboration, which is familiar from *Dracula*.

This chapter has explored how the post-war culture sought to move beyond the traumas and anxieties generated by the war and the way that certain texts have used the Gothic to explore that possibility. A different type of spectrality is generated here from the spectres that we have looked at in previous chapters. The ghosts of M. R. James are often malevolent and thereby indicate a horror that the dead will not leave the post-war world in peace. How to remember as a form of forgetting is suggested in poppies and the sanitised prose of war memorials that James also produced. How to construe the war dead as a matter of historical record underpins E. F. Benson's 'And the Dead Spake –', and his post-war ghost stories are shaped by amoral spectres that are not found in his pre-war ghost stories. How to honour the war dead is also central to Sayers's *The Nine Tailors*, which represents figures such as Deacon, whose disfigured remains are buried in the wrong place and who appear, symbolically speaking, to have been killed by a recollection of shelling that the bells both evoke and work beyond as they too represent a type of British history which has blood on its hands. Wheatley's defeat of black magic reflects the occult vision of spiritualist narratives that were popular in the war. Like them, it is optimistic that the forces of good will triumph but argues that this is an ongoing battle which requires certain spiritual values and reactionary political views, in order to triumph. The recent past of the war retains a presence as a Gothic force of barbarism which poses an ongoing threat to civilisation. The texts discussed in this chapter employ the Gothic as a mode of othering which demonises the past, but this is always tinged with ambivalence. What appears to be truly horrifying is that the trauma of war retains a vestigial presence within the cultural memory that threatens the capacity to envisage a future peacetime world because, for Wheatley, thinking about one war will lead to another.

Notes

1. Changes made in 1968 also replaced the typical patriotic pageant of the ceremony with a new form of observance more palatable to a less militaristic age (Cannadine 1981: 234).
2. Abel Gance's film *J'Accuse* (1919) does something similar as soldier-ghosts return to their communities to see how they have been remembered.
3. She was also the author of 'The Casualty List', published in 1934, which addresses issues about grief in the post-war period.
4. Patrick J. Murphy and Fred Porcheddu, 'Lay of a Last Survivor: *Beowulf*, Great War Memorials, and M.R. James's "A Warning to the Curious"', *The Review of English Studies*, Vol. 66, No. 274, (2014), pp. 205–222.
5. See Murphy and Porcheddu, pp. 211–2.
6. Stephen Ahearne-Kroll *The Psalms of Lament in Mark's Passion: Jesus' Davidic Suffering* (Cambridge: Cambridge University Press, 2007).
7. Also cited by Murphy and Porcheddu, p. 220.
8. Michelle Miranda, 'Reasoning Through Madness: The Detective in Gothic Crime Fiction', Palgrave Communication, 2017. https://www.nature.com/articles/palcomms201745 (last accessed 4 November 2021).
9. Dorothy L. Sayers, in her 'Introduction' to *Great Short Stories of Detection, Mystery and Horror* (London: Gollancz, 1939), pp. 7–47, explores the 'ancient' origins of both forms, p. 7, and the importance of the Newgate novel on a British tradition of detective fiction, p. 22. She also explores the importance of Poe's detective fiction, pp. 13–19, and Le Fanu's 'gift of investing the most mechanical of plots with an atmosphere of almost unbelievable horror' (p. 22).
10. Bryonny Muir, 'Bringing up the Body (Don't Mention the War): Traumatic Return in Dorothy L. Sayers' *The Nine Tailors*,' *English: Journal of the English Association*, Vol. 66, No. 255, Winter 2017, pp. 291–310, 307.
11. At this point, Muir is reflecting on Luckhurst's *The Trauma Question* (London: Routledge, 2008).

12. Muir discusses this in relation to Virginie Renard's essay on 'Reaching Out to the Past: Memory in Contemporary British First World War Narratives', in *British Popular Culture and the First World War*, ed. Jessica Meyer (Leiden: Brill, 2008), pp. 285–305, in Muir at note 19, p. 298.

Conclusion: Ghostly Afterlives

This book has explored how images of spectrality permeated writing about the war from 1914 until the 1930s. The ambition has been to explore how texts from the period drew upon pre-existing Gothic versions of the ghost as a way of managing (or not) the trauma of war. We have seen how ghosts from the Walpolean tradition have influenced formations of spectrality which grant the past an insistent presence that demands, like Hamlet's father's ghost, to be heard. The anti-Enlightenment impulse associated with these figures is in keeping with the irrationality that many associated with the war itself. The uncanny presence of dead undead models of lost, and often shell-shocked, soldiers permeate these tales, even when the ambition is to bring them back to life through the restorative warmth of the emotionally unconflicted family home. Not all ghosts, as we have seen, can be so easily accommodated and they reflect the ongoing feelings of loss, alienation and confusion engendered by the war. The spectres are various but all address ways in which trauma may, or may not, be overcome. The liminal figure of the ghost provided the means through which a culture sought to make visible its fears and anxieties about the dead of the war that they could not leave behind, and which, at times, seemed to haunt the post-war world terrifyingly with an unappeasable resentment. How these issues become addressed in what we might term the neo-First World War writings of Pat Barker will be outlined here, but it is also important to consider the relationship between the First and Second World Wars (as, indeed, Barker does in her *Life Class* trilogy), as this too implicates a model of haunting.

Elizabeth Bowen's 'The Demon Lover' (1945) dramatises a link between the wars as the ghost of a First World War soldier revisits his former lover in a 1940s blitzed London. The principal protagonist is the forty-four-year-old Mrs Drover, who is visiting the abandoned family home to secure possessions to forward on to her new, safer, blitz-free residence. She finds a letter which indicates that she is expected to keep her promise of an anniversary meeting with her former lover, who was killed in 1916. The letter's tone is threatening: 'The years have gone by at once slowly and fast. In view of the fact that nothing has changed, I shall rely upon you to keep your promise' (Bowen 1966a: 84). The home is invaded by his malevolent spirit, which is different to that of those shell-shocked soldiers, discussed earlier in this book, who are brought back to life in domestic spaces. This ghost brings nothing but death, with Mrs Drover noting on her entry into the house that 'Dead air came out to meet her as she went in' (82). The promise to be with him on a certain date twenty-five years after they parted in 1916 was forced out of her at the time. The terrified Mrs Drover believes that she has made good her escape in a taxi, but on recognising the face of the driver, her 'mouth hung open for some seconds before she could issue her first scream', after which 'the taxi, accelerating without mercy, made off with her into the hinterland of deserted streets' (89–90). Bowen's tale is not political in the way that Wheatley's novel is, but addresses in emotionally horrifying terms the effect of the terror of one war upon another. However, as with Wheatley, there is an issue about masculinity. Bowen's spectral soldier represents a frightening, because violent, form of masculinity reflecting the violence of the war itself. From the vantage point of the 1940s, the dead of the earlier war come back because, politically speaking, they ghost the violence of the later conflict.

In more recent accounts of World War One, the reconstruction of the war is used for other purposes but employs images of spectrality which are familiar from critical debates about trauma. Novels which have focused on the Great War include Susan Hill's *Strange Meeting* (1971), Paul Bailey's *Old Soldiers* (1980) and Sebastian Faulks's *Birdsong* (1993), which all reflect on the war in a realist mode. There are also self-consciously Gothic reworkings of the war which use vampires to represent the supposed blood-lust of those involved in the fighting, such as Kim Newman's *The Bloody Red Baron* (1995) and Kate Cary's *Bloodline* (2010), with both texts posing as sequels to *Dracula*.

Pat Barker's *Regeneration* trilogy, *Regeneration* (1991), *The Eye in the Door* (1993) and *The Ghost Road* (1995), explore the type of material that has been examined in this book as the series draws upon models of trauma developed by Freud and nuanced by Rivers. While not Gothic novels, they nevertheless repeatedly employ ghosts that are familiar from the Gothic tradition. These figures are largely psychological (rather than supernatural) in origin, which is in keeping with many of the tales discussed in this book. Barker has, in the main, been faithful to her primary sources and her trilogy is populated by ghosts that are often laid to rest by the psychoanalytical skills of Rivers, who, in decoding his patients' dreams, enables them to return to a semblance of health. The real-world Rivers was not always so successful and Michelle Barrett notes of Barker's trilogy that 'The persistent ghosts in the writing of the First World War are not so easily dispatched' (Barrett 2012: 258). Barker's trilogy, whilst faithful to Rivers's account of his therapeutic method, also makes explicit themes about masculinity which are developed in her representation of the homosocial relationships between Wilfred Owen, Siegfried Sassoon and Robert Graves, combined with some speculation about Rivers's sexuality. Rivers implicates masculinity as a failed trope of the war. Barker's Rivers contemplates the cultural background of his officer-class patients and in *Regeneration* concludes that 'The Great Adventure' promised at the start of the war, which was 'the real life equivalent of all the adventure stories they'd devoured as boys', had, in the reality of war, 'consisted of crouching in a dugout waiting to be killed'. This meant that 'The war that had promised so much in the way of "manly" activity had actually delivered "feminine" passivity, and on a scale that their mothers and sisters had scarcely known. No wonder they broke down' (Barker 1992: 107–8). The foregrounding of issues about masculinity and sexuality may feel like more contemporary concerns but they are intended to challenge ways in which the war has been typically remembered.

The fictitious Billy Prior focalises issues about masculinity. He is working-class, from the north of England and bisexual. He is an officer who does not feel that he belongs to the officer class and is keenly aware of the social iniquities that he sees both in the army and at home. His is a ghost-ridden world in which his projected ghosts require appeasement because they have returned for revenge. In *The Eye in the Door*, it is noted that 'It seemed to him the streets were full of ghosts, grey, famished, unappeasable ghosts, jostling on the pavements, waiting outside homes that had prospered in their absence.' It is an estrangement that he shares: 'He was no more part of the life around him than one of those returning ghosts' (Barker 1994: 97). Like the ghosts in M. R. James, these are not easy to lay to rest and, as with Bowen's ghost in 'The Demon Lover', there is no possibility of recuperation. In the final part of the trilogy, the battle-weary Prior reflects on the precarious nature of front-line friendships, concluding that there were 'ghosts everywhere. Even the living were only ghosts in the making. You learned to ration your commitment to them' (Barker 1996: 46). Ghosts are also memories which haunt and we first encounter Prior, in *Regeneration*, at Craiglockhart hospital where he is under the care of Rivers after developing a form of mutism brought on by a traumatic event that he is initially unable to remember. Rivers retrieves the memory by hypnotising Prior. The traumatic event centres on the death of two soldiers in Prior's section, Sawden and Towers, who are killed in a trench by a shell shortly after Prior had spoken to them. Prior and a sergeant bag up the remains and distribute lime over the parts that cannot be buried. Prior picks up Towers's eyeball, which sits in the palm of his shaking hand, and he asks his sergeant, '"What am I supposed to do with this gob-stopper?"' (Barker 1992: 103), before the sergeant grasps his wrist and tips the eye into the bag with the rest of the remains. Rivers awakens Prior from his trance and explains the reasons behind Prior's earlier mutism, in which the 'gob-stopper' eyeball incident had proved traumatically unspeakable (had stopped his gob) and so became a suppressed memory. Prior's response to the analysis takes Rivers by surprise:

> '*Is that all?*' Prior said.
> He seemed to be beside himself with rage.
> 'I don't know about *all*,' Rivers said. 'I'd have thought that was a traumatic experience by any standards.'
> Prior almost spat at him. '*It was nothing.*' (Barker 1992: 104, italics in original)

This moment has been much discussed by critics and Barrett notes that Prior's anger is generated by the fear that he had been responsible for the men's deaths, rather than by an experience which Prior had come to regard as a commonplace occurrence of war (Barrett 2012: 249). Rivers's reading of the incident is correct, but for Prior this incident is '*nothing*' in comparison to his other wartime experiences, which he can recollect with all too much clarity.

Prior is also a figure who, representationally, makes explicit issues about sexuality which were necessarily largely concealed at the time but which we witnessed in C. H. B. Kitchin's 'Dispossession', discussed in Chapter 1. For Sean Francis Ward, this is the major contribution made by Barker, in which 'the trilogy calls attention to forms of collective life that have not been, and perhaps cannot be, integrated into official British histories or commemorations of the war' (Ward 2016: 321). The trilogy, therefore, especially in relation to Prior's graphic sexual encounters with men and women, makes visible what public memorialisations leave out.[1] How to remember trauma as a way of overcoming it is thus supplanted by another narrative, which reflects more broadly on how the war is culturally remembered. The trilogy is critically regarded as representing anxieties about conflicts from the early 1990s, which have been transposed to a First World War setting. Sharon Monteith and John Brannigan relate the trilogy to the Gulf War, with Brannigan noting that 'the outbreak of the Gulf war of 1991 was reported through images of soldiers waiting in trenches, scrambling for gas masks and huddling from artillery barrages' (Brannigan 2005: 114). In addition, Monteith argues that the trilogy should be seen as a reaction to 'debates about Gulf War Syndrome' (Monteith 2002: 55) and the psychological condition of British combatants. For Ward:

> The history of World War I became a key site of contest and revision during this time. Official histories and state-sponsored memory projects returned to a familiar narrative of the 'Great War' as a harrowing but ultimately triumphant and nationally unifying crisis. Remembering the war – and remembering it *in this way* – was particularly important for Britain's transforming war culture and its late-century martial politics. (Ward 2016: 324, italics in original)

This also coincided with a period when there were few veterans of the Great War left and there emerged a cultural need to remember them in a certain way. Barker's trilogy thus works against this narrative by emphasising what is forgotten in this sanitised act of remembrance. Prior's aggression towards Rivers, in which, at one point, he takes over a psychoanalytical session to imply that Rivers's loss of visual memory might have been due to an incident of child abuse, should be seen as a writing back against those who sought tidy solutions to complex problems.

Barker's Rivers might be spoken back to by Prior but he is also haunted by his own ghosts, with much of *The Ghost Road* focusing on his reflections on his time as an anthropologist working on what Europeans referred to as Eddystone Island (Simbo) in the Solomon Islands. His studies lead him to the conclusion that the supposed ghosts that speak on the island 'had all been asking questions the living people wanted answered' (Barker 1996: 211) and these are the same ghosts he sees projected by his traumatised war patients, in whom 'the questions became more insistent, more powerful, for being projected into the mouth of the dead' (Barker 1996: 212). As we have seen, Walpole's ghosts are similarly insistent as they make visible what is otherwise seemingly concealed by the new dynasty, presided over by Manfred. Walpole's ghosts indicate that the past is defined by unresolved tensions and, according to Barker, ghosts 'are a neat metaphor [...] for whatever in the past we haven't managed to resolve' (cited in Rawlinson 2010: 166). Specifically, in Barker, these are the unabreached ghosts of war that Rivers has worked so hard to make sense of but they are also figures associated with modern-day concerns about 'recovered memory, hidden subjectivities, forgotten stories – the exclusions and elisions of history' (Brannigan 2005: 117), a view which accords with Jonathan

Dent's account of *The Castle of Otranto* and its anti-Enlightenment representations of a barely suppressed violent history. Brannigan summarises how 'the trilogy shows the war and its social contexts to remain alive with troubling questions about the relationships between reality and representation, language and silence, science and ethics, and history and haunting' (Brannigan 2005: 119). Barker returned to these issues in *Another World* (1998), in an account of the elderly Geordie, who carries the scar of a bayonet wound from the Great War and who is haunted by his memories of the fighting. He dies of cancer, but in his own mind he is unsure if his illness is not due to his war wound finally catching up with him. In Barker's *Life Class* trilogy, consisting of *Life Class* (2007), *Toby's Room* (2012) and *Noonday* (2015), she returned to the war, exploring the historical arc examined in this book from the First World War, the 1920s and the 1930s, up to the Second World War.

Life Class again makes explicit ideas about masculinity that would become challenged during the First World War. A pre-war art-school setting provides an opportunity for the student Kit Neville to assert that 'Virility was the essence of great art; effeminacy had to be extirpated at all costs' (Barker 2014: 107). In *Toby's Room*, Neville works as a medical orderly and his views on virility are translated into the war when he sees Toby, a medical officer and the brother of Elinor, an art student that Neville has a romantic attachment to, having sex with one of the men in their regiment. Neville tells the padre, knowing that it will be reported and Toby court-martialled. Neville grudgingly admits his role in this to Paul, who later marries Elinor (and decides not to let her know about Neville's conduct). For Neville, homosexuality is '"just another form of bullying. I hated it at school and I hate it now"' (Barker 2013: 249). Paul reflects on this comment that 'Neville had an extreme hatred of what he described as "effeminacy" or "degeneracy", whether in life or in art' (Barker 2013: 249). Toby is offered a way out by his commanding officer, which is to commit suicide rather than face a court-martial. Toby and Neville traverse a battlefield looking for wounded soldiers, when Toby tells Neville about his plight. Toby stands up and faces the German line, hoping that he will be shot, but when that does not happen puts his revolver in his mouth and shoots himself. The implication is that Toby was aware that Neville was responsible for reporting him and wishes to make him see the consequences of his action. Neville acknowledges to Paul that he knew what would happen to Toby after he had reported him and refers to it as a '"total waste"' but it was '"all because he couldn't keep his dick inside his breeches. But, you know, that was his decision, not mine"' (Barker 2013: 249). The title *Toby's Room* evokes Woolf's *Jacob's Room* (1922), which centres on the loss of Jacob Flanders, who is killed in the war, and the content recalls Brittain's *Testament of Youth* (1933), with its representation of a close bond between sister and brother, including critical suggestions that Brittain's brother, Edward, was outed as gay during the war and was offered a similar deal to Toby to help him avoid a court-martial (Edward died charging Austrian forces in Italy in June 1918). However, the novel is clear that Toby and Elinor have committed incest on at least one occasion and this is the Gothic secret that Elinor maintains while others, such as Neville, harbour their own.

The final novel, *Noonday*, is set during the Second World War, with Elinor still obsessed with Toby and the secret past that she shared with him. She notes of one of her portraits of Toby that 'It caught something of the reality, the power, of that slim, voracious ghost' (Barker 2016: 35). The London of the blitz recalls Bowen's representation of it throughout her collection *The Demon Lover & Other Stories* (1945), with Paul noting that, in the dark, London seemed to come alive when:

> You had a sense on these nights of long-buried bones working their way to the surface: London's dead gurgling up through the drains. Perhaps in these thronging shadows the living and the dead met in fleeting, unconscious encounters. Why not? *How would you know?* (Barker 2016: 119, italics in original)

Bowen, in her Postscript to her 1945 collection, recalls a similar night-time version of London: 'Walking in the darkness of the nights of six years (darkness which transformed a capital city into a network of inscrutable canyons) one developed new bare alert senses with their own savage warnings and notations' (Bowen 1966b: 202). Bowen also states that her typical writerly distance from the world was lost during the war because 'I felt one with, and just like, everyone else. Sometimes hardly knew where I stopped and somebody else began [...] We all lived in a state of lucid abnormality' (Bowen 1966b: 197). As in Barker, reality becomes reconstituted, or as Bowen puts it, reality becomes 'found' in 'small worlds-within-worlds of hallucination – in most cases, saving hallucination' (Bowen 1966b: 200). This is an unreal, ostensibly Gothic world, which is both disorientating and, paradoxically, liberating. The fundamental issue concerns how to represent this state of mind and, within that, the ghost takes on symbolic importance (and there are many ghosts in Bowen's collection), as a way of trying to make sense of this hallucinatory experience which replaces a more confident pre-war reality. That the ghosts of the first global conflict play a role in the second is suggested at the end of *Noonday*.

In *Noonday*, Neville and Elinor have become ambulance drivers and

Neville is killed while trying to help Elinor during an air raid. Neville advances towards Elinor, who is near a building that has been badly damaged. She later recounts to Paul what happened: '"I kept waving at him: Go back, go back [...] he just kept coming, and then the wall came down and all I could see was smoke"' (Barker 2016: 254). Earlier, we have seen this moment from Neville's point of view:

> Elinor was still waving. Jumping up and down now, shouting, but he couldn't hear anything above the roar of the flames. She'd been joined by a young man in army uniform, who looked vaguely familiar, but couldn't be, of course; it was just somebody Elinor had roped in to help carry the stretchers. Well, *good girl*. The more young, male muscle there was around, the better.
> Whoever it was, he was waving too, or beckoning: *Come on, come on*. (Barker 2016: 246, italics in original)

Neville appears to go to his death after being led towards the collapsing building by Toby's ghost, so that, in the end, the ghosts of World War One representationally linger in Barker's account of belated justice.

We have seen throughout this study that trauma poses a problem for representation. However, later accounts such as Barker's freight the Great War with more contemporary preoccupations about gender, sexuality and Gulf War post-traumatic stress disorder. This might sound as if Barker has taken liberties with the war but such a cultural incursion should be seen within the context of cultural memorialisation. How to remember the war poses a different problem from that of how to represent the traumas of those who participated in it. Barker is a political writer who challenges public acts of (mis)remembrance by subverting the dominant historical narrative. Her self-conscious political intervention contrasts with Bowen's view that her hallucinatory stories may stand as an unwitting testimony to the experience of war. Bowen notes of her collection that 'These as wartime stories, are at least contemporary – twenty, forty, sixty years hence they may be found interesting as documents, even if they are found negligible as art' (Bowen 1966b: 202). Fiction becomes transformed into historical documents because they record the mentalities of the moment, rather than verifiable historical facts.

These latter-day ghostly reconstructions of the Great War and its aftermath are reminders of how the conflict poses an ongoing problem about representation and interpretation. While original source material, such as the writings of Rivers and others, has been meticulously researched by Barker, it does not mean that we are looking at an objectively formulated version of the past. The battle is over how the past is represented and the figure of the ghost repeatedly plays a crucial role in that. How to lay memories to rest becomes supplanted by a cultural need to reflect on how we remember. Susan Hill, in the Afterword to *Strange Meeting*, indicates that writing the novel constituted a tacit form of abreaction:

> I cannot now bear to read a word about any aspect of the First World War […] I have lost all interest in it, the whole subject has gone cold on me. I was haunted by it for years and in writing the novel I laid the ghost forever: it was an obsession which I followed to a conclusion and which then left me completely and forever. (Hill 1989: 180)

The Afterword was written in 1989, shortly before the publication of several novels discussed here, which indicates that the war was still very much culturally alive.

Ghosts function as a way of managing forms of traumatic experience because they are associated with the memories which haunt the traumatised subject. This is also true for communities and nations which try to make sense of how to remember a past associated with trauma. We have seen how the Gothic ghost is often culturally redeployed to articulate how both a subject and a society recollect the experience of the First World War. This is an impulse which we still live with. Much of the research for this book took place in 2018 during the centenary commemorations. During this period, the charity Remembrance drew upon the 'There but Not There' memorialisation, which first appeared in 2016 in Penhurst Church in Kent and consisted of fifty-one transparent military figures sitting in pews. The charity aimed to promote the installation of one transparent figure in every church in Britain which had a roll of honour. Finally, the symbolic figure of the ghost, which is there but not there, articulated an explicit act of national remembrance.

Note

1. The issue of sexuality and the war also haunts Helen Dunmore's *The Lie* (London: Windmill Books, 2014), in which her recovering soldier, Daniel Branwell, is confronted by the ghost of his dead friend, Frederick Dennis.

Bibliography

Ahearne-Kroll, Stephen (2007), *The Psalms of Lament in Mark's Passion: Jesus' Davidic Suffering*, Cambridge: Cambridge University Press.
Aldington, Richard (1929), *Death of a Hero*, London: Chatto & Windus.
— (1930a), 'The Case of Lieutenant Hall', in *Roads to Glory*, London: Chatto & Windus, pp. 227–53.
— (1930b), 'Farewell to Memories', in *Roads to Glory*, London: Chatto & Windus, pp. 257–78.
— (1948a), *The Complete Poems of Richard Aldington*, London: Allan Wingate.
— (1948b), '1933', in *The Complete Poems of Richard Aldington*, London: Allan Wingate, p. 338.
— (1948c),'The Blood of the Young Men', in *The Complete Poems of Richard Aldington*, London: Allan Wingate, pp. 119–121.
— (1948d), 'Concert', in *The Complete Poems of Richard Aldington*, London: Allan Wingate, p. 108.
— (1948e), 'The Eaten Heart', in *The Complete Poems of Richard Aldington*, London: Allan Wingate, pp. 275–287.
— (1948f), 'Epilogue', in *The Complete Poems of Richard Aldington*, London: Allan Wingate, p. 148.
— (1948g), 'In Memory of Wilfred Owen', in *The Complete Poems of Richard Aldington*, London: Allan Wingate, p. 302.
— (1948h), 'Meditation', in *The Complete Poems of Richard Aldington*, London: Allan Wingate, pp. 145–6.
— (1948i) 'To One Dead', in *The Complete Poems of Richard Aldington*, London: Allan Wingate, p. 333.
Anon. (1914a), *The Occult Review*, September, Vol. XX, No. 3.
Anon. (1914b), *The Occult Review*, October, Vol. XX, No. 4.
Anon. (1914c), *The Occult Review*, November, Vol. XX, No. 5.
Anon. (1916), *The Occult Review*, January, Vol. XXIII, No. 1.
Anon. (1917), 'What is the Greatest Deed of Valour?', *The Strand*, June–December, pp. 582–7.
Anon. (1918), *The Occult Review*, December, Vol. XXVIII, No. 6.
Ashmead-Bartlett, Ellis (1917), 'Life on a Battleship', *The Strand*, June–December, pp. 563–71.
Atkey, Bertram (1919), 'MacKurd: A Tale of the Aftermath', *The Strand*, July–December, pp. 429–40.

Austin, F. Britten (1919), 'A Point of Ethics', *The Strand*, January–December, pp. 555–64.
Baker, Phil (2011), *The Devil is a Gentleman: The Life and Times of Dennis Wheatley*, Sawtry: Dedalus.
Balaev, Michelle, ed. (2014), *Contemporary Approaches in Literary Trauma Theory*, Basingstoke: Palgrave.
Balmer, Edwin (1919), 'A Case of Lost Memory', *The Strand*, January–June, pp. 426–34.
Barker, Pat (1992), *Regeneration*, Harmondsworth: Penguin.
— (1994), *The Eye in the Door*, Harmondsworth: Penguin.
— (1996), *The Ghost Road*, Harmondsworth: Penguin.
— (1998), *Another World*, London: Viking.
— (2013), *Toby's Room*, Harmondsworth: Penguin.
— (2014), *Life Class*, Harmondsworth: Penguin.
— (2016), *Noonday*, Harmondsworth: Penguin.
Barrett, Michelle (2012), 'Pat Barker's "Regeneration" Trilogy and the Freudianization of Shell Shock', *Contemporary Literature*, Vol. 53, No. 2, pp. 237–60.
Benson, E. F. (2012a), 'And the Dead Spake –', *Night Terrors: The Ghost Stories of E. F. Benson*, Ware: Wordsworth, pp. 199–215.
— (2012b), 'Caterpillars', *Night Terrors: The Ghost Stories of E. F. Benson*, Ware: Wordsworth, pp. 91–98.
— (2012c), 'Expiation', *Night Terrors: The Ghost Stories of E. F. Benson*, Ware: Wordsworth, pp. 451–66.
— (2012d), 'The Face', *Night Terrors: The Ghost Stories of E. F. Benson*, Ware: Wordsworth, pp. 383–95.
— (2012e), 'How Fear Departed from the Long-Gallery', *Night Terrors: The Ghost Stories of E. F. Benson*, Ware: Wordsworth, pp. 77–89.
Bion, Wilfred (1962), *Learning from Experience*, London: Heinemann.
— (1985), *The Long Week-End 1897–1919: Part of a Life*, ed. Francesca Bion, Abingdon: Fleetwood Press.
Blunden, Edmund (1932), *Fall In, Ghosts*, London: The White Owl Press.
— (1936), 'Shakespeare's Significances', in *Shakespeare Criticism, 1919–1935*, ed. Anne Ridler, Oxford: Oxford University Press, pp. 327–42.
— (2015a), *Undertones of War*, ed. John Greening, Oxford: Oxford University Press.
— (2015b), '1964 Introduction to Collins Edition', in *Undertones of War*, ed. John Greening, Oxford: Oxford University Press, pp. 325–8.
— (2015c), 'The Aftermath', in *Undertones of War*, ed. John Greening, Oxford: Oxford University Press, p. 269.
— (2015d), 'Mont de Cassel', in *Undertones of War*, ed. John Greening, Oxford: Oxford University Press, p. 261.
Bonikowski, Wyatt (2005), '*The Return of the Soldier* Brings Death Home', *Modern Fiction Studies*, Vol. 51, Number 3, Fall, 513–35.
Booth, Allyson (1996), *Postcards From the Trenches: Negotiating the Space Between Modernism and the First World War*, Oxford: Oxford University Press.
Bowen, Elizabeth (1966a), 'The Demon Lover', in *The Demon Lover & Other Stories*, Harmondsworth: Penguin, pp. 82–90.

— (1966b), 'Postscript by the Author', in *The Demon Lover & Other Stories*, Harmondsworth: Penguin, pp. 196–203.
Brannigan, John (2005), *Pat Barker*, Manchester: Manchester University Press, 2005.
Breton, André (1978), 'The Automatic Message', in *What is Surrealism? Selected Writings*, ed. Franklin Rosemont, London: Pluto Press, pp. 132–47.
Brittain, Vera (2014), *Testament of Youth*, London: Virago.
Brodie-Innes, J. W. (1918), 'Psychic Help for Soldiers and Sailors', *The Occult Review*, April, pp. 211–21.
Buelens, Gert, Sam Durrant and Robert Eaglestone, eds (2014), *The Future of Trauma Theory: Contemporary Literary and Cultural Criticism*, London: Routledge.
Burrage, A. M. (2009), *War is War* by X-Private X, Chippenham: Anthony Rowe.
Cannadine, David (1981), 'War and Death, Grief and Mourning in Modern Britain', in *Mirrors of Mortality: Studies in the Social History of Death*, ed. Joachim Whaley, Abingdon: Routledge, pp. 187–242.
Cannan, May Wedderburn (1919), 'Women Demobilised', in *The Splendid Days*, Oxford: Blackwell, p. 79.
— (1976), *Grey Ghosts and Voices*, Kineton: The Roundwood Press.
Caruth, Cathy (1995), 'Introduction', in *Trauma: Explorations in Memory*, ed. Cathy Caruth, Baltimore: Johns Hopkins University Press, pp. 3–12.
— (1996), *Unclaimed Experience: Trauma, Narrative, and History*, Baltimore: Johns Hopkins University Press.
Castle, Terry (1995), 'The Spectralization of the Other in The Mysteries of Udolpho', in *The Female Thermometer: Eighteenth-Century Culture and the Invention of the Unconscious*, Oxford: Oxford University Press, pp. 120–39.
Chapman, Guy (1965), *A Prodigious Prodigality: Fragments of Autobiography*, London: MacGibbon & Kee.
Conrad-O'Briain, Helen (2011), 'Providence and Intertextuality: Le Fanu, M. R. James, and Dorothy Sayers' *The Nine Tailors*', *The Irish Journal of Horror Studies*, No. 9, pp. 22–31.
Cook, Tim (2013), 'Grave Beliefs: Stories of the Supernatural and the Uncanny among Canada's Great War Trench Soldiers', *The Journal of Military History*, No. 77 (April), pp. 521–42.
Dante (Dante Alighieri) (2012), *The Divine Comedy: Inferno, Purgatorio, Paradiso*, trans. Robin Kirkpatrick, Harmondsworth: Penguin.
Davies, Owen (2018), *A Supernatural War: Magic, Divination, and Faith During the First World War*, Oxford: Oxford University Press.
Dent, Jonathan (2016), *Sinister Histories: Gothic Novels and Representations of the Past, from Horace Walpole to Mary Wollstonecraft*, Manchester: Manchester University Press.
Dickens, Charles (1985), *American Notes for General Circulation*, ed. John S. Whitely and Arnold Goldman, Harmondsworth: Penguin.
— (2008), *A Christmas Carol*, in *A Christmas Carol and Other Christmas Books*, Penguin: Harmondsworth, pp. 5–84.
Dunmore, Helen (2014), *The Lie*, London: Windmill Books.
Einhaus, Ann-Marie (2013), *The Short Story and the First World War*, Cambridge: Cambridge University Press.

Eliot, T. S. (2001), *The Waste Land*, in *The Waste Land and Other Writings*, intro. Mary Karr, New York: Modern Library, pp. 38–56.

— (2014), 'A Note of Introduction', in *In Parenthesis*, London: Faber and Faber, pp. vii–viii.

Everett, H. D. (2006), 'A Perplexing Case', in *The Crimson Blind & Other Stories*, Ware: Wordsworth, pp. 167–76.

Foley, Matt (2017), *Haunting Modernisms: Ghostly Aesthetics, Mourning, and Spectral Resistance Fantasies in Literary Modernism*, Basingstoke: Palgrave.

Ford, Ford Madox (1982a), *The Last Post*, in *Parade's End*, Harmondsworth: Penguin, pp. 676–836.

— (1982b), *A Man Could Stand Up*, in *Parade's End*, Harmondsworth: Penguin, pp. 503–675.

— (1982c), *Some Do Not ...*, in *Parade's End*, Harmondsworth: Penguin, pp. 3–288.

— (2004), 'War and the Mind', *War Prose*, ed. and intro. Max Saunders, Manchester: Carcanet Press, pp. 42–8.

Freedman, Ariela (2010), 'Dorothy Sayers and the Case of the Shell-Shocked Detective', *Partial Answers: Journal of Literature and the History of Ideas*, Vol. 8, No. 2, 365–87.

Freud, Sigmund (1955), 'Memorandum on the Electrical Treatment of War Neurotics', in *The Standard Edition of the Complete Psychological Works of Sigmund Freud*, trans. James Strachey, Vol. XVII (1917–19), *An Infantile Neurosis and Other Works*, London: Hogarth Press, 211–15.

— (1990a), 'On Transience', in *Art and Literature: Jensen's 'Gradiva', Leonardo Da Vinci and Other Works*, ed. Albert Dickson, Harmondsworth: Penguin, pp. 283–90.

— (1990b), 'The Uncanny', in *Art and Literature: Jensen's 'Gradiva', Leonardo Da Vinci and Other Works*, ed. Albert Dickson, Harmondsworth: Penguin, pp. 339–76.

— (1991a), *Beyond the Pleasure Principle*, in *On Metapsychology*, ed. Angela Richards, Harmondsworth: Penguin, pp. 269–337.

— (1991b), 'Mourning and Melancholia', in *On Metapsychology*, ed. Angela Richards, Harmondsworth: Penguin, pp. 245–68.

— (1991c), 'Thoughts for the Times on War and Death', in *Group Psychology, Civilization and Its Discontents and Other Works*, ed. Albert Dickson, Harmondsworth: Penguin, pp. 57–89.

Fussell, Paul (2009), *The Great War and Modern Memory*, Oxford: Oxford University Press.

Graham, Desmond (1984), *The Truth of War: Owen, Blunden and Rosenberg*, Manchester: Carcanet.

Graves, Robert (1930), 'Postscript to "Goodbye to All That"', in *But It Still Goes On: An Accumulation*, London: Jonathan Cape, pp. 13–56.

— (1967), *Goodbye to All That*, Harmondsworth, Penguin.

— (1984), 'The Shout', in *Roberts Graves: Collected Short Stories*, Harmondsworth: Penguin, pp. 11–30.

— (2003a), 'From Our Ghostly Enemy', in *Robert Graves: The Complete Poems*, ed. Beryl Graves and Duncan Ward, Harmondsworth: Penguin, pp. 219–21.

— (2003b), 'Haunted', in *Robert Graves: The Complete Poems*, ed. Beryl

Graves and Dunstan Ward, Harmondsworth: Penguin, p. 92.
— (2003c), 'The Haunted House', in *Robert Graves: The Complete Poems*, ed. Beryl Graves and Dunstan Ward, Harmondsworth: Penguin, p. 84.
— (2003d) 'No More Ghosts', in *Robert Graves: The Complete Poems*, Harmomdsworth: Penguin, ed. Beryl Graves and Duncan Ward, p. 385.
Hartley, L. P. (1929), 'The Travelling Grave', in *Shudders*, ed. Cynthia Asquith, London: Hutchinson, pp. 9–37.
Haslam, Sara (2014), 'From Conversation to Humiliation: *Parade's End* and the Eighteenth Century', in *Ford Madox Ford's* Parade's End: *The First World War, Culture, and Modernity*, ed. Ashley Chantler and Rob Hawkes, Amsterdam: Rodopi, pp. 37–51.
Hazelgrove, Jenny (2000), *Spiritualism and British Society between the Wars*, Manchester: Manchester University Press.
H. C. (1915), 'What Happens in the Spirit-World over a Battlefield; An Exact Description of What Occurs, as Revealed by Clairvoyant Vision and Higher Sense', *The Occult Review*, June, pp. 352–5.
Hill, Susan (1989), *Strange Meeting*, Harmondsworth: Penguin.
Hobsbawm, Eric (1995), *The Age of Revolution*, London: Weidenfeld and Nicolson.
Holtby, Winifred (2010), *South Riding: An English Landscape*, intro. Marion Shaw, London: Virago.
Hyder, Alan F. (1999), 'A Nightmare', in *True World War 1 Stories*, London: Robinson, pp. 152–8.
Hynes, Samuel (1995), 'The Man Who Was There', *The Swanee Review*, Vol. 103, No. 3, Summer, pp. 394–414.
James, M. R. (1970a), 'A Neighbour's Landmark', in *The Collected Ghost Stories of M. R. James*, London: Edward Arnold, pp. 514–32.
— (1970b), 'The Uncommon Prayer-Book', in *The Collected Ghost Stories of M. R. James*, London: Edward Arnold, pp. 490–513.
— (1970c) 'A View from a Hill', in *The Collected Ghost Stories of M. R. James*, London: Edward Arnold, pp. 533–60.
— (1970d) 'A Warning to the Curious', in *The Collected Ghost Stories of M. R. James*, London: Edward Arnold, pp. 561–87.
Jameson, Storm, ed. (1935), *Challenge to Death*, Boston: E. P. Dutton.
— (1982), *Company Parade*, London: Virago.
Johnson, George M. (2015), *Mourning and Mysticism in First World War Literature and Beyond: Grappling with Ghosts*, Basingstoke: Palgrave.
Jones, David (2014), *In Parenthesis*, London: Faber and Faber.
Keats, John (2018), 'Letter to George and Thomas Keats (Negative Capability)', in *The Norton Anthology, English Literature: The Romantic Period*, Vol. D, New York: W. W. Norton & Co., pp. 1016–17.
Kitchin, C. H. B. (1931), 'Dispossession', in *Shudders: A Collection of New Nightmare Tales*, ed. Cynthia Asquith, Hutchinson: London, pp. 157–79.
Kline, Burton (1919), 'The Living Ghost', *The Strand*, January–June, pp. 449–59.
Ko, Charles (2007), 'Subliminal Consciousness', *The Review of English Studies*, Vol. 59, No. 242, pp. 740–65.
Lankester, Edwin (1880), *Degeneration: A Chapter in Darwinism*, London: Macmillan.

Levenson, Michael H. (1984), *A Genealogy of Modernism: A Study of English Literary Doctrine 1908–1922*, Cambridge: Cambridge University Press.
Leys, Ruth (2000), *Trauma: A Genealogy*, London: University of Chicago Press.
Light, Alison (1991), *Forever England: Femininity, Literature, and Conservatism Between the Wars*, London: Routledge.
Lodge, Oliver (1917a), 'How I Became Convinced of the Survival of the Dead: An Autobiographical Sketch', *The Strand*, January–July, pp. 563–7.
— (1917b), *Raymond*, London: Methuen.
Lott, Monica (2013), 'Dorothy L. Sayers, the Great War and Shell Shock', *Interdisciplinary Literary Studies*, Vol. 15, No. 1, pp. 103–26.
Loughran, Tracey (2017), *Shell-Shock and Medical Culture in First World War Britain*, Cambridge: Cambridge University Press.
Lowndes, Marie Belloc (1931), 'The Unbolted Door', in *When Churchyards Yawn*, ed. Cynthia Asquith, Hutchinson: London, pp. 207–15.
Luckhurst, Roger (2002), *The Invention of Telepathy, 1870–1901*, Oxford: Oxford University Press.
— (2006), 'Introduction' to *Strange Case of Dr Jekyll and Mr Hyde*, in *Strange Case of Dr Jekyll and Mr Hyde and Other Tales*, ed. Roger Luckhurst, Oxford: Oxford University Press, pp. vii–xxxii.
— (2008) *The Trauma Question*, London: Routledge.
— (2010), 'Religion, Psychical Research, Spiritualism and the Occult', in *The Oxford Handbook of Modernisms*, ed. Peter Brooker, Andrzej Gąsiorek, Deborah Longworth and Andrew Thacker, Oxford: Oxford University Press, pp. 429–44.
McCrae, John (1915), 'In Flanders Field', *Punch*, 8 December.
MacCurdy, J. T. (1918), *War Neurosis*, Cambridge: Cambridge University Press,
Machen, Arthur (2010), *The Great God Pan*, in *The Great God Pan, The Shining Pyramid, The White People*, Cardigan: Parthian.
McLoughlin, Kate (2018), *Veteran Poetics: British Literature in the Age of Mass Warfare, 1790–2015*, Cambridge: Cambridge University Press.
Malamud, Randy (1988), 'Frankenstein's Monster: The Gothic Voice in *The Waste Land*', in *English Language Notes*, Vol. 26, No. 1, pp. 41–5.
Manning, Frederic (1999), *Her Privates We*, London: Serpent's Tail.
Martin, Jack (2010), *Sapper Martin: The Secret Great War Diary of Jack Martin*, ed. and intro. Richard Van Emden, London: Bloomsbury.
Mercier, Charles (n.d.), *Spiritualism and Sir Oliver Lodge*, London, Watt's & Co.
Milton, John (2003), *Paradise Lost*, Harmondsworth: Penguin.
Miranda, Michelle (2017), 'Reasoning Through Madness: The Detective in Gothic Crime Fiction', Palgrave Communication. https://www.nature.com/articles/palcomms201745 (last accessed 4 November 2021).
Moberly, L. G. (1917), 'Inexplicable', *The Strand*, June–December, pp. 572–81.
Monteith, Sharon (2002), *Pat Barker*, Tavistock: Northcote House.
Muir, Bryonny (2017), 'Bringing Up the Body (Don't Mention the War): Traumatic Return in Dorothy L. Sayers' *The Nine Tailors*', *English: Journal of the English Association*, Vol. 66, No. 255, pp. 291–310.
Murphy, Patrick J. and Fred Porcheddu (2014), 'Lay of a Last Survivor: *Beowulf*, Great War Memorials, and M. R. James's "A Warning to the Curious"', *The Review of English Studies*, Vol. 66, No. 274, pp. 205–22.

Myers, Charles (1915), 'A Contribution to the Study of Shell-shock: Being an Account of Three Cases of Loss of Memory, Vision, Smell, and Taste, Admitted into the Duchess of Westminster's War Hospital, Le Touquet', *The Lancet*, 13 February, pp. 316–20.

Myers, F. W. H. (1892), 'The Subliminal Consciousness', in the *Proceedings of the Society for Psychical Research*, 7.

— (1903), *Human Personality and Its Survival of Bodily Death*, London: Longmans, Green, and Co.

Myers, Gabrielle (2011), '"Spread Like a Veil Upon a Rock": Septimus and the Trench Poets of World War 1', *English: Journal of the English Association*, Vol. 60, No. 230, Autumn, pp. 212–28

Nordau, Max (1993), *Degeneration*, Lincoln, NE, and London: University of Nebraska Press.

Norman, Taryn (2016), 'Gothic Stagings: Surfaces and Subtexts in the Popular Modernism of Agatha Christie's Hercule Poirot Series', *Gothic Studies*, Vol. 18, No. 1, pp. 85–99.

Owen, Wilfred (2018), 'Strange Meeting', in *The Norton Anthology of English Literature: The Twentieth and Twenty-First Centuries*, Vol. F, New York: W. W. Norton & Co., pp. 166–7.

Pfaff, Richard William (1980), *Montague Rhodes James*, Farnham: Ashgate.

Pividori, Cristina (2010), 'Eros and Thanatos Revisited: The Poetics of Trauma in Rebecca West's *The Return of the Soldier*', *Atlantis*, Vol. 32, No 2, December, pp. 89–104.

Plain, Gill (2001), *Twentieth-Century Crime Fiction: Gender, Sexuality and the Body*, Edinburgh: Edinburgh University Press.

Poe, E. A. (1982), 'The Facts in the Case of M. Valdemar', in *The Complete Tales and Poems of Edgar Allan Poe*, Penguin: Harmondsworth, pp. 96–103.

Poole, W. Scott (2018), *Wasteland: The Great War and the Origins of Modern Horror*, Berkeley: Counterpoint.

Rawlinson, Mark (2010), *Pat Barker*, Basingstoke: Palgrave.

Reid, Fiona (2010), *Broken Men: Shell Shock, Treatment and Recovery in Britain 1914–1930*, London: Continuum.

Renard, Virginie (2008), 'Reaching Out to the Past: Memory in Contemporary British First World War Narratives', *British Popular Culture and the First World War*, ed. Jessica Meyer, Leiden: Brill Academic, pp. 285–305.

Riquelme, John Paul, ed. (2008), *Gothic and Modernism*, Baltimore: Johns Hopkins University Press.

— (2014), 'Modernist Gothic', in *The Cambridge Companion to the Modern Gothic*, ed. Jerrold E. Hogle, Cambridge: Cambridge University Press, pp. 20–36

Rivers, W. H. R. (1922a), *Instinct and the Unconscious: A Contribution to a Biological Theory of the Psycho-Neuroses*, Cambridge: Cambridge University Press.

— (1922b), 'A Case of Claustrophobia', in *Instinct and the Unconscious: A Contribution to a Biological Theory of the Psycho-Neuroses*, Cambridge: Cambridge University Press, pp. 170–84.

— (1923), *Conflict and Dream*, New York: Harcourt, Brace & Co.

Roper, Michael (2009), *The Secret Battle: Emotional Survival in the Great War*, Manchester: Manchester University Press.

Ruickbie, Leo (2108), *Angels in the Trenches: Spiritualism, Superstition and the Supernatural During the First World War*, London: Robinson.
Sassoon, Siegfried (1936), *Sherston's Progress*, London: Faber and Faber.
— (1997), *Memoirs of an Infantry Officer*, London: Faber and Faber.
— (1999), *The War Poems*, intro. Rupert Hart-Davis, London: Faber and Faber.
Sayers, Dorothy L. (1939), 'Introduction', in *Great Short Stories of Detection, Mystery and Horror*, London: Gollancz, pp. 7–47.
— (1984), *The Nine Tailors: Changes Rung on an Old Theme in Two Short Touches and Two Full Peals*, Sevenoaks: New English Library.
Scanlon, Mara (2017), 'Gender Identity and Promiscuous Identification: Reading (in) Rebecca West's *The Return of the Soldier*', *Journal of Modern Literature*, Vol. 40, No. 3, Spring, pp. 66–83.
Shakespeare, William (1984), *Hamlet*, ed. T. J. B. Spencer, Harmondsworth: Penguin.
Shephard, Ben (2000), *A War of Nerves: Soldiers and Psychiatrists, 1914–1994*, London: Cape.
Showalter, Elaine (1992), *Sexual Anarchy: Gender and Culture at the Fin de Siècle*, London: Virago.
— (2019), 'Introduction', in *Mrs Dalloway*, Harmondsworth: Penguin, pp. xi–xlviii.
Sinnett, A. P. (1914), 'Super-Physical Aspects of the War', *The Occult Review*, December, Vol. xx, No. 6, pp. 346–53.
Skirth, Ronald (2010), *The Reluctant Tommy*, ed. Duncan Barrett, Basingstoke: Macmillan.
Smith, Andrew (2010), *The Ghost Story 1840–1920: A Cultural History*, Manchester: Manchester University Press.
Smith, Andrew and Jeff Wallace, eds (2002), *Gothic Modernisms*, Basingstoke: Macmillan.
Spooner, Catherine (2010), 'Gothic and Crime', in *A Companion to Crime Fictions*, ed. Charles J. Rzepka and Lee Horsley, Oxford: Wiley-Blackwell, pp. 245–57.
Stevenson, Robert Louis (2006), *Strange Case of Dr Jekyll and Mr Hyde*, in *Strange Case of Dr Jekyll and Mr Hyde and Other Tales*, ed. Roger Luckhurst, Oxford: Oxford University Press, pp. 1–66.
Stoker, Bram (1996), *Dracula*, ed. Maud Ellmann, Oxford: Oxford University Press.
Stuart, Gerald Villiers (1920), 'The Mirror and the Incense', *The Strand*, January–June, pp. 120–30.
Summers, Montague (1918), 'Mystical Substitution', *The Occult Review*, October, pp. 215–20.
Thurston, Luke (2012), *Literary Ghosts from the Victorians to Modernism: The Haunting Interval*, London: Routledge.
Townshend, Dale (2008), 'Gothic and the Ghost of Hamlet', in *Gothic Shakespeares*, ed. John Drakakis and Dale Townshend, Abingdon: Routledge, pp. 60–97.
Tropp, Martin (1990), *Images of Fear: How Horror Stories Helped Shape Modern Culture*, Jefferson NC: McFarland.

Tudor Pole, Wellesley (1966), *Private Dowding: The Personal Story of a Soldier Killed in Battle*, London: Neville Spearman.

Walpole, Horace (1998), *The Castle of Otranto*, ed. Emma Clery, Oxford: Oxford University Press.

Ward, J. S. M. (1919), *A Subaltern in Spirit Land: A Sequel to 'Gone West'*, London: Psychic Book Club.

Ward, Sean Francis (2016), 'Erotohistoriography and War's Waste in Pat Barker's *Regeneration* Trilogy', *Comparative Literature*, Vol. 57, No. 3, Fall, pp. 320–45.

West, Rebecca (1987), *The Return of the Soldier*, in *All Passion Spent; The Return of the Soldier; Two Days in Aragon*, Virago Omnibus III, London: Virago, pp. 183–281.

Wheatley, Dennis (1965), *The Devil Rides Out*, London: Arrow.

Wilt, Judith (2001), 'The Ghost and the Omnibus: The Gothic Virginia Woolf', in *Gothic Modernisms*, ed. Andrew Smith and Jeff Wallace, Basingstoke: Palgrave, pp. 62–77.

Winter, Jay (1995), *Sites of Memory, Sites of Mourning: The Great War in European Cultural History*, Cambridge: Cambridge University Press.

Woolf, Virginia (1980), *The Diary of Virginia Woolf*, Vol. 2 1920–1924, ed. Anne Olivier Bell, New York: Harcourt Brace Jovanovich.

— (2000), *Jacob's Room*, London: Vintage.

— (2019), *Mrs Dalloway*, Harmondsworth: Penguin.

Zilcosky, John (2103), 'Savage Science: Primitives, War Neurotics, and Freud's Uncanny Method', *American Imago*, Vol. 70, No. 3, Fall, pp. 461–86.

Index

Aldington, Richard, 19, 158, 162
   'Concert', 152
   Death of a Hero, 83, 87, 105
   'Epilogue', 152
   Farewell to Memories, 156n13
   'In Memory of Wilfred Owen', 153
   Images of Desire, 152, 153
   Images of War, 151, 152, 153
   'Meditation', 153
   'The Blood of the Young', 153
   'The Case of Lieutenant Hall', 78–53, 86, 87, 108, 153
   The Complete Poems, 151
   The Eaten Heart, 153
   'To One Dead', 153–4
Ahearne-Kroll, Stephen, 170
Atkey, Bertram, 'MacKurd: A Tale of the Aftermath', 54–7
Austin, F. Britten, 'A Point of Ethics', 41–4, 45, 46, 47–8

Bailey, Paul, *Old Soldiers*, 202
Baker, Phil, 197
Balmer, Edwin, 'A Case of Lost Memory', 32–4, 36, 54, 57
Barker, Pat, 197, 198, 201, 205
   Another World, 206
   Life Class, 206
   Noonday, 206, 207–8
   Regeneration, 202, 204
   The Eye in the Door, 202, 203
   The Ghost Road, 202, 203, 206
   Toby's Room, 206–7
Barrett, Michelle, 203, 204
Bayfield, M. A., 123

Benson, E. F., 19, 96, 154, 178–84
   'And the Dead Spake – ', 180–3, 198
   'Caterpillars', 179
   'Expiation', 180
   'How Fear Departed from the Long-Gallery', 178–9
   'The Face', 179, 187
Bion, Wilfred, 73, 82, 92, 108
   Learning from Experience, 74
   The Long Week-End 1897–1919: Part of a Life, 74–5, 78
Blackwood, Algernon, 95, 109n5
Blunden, Edmund, 18, 86, 102, 107, 162, 170
   Fall In, Ghosts, 92
   'Mont de Cassel', 92
   'Shakespeare's Significances', 93
   'The Aftermath', 87
   Undertones of War, 1–2, 87–93, 94, 95, 96, 106, 107
Bonikowski, Wyatt, 59, 61
Booth, Allyson, 143, 147
Bowen, Elizabeth, 207, 208
   'The Demon Lover', 201–2, 203
Bradley, F. H., 146
Brannigan, John, 204–5, 206
Breton, André, 136
Brittain, Vera, 18, 102, 162, 163, 170
   Testament of Youth, 1–2, 33, 93–6, 99, 106, 207
Brodie-Inness, J. W., 119–20
Burke, Edmund, 3
Burrage, A. M., *War is War*, 87–8

Caruth, Cathy, 7–8, 20n5, 79, 81
Cannadine, David, 158
Cary, Kate, *Bloodline*, 202
Chapman, Guy, *A Passionate Prodigality: Fragments of Autobiography*, 89–90, 94
Christie, Agatha, 84, 185, 193, 195, 198
Conrad-O'Briain, Helen, 186
Cook, Tim, 16–17

Dante, *Purgatorio*, 134, 139
Davies, Owen, 17, 109n3, 155n3, 155n4, 155n6, 155n8
Dent, Jonathan, 10–11, 27, 33, 111, 205
Dickens, Charles, 108, 126
Dunmore, Helen, *The Lie*, 209n1

Einhaus, Ann-Marie, 23
Eliot, T. S., 18, 147–8, 151
  The Waste Land, 136, 143–7, 193
Everett, Henrietta Dorothy, 63n7
  'A Perplexing Case', 48–50, 54, 195

Faulks, Sebastian, *Birdsong*, 202
Foley, Matt, 112, 135, 137, 138, 139, 140, 141, 142, 151, 155n1
Ford, Madox Ford
  Parade's End, 103–6
  'War and the Mind', 89
Freedman, Angela, 192
Freud, Sigmund
  Beyond the Pleasure Principle, 4–7, 10, 11, 70, 75, 77, 78, 97
  'Memorandum on the Electrical Treatment of War Neurotics', 66
  Mourning and Melancholia, 4, 138, 140–1, 195
  'On Transience', 65
  The Interpretation of Dreams, 10
  'The Uncanny', 2, 3–4, 7, 10, 11, 13, 17, 22–63, 67, 71, 74, 81, 85, 100, 138

'Thoughts for the Times on War and Death', 66, 86
Fussell, Paul, 103, 105–6, 158–9

Gance, Abel, *J'Accuse*, 199n2
Graham, Desmond, 92–3
Graves, Robert, 18, 19, 158, 163, 167, 170, 184, 203
  'From Our Ghostly Enemy', 159–60
  Goodbye to All That, 1–2, 106, 107, 173
  'Haunted', 106
  'No More Ghosts', 160–1
  'Postscript to "Goodbye to All That"', 107
  'The Haunted House', 107
  'The Shout', 172–4, 188
Greening, John, 93

Hardy, Thomas, 104
Hartley, L. P., 'The Travelling Grave', 83–6
Haslam, Sara, 104, 105
Hawthorne, Nathaniel, *The Scarlet Letter*, 94
Hazelgrove, Jenny, 119
Hill, Susan, 202
  Strange Meeting, 209
Hitchcock, Ethan Allen, *The Story of the Red Book of Appin*, 196
Hoffmann, E. T. A., 'The Sandman', 23, 24, 30
Holtby, Winifred, 96, 163, 199n3
  South Riding, 163–4, 172
Horace, *Odes*, 123
Hume, David, *The History of England*, 11
Hyder, Alan F., 'A Nightmare', 76–8, 80, 81, 88
Hynes, Samuel, 65

James, Henry, 141
James, M. R., 19, 90, 154, 167–78, 180, 183, 184, 186, 191, 198, 203
  'A Neighbour's Landmark', 171–4, 175, 176, 188
  'A View from a Hill', 174–77, 192

'A Warning to the Curious', 165, 168, 175, 178, 187
'The Uncommon Prayer-Book', 167–71, 174, 175, 176, 189, 190
The Wanderings and Homes of Manuscripts, 170
James, William, 136
Jameson, Storm, *Company Parade*, 90, 98–102, 105, 106
Johnson, George M., 16
Jones, David, 18
In Parenthesis, 147–51, 152
Joyce, James, 135

Keats, John, 75
Kitchin, C. H. B., 83
'Dispossession', 50–4, 56, 57, 80, 204
Kline, Burton, 'The Living Ghost', 28–30
Ko, Charles, 135

Le Fanu, Sheridan, 186
Le Queux, William, *The Invasion of 1910*, 114
Levenson, Michael, 147
Leys, Ruth, 20n4
Light, Alison, 185
Lodge, Oliver, 119, 180, 182
Raymond, 18, 122–6, 130, 133, 146
Lott, Monica, 192
Loughran, Tracey, 44–5, 50, 63n6
Lowndes, Marie Belloc, 63n4
'The Unbolted Door', 34–6, 43
Luckhurst, Roger, 15, 20n5, 20n8, 136

Machen, Arthur, 95, 109n5
'The Bowmen', 92
The Great God Pan, 14–15
McCrae, John
'In Flanders Field', 158–9
McLoughlin, Kate, 13–14, 30, 58–9, 62, 75, 155n11
Malamud, Randy, 146
Manning, Frederic, *Her Privates We*, 69–72, 79, 89, 92

Martin, Jack, 69, 70, 71
Mercier, Charles, 125–6
Milton, John, *Paradise Lost*, 114
Miranda, Michelle, 185
Moberly, L. G., 'Inexplicable', 24–6, 27, 66
Montieth, Sharon, 204, 205
Mortley, Alice, 128
Muir, Bryonny, 190–1, 192, 199n11, 200n12
Murphy, Patrick J., 165–6, 167, 169, 178, 199n5, 199n7
Myers, Charles, 44
Myers, F. W. H., 113–14, 120, 122, 123, 135, 136
Myers, Gabrielle, 140, 142

Newman, Kim, *The Bloody Red Baron*, 202
Nordau, Max, 65, 115
Norman, Taryn, 185

Occult Review, The, 18, 112–22, 126, 128
Owen, Wilfred, 16
'Strange Meeting', 82, 83, 87, 135, 203

Pfaff, Richard, 166, 170
Piper, Leonora, 122–3
Pividori, Cristina, 59–60
Plain, Gill, 185, 186, 193
Poe, Edgar Allan, 186
'The Facts in the Case of M. Valdemar', 120
Poole, Scott W., 17, 19n2, 63n2
Porcheddu, Fred, 165–6, 167, 169, 178, 199n5, 199n7

Radcliffe, Ann, 83, 189, 192
Radziwill, Catherine, 121
Reid, Fiona, 44, 63n8
Riquelme, John Paul, 111, 113, 116, 135, 145, 155n9
Rivers, W. H. R., 14, 97, 203, 204, 208
'A Case of Claustrophobia', 67–8, 69, 72, 73, 77, 78, 81, 108

Rivers, W. H. R. (*cont.*)
   Conflict and Dream, 66
   Instinct and the Unconscious, 42, 44–8, 52, 62, 66, 67, 69, 70, 73, 99
Roper, Michael, 74, 75–6
Ruickbie, Leo, 20n9, 155n2

Sassoon, Siegfried, 18, 63n3, 90, 104, 155n12, 162, 203
   Memoirs of an Infantry Officer, 1–2, 31, 88–9
Sayers, Dorothy L., 186, 199n9
   The Nine Tailors, 19, 158, 172, 184–93, 198
Scanlon, Mara, 61–2
Shakespeare, William, *Hamlet*, 9–10, 15, 70, 131–2, 139
Shelley, Mary, *Frankenstein*, 14, 68, 110, 111, 116, 124, 127, 129, 136, 143, 144, 145, 146, 148, 150, 154, 181, 182, 185–6, 193
shell-shock, 41–63
Shephard, Ben, 62n5
Showalter, Elaine, 140, 142
Sinnett, A. P., 113–1, 119
Skirth, Ronald, *The Reluctant Tommy*, 97, 99, 109n6
Smith, Andrew, 155n8, 155n9
spiritualism, 16, 18, 110–37, 143, 146, 154, 180, 181–2, 185, 197, 199
Spooner, Catherine, 185, 190
Stevenson, Robert Louis, *Strange Case of Dr Jekyll and Mr Hyde*, 14–15, 65, 69, 99, 100, 115, 118, 128, 185
Stoker, Bram, *Dracula*, 14, 110, 111, 115, 116, 118, 120, 124, 127, 129, 143, 144, 146, 154, 157, 183, 185, 193, 194, 198, 202
Strand, The, 17, 24, 28, 37, 41, 54, 170

Stuart, Gerald Villiers, 'The Mirror and the Incense', 37–41, 44
Summers, Montague, 120–1

Thurston, Luke, 26, 27, 36
Townshend, Dale, 9–10, 15, 27, 30, 132, 137–8
Tropp, Martin, 15–16
Tudor Pole, Wellesley, *Private Dowding*, 126–31, 133, 137, 139, 145

Verrall, Margaret, 122–3

Wallace, Jeff, 155n9
Walpole, Horace, 21, 23, 29, 33, 35, 83, 101, 141, 148, 150, 152, 153, 154, 157, 158, 163, 164, 180, 182, 185, 189, 191, 192, 201
   The Castle of Otranto, 2, 9–13, 26, 27, 28, 104, 111, 131–2, 139, 149, 150, 161, 173, 174, 176, 205
Ward, J. S. M., *A Subaltern in Spirit Land*, 131–4, 136, 137, 196
Ward, Sean Francis, 204, 205
Wells, H. G., 117, 181
   The War of the Worlds, 114
West, Rebecca, 13, 102
   The Return of the Soldier, 58–63, 73, 78
Wheatley, Dennis, *The Devil Rides Out*, 19, 158, 184, 193–8, 202
Wilde, Oscar, 99, 100
Wilt, Judith, 140, 141, 143
Winter, Jay, 110, 119
Woolf, Virginia, 13, 16, 18, 26, 151
   Jacob's Room, 206
   Mrs Dalloway, 138–43

Young, Edward,
   Night Thoughts, 89, 91

Zilcosky, John, 25–6

EU representative:
Easy Access System Europe
Mustamäe tee 50, 10621 Tallinn, Estonia
Gpsr.requests@easproject.com

www.ingramcontent.com/pod-product-compliance
Lightning Source LLC
Chambersburg PA
CBHW070351240426
43671CB00013BA/2464